WOMEN
and
EDUCATION

THE NATIONAL SOCIETY
FOR THE STUDY OF EDUCATION

Series on Contemporary Educational Issues
Kenneth J. Rehage, Series Editor

The 1984 Titles:

Women and Education: Equity or Equality?, Elizabeth Fennema
and M. Jane Ayer, editors
Curriculum Development: Problems, Processes, and Progress,
Glenys Unruh and Adolph Unruh

The National Society for the Study of Education also publishes
Yearbooks which are distributed by the University of Chicago Press.
Inquiries regarding all publications of the Society, as well as
inquiries about membership in the Society, may be addressed to the
Secretary-Treasurer, 5835 Kimbark Avenue, Chicago, IL 60637.
Membership in the Society is open to any who are interested in
promoting the investigation and discussion of educational
programs.

WOMEN

and

EDUCATION

EQUITY OR EQUALITY?

Edited by

Elizabeth Fennema

University of Wisconsin — Madison

and

M. Jane Ayer

University of Wisconsin — Madison

McCutchan Publishing Corporation
2526 Grove Street
Berkeley, California 94704

ISBN 0-8211-0507-8
Library of Congress Catalog Card Number 83-62772

Printed in the United States of America

Cover design by Terry Down, Griffin Graphics
Typesetting composition by Delmas

Series Foreword

The essays in this volume address an issue of genuine concern. As the editors, M. Jane Ayer and Elizabeth Fennema, note in the preface, it is time to bring scholarship to bear on the role and position of women in education. This book is one such effort. The several contributors bring their scholarly talents to the complementary tasks of illuminating the situation and pointing toward solutions.

The National Society for the Study of Education is pleased to include this book in its series on Contemporary Educational Issues. We are grateful to Dean Ayer and Professor Fennema for their careful planning and for their sustained effort over a considerable period of time. We are indebted to each of the contributors for preparing the significant papers that comprise the volume. As distinctive contributions to the field of education, the chapters in this book will surely stimulate discussion and serious thought about the various subjects with which they deal.

Kenneth J. Rehage

for the Committee on the Expanded
Publication Program of the National
Society for the Study of Education

Contributors

Helen S. Astin, University of California, Los Angeles

M. Jane Ayer, University of Wisconsin-Madison

Ann H. Barbee, Stanford University

Anne Bennison, University of Wisconsin-Madison

Lisa J. Crockett, University of Chicago

Elizabeth Fennema, University of Wisconsin-Madison

Maxine Greene, Teachers College, Columbia University

Shirley Jane Kaub, East High School, Madison, Wisconsin

Marlaine E. Lockheed, Educational Testing Service

Cora Bagley Marrett, University of Wisconsin-Madison

Vandra Masemann, University of Wisconsin-Madison

Westina Matthews, Chicago Community Trust

Karen Merritt, University of Wisconsin System

Anne C. Petersen, Pennsylvania State University

Penelope Peterson, University of Wisconsin-Madison

Susan E. Searing, University of Wisconsin System

Pauline S. Sears, Stanford University

Mary Beth Snyder, University of California, Los Angeles

Louise Cherry Wilkinson, University of Wisconsin-Madison

Contents

Preface

This collection represents an evolving generation of scholarship on the role and position of women in education. The political rhetoric of the early 1970s served well the purpose of marshalling forces against sexism; perhaps now we can move on to more fundamental scholarship and to seek solutions to the problems that have been so well identified. An examination of the problems and issues confronting females in education reveals sets of interwoven variables and situations, some which fit neatly within one model or theory, and some which appear to have no best fit. Many variables often describe situations or elements that result from an interaction or interplay between persons, events, and situations. It is obvious that throughout the literature not enough attention has been paid to conceptual development or to the application and testing of theoretical constructs. So elementary is this step to the proper analysis of social change that one is shocked by the failure of social scientists who have made so little serious effort to develop true conceptual models applicable to the processes evident within the feminist movement, particularly with regard to the educational status of women.

By positing the four conceptual approaches of pluralism, assimilation, deficit, and social justice, Bennison et al. (Chapter One) have offered four theoretical models for considering the role and place of women in education. Does one strive for assimilation and become a part of the governing structure by becoming the same as those who govern, or does one seek to make a pluralistic home within the established setting and gain a position of influence and power because of one's differences? Is it possible to do this? Faculty competence and skills and the reward structure of academe are based upon an assimilationist model with peer review as the major instrumentation. The support of commonly shared academic values and the enforcement of academic standards often overshadow a more hidden set of criteria for admission to the academy through tenure. These criteria are the folkways and mores of the institutional structure.

One comes to belong only by learning those behaviors, languages, and styles that are consistent with the dominant social system, regardless of other skills and credentials. Salary analyses show that experiences which do not serve to develop appropriate skills will be of little help to females in search of salary equity. That is to say, for women to attain parity, their vita must be longer and the catch-up phase for the social scientist begins after approximately forty-four years of experience. Assimilation is a very slow process for the aspirant seeking entry to the greater structure and slow as well for individuals singly or collectively to have an impact upon the existing structure. It is only when that impact can be felt that the established dimensions for assimilation will be changed to allow freedom of access to the academy.

Within the field of professional education let us assume that there are no discrepancies among the professional cadre and we need not concern ourselves with the deficit model. Federal rulings such as Executive Order 11246 and Title IX have legally defined conditions of social justice. Why then do we continue to find conditions of employment for women that show no improvement? More than 46 percent of high school teachers are female, but only 5 percent of school administrators are women. One school board member in five is a woman, and boards of directors in the private sector reflect only a slightly improved pattern of membership by sex. Not only are women directed away from leadership roles, but they are counseled into specializations that do not lead naturally into positions of power, decision making, and budget control. Women continue to occupy such traditional roles as counselors, teachers, and educational specialists.

In contrast with male expectations, females cannot assume a natural progression from entry-level positions to academic or administrative leadership without gaining knowledge of ways to circumvent institutional barriers and without meeting criteria that include the folkways and mores of an institution. A necessary strategy is the deliberate choice of areas of study and positions that will help move an individual from level A to level B, bridging positions in a manner carefully considered and plotted.

Under existing social conditions, once a woman has identified her goals she must adopt a strategy that will bring about her acceptance within an assimilationist value structure. Social protests of recent years have reflected attempts to force a more pluralistic social structure, but until the institutional power base itself becomes more pluralistic (assuming this will occur to some extent because of social pressure), conditions for assimilation will continue to prevail. The perils are well known; women who seek to enter must by definition adopt masculine values of intellectual aggressiveness, dominance, and authority, and sublimate traits identified as feminine and, therefore, come to be viewed as inappropriate.

Yet, it is only from within the institutionalized social structure that more rapid change will occur and, given the difficulties in effecting change as shown in the civil rights and feminist movements, women will deliberately have to seek increased decision-making power. By increased use of complementary characteristics, concepts of pluralism and assimilation can be merged to bring about a system that serves all and which cannot be manipulated by the few who will not recognize that the principles of the human rights movements can no longer be termed invalid.

M. Jane Ayer
Elizabeth H. Fennema
University of Wisconsin-Madison
June 1983

1

Equity or Equality: What Shall It Be?

Anne Bennison, Louise Cherry Wilkinson, Elizabeth Fennema, Vandra Masemann, and Penelope Peterson

Free public education for all citizens is one of the beliefs basic to American values. American educators proudly trace this belief from the Old Deluder Satan Law of 1647 through the early nationhood days of Jefferson up to the present time. However, since World War II and increasingly during the 1960s and 1970s, there has been closer examination of what this belief has meant to various groups of people and whether equality or equity of education should be provided. Some people are suggesting that equality of education should be provided, meaning identical educational opportunities for all learners. Others are promoting equity of education, meaning the provision of varied educational opportunities in order to achieve specified goals.

The decision of the Supreme Court in *Brown* v. *Board of Education of Topeka* (1954) was a major impetus for the examination of the equity or equality issue. This decision stated that separate schools for blacks were inherently unequal, raising the question of equality in education for many other groups such as females, other ethnic minorities, the developmentally disabled, and the gifted. Not only are questions being asked, but changes have

1

occurred. Educational programs have been designed to provide
equitable education for a variety of groups funded by private
foundations, the federal government, and local educational
agencies. These programs include a range of activities: tutoring to
help learners overcome mathematics deficiencies and multimillion
dollar endeavors to change attitudes and behaviors of learners and
teachers, redesign curricula, and in some cases to restructure the
entire educational environment of a community.

The premise of some programs is the assertion that identical and
equal experiences must be provided for all learners in order to
provide equitable education. Because identical experiences are
provided, it is assumed that equity of education is assured. Other
programs are based on the assertion that intervention programs
must be provided to compensate for deficiencies the learners bring to
school. The basic assumption is that equality of educational
opportunity does not provide equity, but that equity is achieved
only when the outcomes of schooling are the same for all groups.
Other programs support the assertion that the strength of American
education and the strength of the United States is in diversity.
Therefore, individual or group strengths—which may be
different—should be developed with equitable education so that
cultural and individual diversity can result. This position often
reflects the belief that because the societal roles of various ethnic
groups and the sexes are different, education should take into
consideration this role differentiation and provide appropriate
education.

Each one of these positions rests on assumptions that are seldom
explicated and often go unrecognized. The purpose of this essay is to
provide a framework that will clarify assumptions underlying
programs designed to provide equality or equity in education for
females and males. Perhaps if such assumptions are understood,
programs may be better designed so that equity in education can
become a reality for all people.

PHILOSOPHICAL MODELS FOR ACHIEVING EDUCATIONAL EQUITY

The primary assumptions that differentiate such programs fall
within three categories: (1) assumptions about what the
characteristics of learners are, (2) assumptions about what the goals

of education for different groups and individuals should be, and (3) assumptions about how programs should be structured to achieve educational equity.

Four models for achieving educational equity will be discussed in this chapter. The *assimilationist* model, currently in practice in most public schools, is based upon the assumption that the salient characteristics of female and male learners are basically the same. It is further assumed that the results of the educational process for males and females should and will be the same because the goals are the same, and identical educational opportunities are provided. The *deficit* model assumes that while the goals and results of the educational process should be the same for females and males, either sex might enter the educational process deficient in some way. In order to reach the same goals, educational programs must be structured that will compensate for the deficits.

The *pluralistic* model is based on yet a third set of assumptions, primarily that the goals of education should differ for different groups. While the salient characteristics of learners from certain groups are different, these differences are not believed to be deficits. The educational environment should be structured with these differences in mind so that the end result is greater diversity among learners. A fourth model is that of *social justice*, which addresses some issues not incorporated in the previous three models. The assumptions within this framework are that people are alike in some ways and different in other ways; and, thus, people should be treated identically in ways they are alike and differently in ways they are not alike. Relevant differences are respected and treated fairly, and justice is achieved.

Assimilationism

The assimilationist model is based on the assumption that girls and boys have similar abilities to learn when they enter school, that they should be given the same or equal opportunities to learn, and that the result will be equal educational outcomes for all children. An important principal is that sex is not a salient characteristic on which to group people for purposes of learning; the assimilationist position assumes that there are no differences between the sexes relevant to the educational process. Consider the following statement by Grady about sex-related differences:

It is no longer reasonable to hypothesize subject sex differences in fundamental psychological processes. It seems clear that given the same social situation, the same reinforcement contingencies, the same expectancies, both sexes will react similarly. Men and women are basically alike (Grady 1975, p. 7).

Certain beliefs are adhered to in the assimilationist position. While some biological sex differences exist, such as differences in genitalia, physique, and physiological processes, these differences are considered irrelevant to the educational process. On the other hand, there may be some sex-related differences that are salient to the educational process. Possible sex-related differences are: verbal, mathematical, and visual-spatial skills (Maccoby and Jacklin 1974), but these dissimilarities are not of the same order as are biological differences. The biological differences between female and male are absolute in some cases (genitalia) and of large magnitude in others (such as strength). Differences in the educationally salient characteristics, however, are of small magnitude and represent average differences with tremendous overlap between the groups in question. These differences are sex-related but not sex-determined as are the biological differences. Because the salient educational differences are not sex-determined, and because the overlap in performance is so great, sex is not a relevant educational difference; and females and males should be considered the same for educational purposes. Accordingly, because learners are considered the same in all educationally relevant attributes, it follows that they should be given the same educational opportunities, including curricular choices, instructional treatments, courses of study, as well as the same attention by teachers, principals, and counselors. If learners are treated the same, they will achieve the same educational outcomes—outcomes that are considered desirable for all children in our society to achieve regardless of their sex.

Traces of the assimilationist position might be found in the statements by the coeducation proponents at the beginning of the twentieth century. It was deemed philosophically desirable for all citizens in our society to learn basic skills such as reading and writing, and it was assumed that females as well as males of all ethnic backgrounds had the same abilities to learn these skills and that they should be given the same educational opportunities to do so.

This pattern of belief exists still. Females and males attend elementary schools where they overtly participate in the same educational activities taught by the same teachers. Courses are open to both sexes in secondary schools where great emphasis is placed on an intelligent selection of subjects so that individuals will acquire the essentials of education while at the same time exploring a variety of options for future planning.

In practice, however, many contradictions exist within the assimilationist model. While females and males have overtly been exposed to the same educational experiences, in reality they have not been considered the same, have not been given the same educational opportunities, and have not been expected to achieve the same outcomes. Maccoby and Jacklin (1974) have pointed out the unfounded myths about how the sexes differ. Others, such as Kemer (1965), have shown that teachers describe the good male students quite differently than good female students. Furthermore, boys and girls are treated differently in the educational process and are expected to achieve different goals as a result of education (Frazier and Sadker 1973; Stacey, Bereaud, and Daniels 1974; Good, Sikes, and Brophy 1973).

Currently the assimilationist model for achieving equity in education is best represented by proponents of androgyny and the goals they espouse for education. (See, for example, Kaplan and Bean 1976.) Androgyny is considered to be the ultimate outcome desired as a result of the socialization process, in general, and of the educational process in particular. Androgyny is a nonstereotypic sex-role identity that incorporates positively valued masculine characteristics and positively valued feminine characteristics. Androgynous individuals are assertive as well as yielding, ambitious and compassionate, self-sufficient yet able to sooth hurt feelings, forceful but understanding (Bem 1974). They are able to achieve similarly in cognitive areas such as mathematics and science, as well as in the verbal areas of reading, language, and communication. Both sexes have the potential to become androgynous. As Kaplan and Bean state:

> The diversity of humanness would be based more on individual temperaments than on sex-typed expectations. We envision that the future effect of sex on behavior will become as innocuous as current reactions to hair color. There are still some lingering stereotypes about hot-tempered redheads and sexy blonds, but one would scarcely make a personnel decision or build a relationship on the

basis of these characteristics alone. Our position is premised on the
argument . . . that researchers in the biological sciences have not demonstrated a
causal link between biological sexual dimorphism and existing behavioral sex
differences (Kaplan and Bean 1976, p. 384).

The way to achieve androgyny is by providing truly equal
educational opportunities to girls and boys. Such provisions
include eliminating sex-role stereotypes in textbooks and other
curriculum materials; changing the teaching and advising practices
of teachers, administrators, and school counselors; and having
similar expectations of success for both sexes. Studies such as
Women on Words and Images (1972) have led to the adoption of
nonsexist guidelines for textbooks by some textbook publishers.
Other efforts such as the production of films on sex-role
stereotyping in the schools by Golden and Hunter (1974) have been
aimed at changing the stereotyped practices of teachers,
administrators, and counselors to provide equal educational
opportunities to boys and girls.

The Deficit Approach

The deficit model is characterized by the assumption that
differences among groups of learners exist which render them
unequal in ways that are important to the educational process. For
example, there may be sex-related deficits in cognitive areas, such as
verbal or spatial skills. It is sometimes believed that these deficits are
the result of genetic and environmental influences, but most often it
is believed that the deficit is the result of socialization processes. Cole
and Bruner have provided one version of the deficit hypothesis with
regard to social causes of ethnic differences in abilities:

It rests on the assumption that a community under conditions of poverty (for it is
the poor who are the focus of attention, and a disproportionate number of the
poor are members of minority ethnic groups) is a disorganized community, and
this disorganization expresses itself in various forms of deficit (Cole and Bruner
1971, p. 867).

The values placed upon these differences in abilities are
determined by the dominant culture, specifically by members of
society who are in a position to make and communicate evaluative
judgments. For example, if literacy is highly valued as a skill in the

culture, then verbal skills are highly valued as a product of schooling.

The role and function of education within the deficit model are to ensure equal educational outcomes for all. This goal usually requires different educational environments for children with deficits, that is, compensatory education. Learners will develop the same skills and abilities as a result of the educational process if they are provided with educational environments that aim specifically to compensate for or remedy a deficit.

The basic assumptions of the deficit model, that some children are deficient in some abilities and that these deficiencies are results of environmental influences, have received some support from empirical studies. But evidence also suggests that there are sex-related differences in verbal, mathematical, and spatial skills. These skills are highly valued in this society because they are a prerequisite for many prestigious occupations.

The role and function of educational institutions using a deficit approach are to provide educational opportunities for all children to help them compensate for deficits that society identifies as important. Compensatory education refers to educational interventions designed to remedy failure in school for children who suffer from environmental deficiencies. The major rationale for compensatory education is the deficit model. For example, Fox reports on attempts to improve the mathematical skills of precocious females who exhibit deficits. This deficit developed because of the effect of differential environments upon males and females. Females failed to seek stimulation in mathematics and the sciences and were less likely to take advantage of special educational opportunities provided by intervention programs, such as the one designed by Fox and her colleagues. Fox concluded:

> Girls are reluctant to try skipping a grade, taking a college course such as computer science, or enrolling in special accelerated mathematics programs, and are less critical of school. The reason seems to be that girls are afraid to try things which might make them appear different in relation to their peers (Fox 1975, p. 7).

A number of compensatory education programs were designed in the 1960s to increase the intelligence and school achievement scores of poor children. The consensus seems to be that these programs have failed to increase minority children's tested intelligence scores. Critics differ on the interpretation of this fact as well as on recommendations for further attempts to remedy the deficit. Jensen (1969) has argued that compensatory education has failed because intelligence is primarily determined by inherited factors, not environmental factors. In contrast, Baratz and Baratz have argued that "this clearly indicates that critical intervention must be done, but on the procedures and materials used in the schools rather than on the children those schools service" (Baratz and Baratz 1970, p. 41).

The outcomes of the deficit model depend on the design of the educational interventions. If attempts to remedy deficiencies were successful, there would be no lasting sex-related or ethnic group differences in schooling outcomes.

The Pluralist Model

The pluralist model assumes that children who enter school have important differences in their cultural background or in gender and that these variations are best served by different educational experiences which result in unique outcomes and goals. At various times in American history, several of these differences have been accentuated. Diverse types of schools have been established that emphasized religious or religious-ethnic differences (Andersson and Boyer 1971), ethnic differences as in the case of Bureau of Indian Affairs Schools for Native Americans (Fuchs and Havighurst 1973), racial differences, or sex-role differences. One of the most important aspects of the pluralist model is its dialectical relationship to the assimilationist model, such that any gains by the dominated groups who claim pluralism are generally seen as a threat to the assimilationist-minded dominators. The realities of the power relationships between the dominators and the dominated, whether on the basis of religion, race, ethnicity, or sex, cannot be lightly discounted in any discussion of educational opportunities for minorities and women.

It is being argued that the pluralist model recognizes only cultural differences among groups, but it must be acknowledged that this has not always been so. At its most extreme, the pluralist model espouses inherited race-related differences, a position that continues to be used to justify racist political regimes. Biological determinism has been evoked as a rationale for subordinating women and various ethnic groups, including Native Americans and white immigrant groups. For example, at the turn of the century, certain physical characteristics of women and subordinate ethnic groups were viewed as related to their ability to be docile, dogged workers, "twelve hours to the day, day after day, through the three hundred and sixty-five days, excepting Sundays, Thanksgiving, and Fast-days" (Melville, as quoted in Greene, p. 24 of this volume). Any biological explanation generally buttressed the claims of the majority for power and control of the labor and lives of minority groups.

The major shift surrounding the pluralist model is the change from a biological focus on inherited differences to an emphasis on childhood socialization and learned cultural differences (Ellis 1976). Anthropologists have documented the innumerable kinds of learning and socialization in various cultural milieux (see Williams 1972, Spindler 1974, Mead 1937, Middleton 1976). When a cultural explanation is applied to minority group concerns, it then requires that those in the majority acknowledge relevant differences in educational goals and create a pluralistic framework in which minority group rights to live differently are upheld. This problem forms the core of the debate on political and educational pluralism in America.

While this delineation appears to apply only to ethnic, racial, or religious minorities, it has also been extended in anthropological literature to gender-role and the problem of "women's culture." Edwin Ardener, a British anthropologist, delineates the problem. Men and women in any society have their own symbolic universes which overlap to some extent in the male-defined institutional social order. Researchers such as anthropologists or sociologists, who are themselves the product of their own male-defined epistemology, are able to describe the "male culture" of the society they are studying but are not able to hear or understand that part of the social order pertaining to women. This occurs as the voice of women is muted "because it does not form part of the dominant communicative system of the society" (Ardener 1975, p. 22), either the one being studied or the society of the researcher. The compelling conclusion here is that women's culture should not be ignored simply because it has not been salient in the discussions of male-dominated educational systems; moreover, it should be possible to develop a female-based epistemology that would perceive and acknowledge the reality of women's lives. This viewpoint conflicts strongly with androgynous solutions to the gender problem.

To return briefly to the question of dominator-dominated relations, the pluralist model emphasizes the right of dominated groups—whether ethnic, racial, religious, or female—to have a perspective that is not completely muted by the perspective of the dominant group. Assimilationist and deficit models deny the validity of any muted perspective.

The role and function of education in a pluralistic framework depend on the extent to which pluralism is fostered or allowed. There is historical evidence that schools in America have fostered assimilation rather than pluralism, and the pluralism has been allowed only when it presented no clear threat to the power of dominant groups. Thus, parochial ethnic schools flourished in the 1800s but declined with the Americanization and deethnicization of religion in this century (Dinnerstein and Reimers 1975, p. 145). Separate schooling for females, which stressed homemaking skills and the virtues of passivity, docility, and obedience in a male-dominated society, was clearly not a threat to the dominant social order.

To members of some minority groups, education plays a crucial role in fostering what are considered to be relevant differences. For some religious minorities such as the Amish, the solution has been a completely separate school system that teaches the traditional religious value system (Keim 1975). In the public school system, the two most notable pluralistic programs are multicultural education and bilingual-bicultural education. Margaret Gibson (1976, p. 16) outlines five main approaches to these programs: (1) education of the culturally different, or benevolent multiculturalism; (2) education about cultural differences or cultural understanding; (3) education for cultural pluralism; (4) bicultural education; and (5) multicultural education as the normal human experience. She demonstrates that many programs appearing to be pluralistic are in fact based on assumptions of majority group dominance and that educational pluralism is the only model which has as a goal the increased power of minority groups.

An examination of the papers in this volume reveals very little evidence of a pluralistic stance when viewing women's culture even today. Some of Horace Mann's dicta quoted in Greene's chapter hint at it, but his views are primarily based on biological determinism. A quotation from Willard Waller summarizes the position even in 1932: "It has been said that no woman and no Negro is ever fully admitted to the white man's world" (Waller, as quoted in Greene, p. 33 of this volume). The chapter by Sears and Barbee (Chapter Three) contains, hidden between the lines, stories of gifted women who found great satisfaction in aspects of their lives that comprise a woman's existence. It is also apparent in this paper that women either who chose or who were compelled to work in a male-dominated occupational sphere were also compelled to give up some other life satisfactions. Astin and Snyder (Chapter Eight) favor changing some of the institutional restrictions on the definitions of women's participation, whether as reflected in instructional materials or as exemplified in program and policy planning. This paper rests on the assumption, however, that it is the male-articulated world that should be opened up to the mute disadvantaged females. There is no hint that women's symbolic universe may constitute a separate, and equally valid, reality.

The outcomes and goals of a pluralistic approach to education are diverse and by no means homogeneous in our complex society. The single most acceptable goal in an ideal pluralist philosophy would be heterogeneity. This ideal would have to be upheld by those having the power to define social norms (Dahrendorf 1969). Thus, diverse ethnic, racial, or religious groups would not be subordinated on the basis of their relative distance from those who define heterogeneity as a norm. The concept of minority group itself would undergo a change.

When one examines this pluralistic stance in relation to gender role, it theoretically becomes less possible. Perhaps the reason is that in ethnic groups, cultures can perpetuate themselves through socialization of children, by the use of the language which sets them apart from those of other cultures. However, for males and females in one culture, the problem is less easily solved since they cannot perpetuate themselves without associating with the other sex, and thereby become aware of an articulated part of each other's universe which they can never fully comprehend (Ardener 1975, pp. 14-15). If the resolution is to discard worries about the realities they cannot share and to concentrate on the articulated institutionalized world where their universes overlap, it turns out to be a male-dominated universe where men control the higher-level knowledge of science and technology on which Western culture rests.

In education, this command of institutionalized knowledge is often expressed in achievement scores. In a pluralist model, any other criteria considered valid by peripheral groups could be considered worthy, although criteria are easily discarded as trivial or as irrelevant by those who frame institutionalized knowledge. Religious minorities may see eternal life as the desired outcome of worthwhile learning (Keim 1975), and command of religious knowledge is stressed in their schools. For Native Americans, the primordial attachment to the land may outweigh all other goals (Fuchs and Havighurst 1973), and community control of schools may ensure the perpetuation of this attachment. For various ethnic groups, the preservation and transmission of a culture and language in schools may be all-important. For women the cultivation and enhancement of the tasks of childrearing may be the most worthy goal, as stressed, for example, in traditional home economics courses. In all cases, to the extent to which any of these goals pose a threat to institutionalized norms or definitions of the dominant, they will be rendered mute. Thus, separatist religious enclaves and Native Americans are left alone in geographical isolation, and militant ethnic group demands are treated with grave suspicion or are muted by a bureaucratic blanket of proposals for multicultural programs. The elaboration of the domesticated female role is enthusiastically received by television advertisers and other advocates of consumption while demands by women for more meaningful participation in the male-controlled institutions of higher learning meet with entrenched resistance.

The problem of participation in a man's world has never been fully articulated for women. Ethnic minorities have their own languages. Women in America speak a language that resembles the language men speak. Lakoff (1975) has called women academics "bilinguals" who may never really master socially correct usage of the male professional career language. Most equity action policy is based on the assumption that women can learn to speak the male version of a language and that equality of educational opportunity and outcome requires increased participation by women in and elucidation of a male world. A pluralistic perspective suggests that it is the women's world that needs to be decolonized and articulated. Until that world is articulated, we have not begun to speak about either equality or equity.

The Justice Model

The justice model is of a different order than are the other models discussed. It is a philosophical approach and includes portions of each of the preceding three models. Using justice as a basis for making educational decisions has been at the heart of many recent controversies such as busing for racial integration and reverse discrimination suits in graduate or professional school admissions. The justice model assumes that persons are both alike and different, and that people should be treated identically when equal and differently when unequal in some relevant way. In other words, in order to have justice in education, sometimes equal and the same opportunities are needed and at other times different opportunities are required to provide equity.

How is justice defined in this approach? To some, justice involves the distribution of or access to certain broadly conceived social goods for individual members of a society.

> Justice, whether social or not, seems to have at its center the notion of an allotment of something to persons—duties, goods, offices, opportunities, penalties, punishments, privileges, roles, status, and so on. Moreover, at least in the case of distributive justice, it seems centrally to involve the notion of comparative allotment (Frankena 1962, p. 9).

Others have conceptualized justice somewhat differently. Vlastos suggests that "an action is just if, and only if, it is prescribed exclusively by regard for the rights of all whom it affects substantially" (Vlastos 1962, p. 53). The rights he speaks of are human rights of well-being (which include the right to welfare, medical care, education, and leisure) and the rights of freedom (which include among others, freedom of movement, religion, suffrage, speech, choice of employment, and thought). Justice is based on conceiving a definition of human worth in which an individual can live a life with personal meaning and dignity rather than basing personal worth on usefulness or merit. However, Williams links the words *justice* and *fairness* with the notion of equality in unequal circumstances. He speaks of the notion of equality being "invoked not only in connections where men are claimed in some sense all to be equal, but in connections where they are agreed to be equal, and the question arises of the distribution of, or access to, certain goods to which their inequalities are relevant" (Williams 1967, p. 120). It is this issue of *relevant differences* that is important.

When justice is used as a basis for organizing education, certain assumptions are made. Human beings are similar in their right to certain social goods such as the right to self-respect and the right to well-being and freedom. Differences such as sex, race, or ethnicity are irrelevant in terms of a person's right to the goods of society no matter which basic goods are considered most important. However, as Williams suggests:

> There is a distinction between a man's rights, the reasons why he should be treated in a certain way, and his power to secure those rights, the reasons why he can in fact get what he deserves.... We are concerned not with the abstract existence of rights, but with the extent to which those rights govern what actually happens (Williams 1967, p. 122).

Differences in educational treatment can best be justified in terms of how such differences enable people to secure their basic human rights and allow equal access to social goods. Education is relevant in helping a person secure individual rights, and some basic education is necessary in order for a person to exercise freedom of speech, suffrage, thought, or choice of employment.

In education then, how would one justify, or could one justify, unequal treatment of students on the basis of sex? In a truly just society, differences of sex would not prevent people from securing their rights or their opportunity for access to the available social goods and, therefore, unequal *treatment* would not be present. However, justice requires treating people identically in ways in which they are equal and differently when they are unequal in some relevant way. The issue is that in an unjust society in which disadvantages and inequalities in power can be linked to sex, these characteristics are no longer irrelevant differences. For example, one might say that the sex of a person selected to study medicine is totally irrelevant and this would be true in a just society in which access to opportunities was truly open. However, if it could be shown that there were no qualified female applicants because they had been systematically discouraged and/or eliminated from pursuing school subjects that would allow them equal access to medical schools, sex would appear to be a relevant difference in selection.

Perhaps the best contemporary example of the complexity of issues and arguments concerning education and justice is the argument about reverse discrimination where admission to educational programs may be partially determined by an affirmative action program. First of all, can affirmative action programs be justified when they are based explicitly on minority differences? Writing in *The New York Review of Books*, Dworkin argued:

> Affirmative action programs use racially explicit criteria because their immediate goal is to increase the number of members of certain races in these professions. But their long-term goal is to reduce the degree to which American society is overall a racially conscious society (Dworkin 1977, p. 11).

In the same article Dworkin summarizes arguments for affirmative action by Archibald Cox:

> A racially conscious test for admission, even one that sets aside certain places for qualified minority applicants exclusively, serves goals that are in themselves unobjectionable and even urgent. Such programs are, moreover, the only means that offer any significant promise of achieving these goals (p. 12).

The answer as to whether affirmative action programs can be justified seems to be in terms of their long-range goals. Different treatment may result in more women obtaining professional status, which may result in a reduction of the differences presently existing between female and male aspirants. In other words, different treatment at certain times can be justified if it leads toward a greater degree of equality in society. This would be similar to Rawls's position that "an inequality of opportunity must enhance the opportunities of those with the lesser opportunity" (Rawls 1971, p. 303).

The second issue and a conflicting claim for justice is the violation of the constitutional rights of those denied opportunities to pursue a particular form of education. Can this be justified on the grounds that one person's loss may be balanced by results in benefits to society as a whole? Is the experiment of taking the risk to establish a more just social system justifiable if it impinges upon the personal rights of even one individual?

Using justice as a basis for making educational decisions has led to a curious predicament, and it is almost impossible to generalize outcomes. At best, it can be stated that in *each* case where unequal or different educational treatment is suggested, the justification must be based upon clearly relevant differences, and these differences cannot be categorically specified because they may be only temporarily relevant or relevant in one situation and irrelevant in another. Decisions as to what is relevant can be aided by using as the ultimate criteria a more just society in which all people have secured the right to well-being and freedom and true access to the broadly defined social goods. In other words, if one can hold as a standard a vision of a truly just society, each new claim for unequal treatment can be measured against this standard. If the differences do not appear to be relevant to the ultimate goal sought, then no difference in treatment should be allowed.

REFERENCES

Andersson, Theodore, and Boyer, Mildred. *Bilingual Schooling in the United States,* 2 vols. Austin, Texas: Southwest Educational Development Laboratory, 1971.

Ardener, Edwin. "Belief and the Problem of Women," and "The 'Problem' Revisited." In *Perceiving Women,* edited by Shirley Ardener. London: Malaby Press, 1975, pp. 1-18 and 19-27.

Baratz, Stephen S., and Baratz, Joan C. "Early Childhood Intervention." *Harvard Educational Review* 40 (February 1970): 29-50.

Bem, Sandra L. "The Measurement of Psychological Androgyny." *Journal of Consulting and Clinical Psychology* 42 (April 1974): 155-62.

Cole, Michael, and Bruner, Jerome S. "Cultural Differences and Inferences about Psychological Processes." *American Psychologist* 26 (October 1971): 867-76.

Dahrendorf, Rolf. "On the Origin of Social Inequality." In *The Concept of Equality,* edited by William T. Blackstone. Minneapolis, Minn.: Burgess Publishing Co., 1969.

Dinnerstein, Leonard, and Reimers, David M. *Ethnic Americans: A History of Immigration and Assimilation.* New York: Dodd, Mead and Co., 1975.

Dworkin, Ronald. "Why Bakke Has No Case." *New York Review of Books* 34 (10 November 1977): 11-15.

Ellis, H.G. "Theories of Academic and Social Failure of Oppressed Black Students: Source, Motives, and Influences." In *The Anthropological Study of Education,* edited by Craig J. Calhoun and F.A.J. Ianni. The Hague: Mouton, 1976.

Fox, Lynn H. "Mathematically Precocious: Male or Female?" In *Mathematics Learning: What Research Says about Sex Differences,* edited by Elizabeth

Fennema. Columbus, Ohio: ERIC Center for Science, Mathematics, and Environmental Education, College of Education, Ohio State University, 1975.

Frankena, William K. "The Concept of Social Justice." In *Social Justice*, edited by Richard B. Brandt. Englewood Cliffs, N.J.: Prentice-Hall, 1962.

Frazier, Nancy, and Sadker, Myra. *Sexism in School and Society*. New York: Harper & Row 1973.

Fuchs, Estelle, and Havighurst, Robert J. *To Live on This Earth: American Indian Education*. New York: Anchor Press/Doubleday, 1973.

Gibson, Margaret. "Approaches to Multicultural Education in the United States: Some Concepts and Assumptions." *Anthropology and Education Quarterly* 8, no. 4 (1976): 7-18.

Golden, Gloria, and Hunter, Lisa. *In All Fairness: A Handbook on Sex Role Bias in Schools*. San Francisco, Calif.: Far West Laboratory for Educational Research and Development, 1974.

Good, Thomas L.; Sikes, J. Neville; and Brophy, Jere E. "Effects of Teacher Sex and Student Sex on Classroom Interaction." *Journal of Educational Psychology* 65 (August 1973): 74-87.

Grady, Kathleen E. "Androgyny Reconsidered." Paper presented at the Eastern Psychological Association Meetings, New York City, April 1975.

Greene, Maxine. "The Impacts of Irrelevance: Women in the History of American Education." Chapter Two in this volume.

Jensen, Arthur. "How Much Can We Boost IQ and Scholastic Achievement?" *Harvard Educational Review* 39 (Winter 1969): 1-123.

Kaplan, Alexandra G., and Bean, Jean P. *Beyond Sex-Role Stereotypes: Readings toward a Psychology of Adrogyny*. Boston: Little, Brown, & Co., 1976.

Keim, Albert N. *Compulsory Education and the Amish: The Right Not to Be Modern*. Boston: Beacon Press, 1975.

Kemer, B.J. "A Study of the Relationship between the Sex of the Student and the Assignment of Marks by Secondary School Teachers." Doctoral dissertation, Michigan State University, 1965.

Lakoff, Robin. *Language and Women's Place*. New York: Harper & Row, 1975.

Maccoby, Eleanor E., and Jacklin, Carol N. *The Psychology of Sex Differences*. Stanford, Calif.: Stanford University Press, 1974.

Mead, Margaret. *Cooperation and Competition among Primitive Peoples*. Boston: Beacon Press, 1937.

Middleton, John. *From Child to Adult*. Austin, Texas: University of Texas Press, 1976.

Rawls, John. *A Theory of Justice*. Cambridge, Mass.: Harvard University Press, 1971.

Spindler, George. *Education and Cultural Process*. New York: Holt, Rinehart & Winston, 1974.

Stacey, Judith; Bereaud, Susan; and Daniels, Joan, eds. *And Jill Came Tumbling After: Sexism in American Education*. New York: Dell Publishing Co., 1974.

Vlastos, Gregory. "Justice and Equality." In *Social Justice*, edited by Richard B. Brandt. Englewood Cliffs, N.J.: Prentice-Hall, 1962.

Williams, Bernard. "The Idea of Equality." In *Philosophy, Politics, and Society*, edited by Peter Laslett and W.G. Runciman. Oxford: Basil Blackwell, 1967.

Williams, Thomas R. *Introduction to Socialization: Human Culture Transmitted*. St. Louis, Mo.: C.V. Mosby Co., 1972.

Women on Words and Images. *Dick and Jane as Victims: Sex Stereotyping in Children's Readers*. Princeton, N.J.: Women on Words and Images, P.O. Box 2163, 1972.

2

The Impacts of Irrelevance: Women in the History of American Education

Maxine Greene

"The notion basic to justice," writes R.S. Peters, "is that distinctions should be made if there are relevant differences and that they should not be made if there are no relevant differences or on the basis of irrelevant differences."[1] The history of women's education in the United States is a history of distinctions made "on the basis of irrelevant differences." That means it is a history of unfairness and inequity. Women were denied equality of consideration over the years; those who denied them that equality felt no obligation to justify what they did. This was because of the way they selected out factors to be considered relevant and because of the way official notions of relevance were imposed and internalized. Righteously and with perfect self-assurance, those in positions of power did what they could to perpetuate the existence of a separate (and subordinate) female sphere.

There is no need to summon up evocations of ancient myths and

Reprinted by permission of the publisher from Maxine Greene, *Landscapes of Learning* (New York, Teachers College Press, © 1978 by Teachers College, Columbia University. All rights reserved), pp. 225-43.

illusions to explain the exclusion of women from the universe of
"all men" presumably "created equal." Natural rights theory,
which gave rise to so much of the American belief system, was itself
qualified by such remarks as Rousseau's that, "The whole education
of women ought to be relative to men."[2] Great apostles of the
enlightenment like Dr. Benjamin Rush called for "a peculiar and
suitable education" for "our ladies." The institutions of liberty and
equality gave women a special responsibility: they were appointed
to instruct "their *sons* in the principles of liberty."[3]

According to the governing construct, women had duties but few
rights. It was not only that they were considered mentally inferior
and that the "dictates of nature" (as one woman explained) required
the home to be each woman's "appropriate and appointed sphere of
action."[4] In a country where, for a moment, almost anything seemed
possible, where what was thought to be civilized could at any time be
abandoned for life on the frontier or in the wilderness, where
violence and anarchy seemed always incipient,[5] there was a felt need
for a moral anchor—a place where order reigned, along with
propriety and control. That, of course, was the responsibility of
women: to establish in the home a counterweight to temptation, to
maintain moral norms. If females were to be educated, it was (as
Catharine Beecher was to say) to fulfill their "peculiar
responsibilities."[6] The fact that they were barred from civil and
political affairs, the fact that they had no legal identity, the fact that
they were, in effect, the chattels of their husbands, all this was
compensated for because precedence was given to them "in all the
comforts, conveniences, and courtesies of life."

When de Tocqueville visited the United States in 1830-31, he was
impressed by the discovery that, here, "The independence of woman
is irrecoverably lost in the bonds of matrimony. . . ." He spoke of the
many ways in which democracy seemed to modify social
inequalities and then made the point that Americans made an
exception when it came to equality between the sexes.

> They admit, that as nature has appointed such wide differences between the
> physical and moral constitution of man and woman, her manifest design was to
> give a distinct employment to their various faculties; and they hold that
> improvement does not consist in making beings so dissimilar do pretty nearly
> the same things, but in getting each of them to fulfill their respective tasks in the
> best possible manner. The Americans have applied to the sexes the great

principle of political economy which governs the manufactures of our age, by carefully dividing the duties of man from those of woman, in order that the great work of society may be the better carried on.[7]

There is some suggestion of economic determinism here, but it must be pointed out that even before the development of the factory system the same division was assumed to exist. This was so despite the shared labors characteristic of domestic industry. As on the frontier, women performed many of the chores usually allotted to men; when left alone, they did whatever they needed to do to survive: ran shops, pushed plows, and repaired machinery. Nevertheless, the traditional notion was stubbornly held in mind. Women were considered predominantly spiritual creatures, emotional and delicate; if they were to be educated at all, the purpose was to educate them for dutiful and dependent lives—for subordination and powerlessness.

When, in the 1830s, the reform movement (which included campaigns for abolition, women's rights, war resistance, and prison reform) began to focus on education rather than "conversion," the notion of subordination was made surprisingly explicit. In the first place, the effort to consolidate existing schools and establish an effective school system was fueled by dread of lawlessness. Not only was it necessary to socialize a great diversity of children into a way of life increasingly dominated by industry, it appeared essential as well to Americanize, through schooling, those who had no experience with freedom—and who seemed all too prone to confuse liberty with license.[8] Whether the dominating concern was to create a literate and disciplined working class. To impose a middle-class and Protestant *ethos*, or to erect barriers against corruption and disorder, the expressed commitment was to "social control." This meant, of course, the internalization of respect for the laws of righteousness and for existing social authorities. Antisocial energies and appetites were to be tamped down; "impetuosity" was to be subordinated to "voluntary compliance."[9] The entire effort and the prevailing atmosphere were thought of as redemptive, humane, and benign.

The teachers in those early schools were largely female. Seldom, if ever, provided with more than an elementary school education themselves, they were granted little status, and their wages were abysmally low. But then it was acceptable to hire young women, who would otherwise be totally dependent as daughters or sisters or wards and pay them less than an ordinary clerk received. Most of them were thought of as spinsters, and, in any case, they were expected to remain unmarried if they hoped to remain in the schools. Few communities could afford better teaching for the younger children, and it is clear enough that women's second-class position allowed school committees, without apology, to tap the pool of the cheapest labor while keeping the lamp of morality alight. After all, who was better equipped to trim that lamp and shelter it from the wind? Henry Barnard, the Connecticut school reformer, was only one of many when he talked of how well prepared such women were—because they were persons "in whose own hearts, love, hope, and patience have first kept school."[10]

Horace Mann, in his Tenth Report as Secretary of the Massachusetts Board of Education, asked his readers to picture the model teacher. Can you imagine a person, he said,

> whose language is well selected, whose pronunciation and tones of voice are correct and attractive, whose manners are gentle and refined, all whose topics of conversation are elevating and instructive, whose benignity of heart is constantly manifested in acts of civility, courtesy, and kindness, and who spreads a nameless charm over whatever circle may be entered? Such a person should the teacher of every Common School be.[11]

Constant emphasis was placed on gentility and docility, the virtues long associated with the female sphere. What is interesting is the consonance between these virtues, the virtues normally linked to hearth and home, and what was thought desirable in the common school. Women teachers were seldom hired to teach older children nor to deal with more than elementary literacy. Their minds were not considered acute enough to handle mathematics or the natural sciences. Their assigned role, indeed their fate, was to mold other people's children, to bind them to respectability and virtue with cords they could not easily break. They were genteel, intrusive models; they were stern mother surrogates; delegated to impose social control, they often ran their classrooms with iron hands.

Nevertheless, they knew—and the community knew—that they were strictly subordinated to the men who administered the schools. The principals and superintendents were male; they were responsible for the curriculum, for discipline, for the moral regimen the teachers were to carry out, and even for the ways in which the classrooms were arranged. David Tyack quotes a journal article stating that, "Women teachers are often preferred by superintendents because they are more willing to comply with established regulations and less likely to ride headstrong hobbies." And then:

> If teachers have advice to give their superior, said the Denver superintendent of schools, "it is to be given as the good daughter talks with the father.... The dictation must come from the other end." In 1841, the Boston school committee commended women teachers because they were unambitious, frugal, and filial: "they are less intent on scheming for future honors or emoluments.... As a class, they never look forward, as young men almost invariably do, to a period of legal emancipation from parental control."[12]

The primary concern of the common school was to move all children, boys *and* girls, to "voluntary compliance"; it is not hard to imagine the special lessons in compliance taught to girls. The image of the obviously subordinate woman must have been powerful enough, but when this was linked to the materials in, say, the McGuffey Readers—with their almost exclusive emphasis on "the good boy," "the poor boy," the boy who stood on the burning deck, and the rest[13]—the construct of the second sphere (the inferior sphere) can only have been continuously confirmed.

There were ordinary young women, however, apart from the early feminists, who did break the pattern of submission and conformity—or, at least, who thought they did. They were the mill girls, who left home to work for wages only to find that they were discriminated against in the factories as much as anywhere else. Not only did they have to work from twelve to sixteen hours a day, they were paid far less than men. Frequently they were compelled to live in company dormitories and submit to rigid discipline. This may well be considered to be still another mode of female education: values and skills were intentionally transmitted, not to mention a whole structure of attitudes and beliefs. Lucy Larcom, who first had wanted to "keep school" as her aunt had done, went to work in the Lowell mills in 1835, when she was about thirteen; she wrote that she thought it a good thing for so many strange girls to leave their homes and go to Lowell, because "it taught them to go out of themselves and enter into the lives of others"[14] and because it appeared to be a way of belonging to the world.

The Lowell mills, in fact, became a tourist attraction, largely due to such girls. Charles Dickens and Harriet Martineau both commented on the self-respect, the good clothes, the fine manners of the thousands of young women who worked there for less than three dollars a week on five-year stints. The operatives had libraries and their own newspapers, but they worked seventy hours a week, and payments for their food and lodging were deducted from their wages. Their "education" included regular church attendance, Sunday School classes, and occasional classes in the fundamentals of literacy; they were required to avoid card games as well as "ardent spirits" and to refrain from all modes of dissolute behavior.[15] Their "intelligence" and contentment were widely advertised, but it is obvious that they were being cared for by the factory managers, puritanical father surrogates who could allow little leeway for spontaneity or choice of self. There were male operatives in some mills and male inhabitants of company towns, but there is no evidence of such protective behavior on their behalf, perhaps because working men, though subordinate, belonged to the sphere where protection and care were not required.

Herman Melville, having visited the Lowell mills and seen the workers there, wrote a story about a paper mill based upon his experience. He called it "The Tartarus of Maids"; it deals with blue-white girls sorting rags, serving iron machines, folding paper, moving through the "consumptive pallors of this blank, raggy life...." Near the end, the narrator speaks with the principal proprietor about his machines and his girls:

> "The girls," echoed I, glancing around at their silent forms. "Why is it, sir, that in most factories, female operatives, of whatever age, are indiscriminately called girls, never women?"
> "Oh! as to that, why, I suppose, the fact of their being generally unmarried—that's the reason, I should think. But it never struck me before. For our factory here, we will not have married women; they are apt to be off-and-on too much. We want none but steady workers: twelve hours to the day, day after day, through the three hundred and sixty-five days, excepting Sundays, Thanksgiving, and Fast-days. That's our rule. And so, having no married women, what females we have are rightly enough called girls."[16]

The girls are compared at the conclusion with the bachelors the narrator had met near London's Temple bar, in a "very perfection of quiet absorption of good living, good drinking, good feeling, and good talk,"[17] men who knew nothing of suffering and loneliness.

These are the two extremes—a Paradise and a Tartarus—but the distinction between the spheres is highlighted in a kind of lurid glare. Melville was able to make a second, more ambiguous distinction as well: between women and girls—those in the protective circle of domestic life and those infantilized by factory managers, bent (like grateful and virtuous daughters) over work tables and looms.

Infantilization and segregation were too often linked with education in the lives of nineteenth century women. It is true that the fiction of the happy, well-cared-for Lowell girls was to a degree destroyed when a Lowell Female Labor Reform Association was organized, in time to be led by Sarah Bagley, who wrote of herself as "a common schooled New England female factory operative...."[18] They engaged in a petition campaign in an unsuccessful effort to move the legislature to enact a ten-hour day. They could not vote, but they tried to exert pressure at election time to defeat unsympathetic legislators. They did not win what they wanted; they were held back by male union members as well as by the factory managers; they continued to be treated as "girls." But the very fact that they moved together for a while suggests that they had not fully internalized the official view of themselves as helpless, docile, and insistently happy. They were schooled, but not well schooled.

Catharine Beecher, daughter of Lyman Beecher and sister of Harriet Beecher Stowe, was perturbed by the spectacle of women going to work in factories and, because so many eligible men were going west to the frontier, an increasing number of "surplus" females were being forced to earn their own living—more often than not as operatives. After conducting a seminary for young women at Hartford (where "*intellectual* culture" was deliberately subordinated to "the formation of that character which Jesus Christ teaches to be indispensable to the *eternal* well being of our race" and where girls were taught their social duty in the world[19]), Miss Beecher turned, in 1827, to female improvement generally. Struck by the disproportion between the number of people who wanted to hire domestic servants and the number of women who wanted to go into domestic service (because of the larger compensation offered by "our manufactories") and impressed also by the importance of the common schools, she began to elaborate on her Christian notions of women's highest calling:

When all the mothers, teachers, nurses and domestics are taken from our sex, which the best interests of society demand, and when all these employments are deemed respectable and are filled by well-educated women, there will be no supernumeraries found to put into shops and mills or to draw into the arena of public and political life.[20]

Beecher's contribution to women's education was to suggest that household work demanded intellectual skills and that women of all classes deserved a well-rounded education in such areas as physiology, hygiene, nutrition, and applied mathematics. Women had their "proper work" to do, she was saying, but that work should be viewed as dignified.[21] Nevertheless (and this must be stressed), she continued to assert that "certain relations" had to be maintained "which involve the duties of subordination.... There must be the relations of husband and wife, parent and child, teacher and pupil, employer and employed, each involving the relative duties of subordination."[22] Her efforts to establish normal schools for teachers, important as they were, were equally permeated with the notion that it was more important "that women be educated to be virtuous, useful, and pious, than that they become learned and accomplished...."[23]

Emma Hart Willard, who herself had received an advanced education, saw the problem of intellectual development quite differently. Largely due to her own fascination with higher mathematics and the frustration she experienced at not being allowed to attend the men's examinations at the University of Middlebury, the Troy Female Seminary she established in 1821 not only included courses in advanced algebra and geometry but more explicit courses in physiology than had yet been offered. This did not mean that she neglected religious training nor the "truths" of the Scriptures. Nor did it mean that she challenged the "service" obligations of women.[24] She did, however, provide high school opportunities at a time when no high schools were open to females; as significantly, she began—at least by indirection—to erode the conventional belief that there were differences in mental capacity between men and women.

She did not, and undoubtedly could not, go as far as the Scotch feminist, Frances Wright, who arrived in the United States in 1819 and launched her campaign for educational emancipation and social justice. An associate of the utopian thinker Robert Owen, she worked at New Harmony, edited a newspaper, and lectured to audiences of workingmen throughout the East and Middle West. Not only did she demand equal education for women, she launched a critique of religious dogmas and, like other Owenites, called for the establishment of free boarding schools to promote the eradication of class differences and class control.[25] Probably of most importance was her continual demand that people begin thinking for themselves. Like Henry David Thoreau, she called on men and women to examine the *grounds* of their beliefs, to open their eyes and inquire; unlike Thoreau and his transcendentalist contemporaries, she spoke directly to those who were subordinated in society, to those—women and workers both—she thought to be oppressed.

And, indeed, the oppression was multifaceted. The maintenance of the two spheres made it immeasurably difficult for women to overcome the feeling that they were the creatures of outside authorities. Harriet Martineau, after one of her visits, spoke directly to the problem when she described the ways in which American women were even deprived of the right to determine what precisely their duties were:

> If there be any human power and business and privilege which is absolutely universal, it is the discovery and adoption of the principle and laws of duty. As every individual, whether man or woman, has a reason and a conscience, this is a work which each is thereby authorized to do for himself or herself. But it is not only virtually prohibited to beings who, like the American woman, have scarcely any objects in life proposed to them; but the whole apparatus of opinion is brought to bear offensively upon individuals among women who exercise freedom of mind in deciding upon what duty is, and the methods by which it is to be pursued.[26]

Emma Willard, Elizabeth Peabody, Margaret Fuller, and the others who were courageous enough to identify themselves and their commitments belonged, it must be recalled, to a privileged class. In most cases, they were admired or indulged or sustained by their fathers or by interested male friends. It was *possible* for them to demand, as Margaret Fuller did, total fulfillment,[27] to reject renunciation, and to enter and enjoy "the Paradise of thought."[28] Numerous others, middle-class and working-class women alike, retained the image of themselves as destined to subordination and dependence; the schools, with few exceptions, reinforced what they had internalized from their earliest days.

Even Mary Lyon, who tried so hard to provide the female students at Mount Holyoke Seminary with the same academic education men were receiving, wrote to her mother, "O how immensely important is this work of preparing the daughters of the land to be good mothers!"[29] Convinced as she was of the importance of domestic knowledge, she herself worked desperately hard outside the domestic sphere. It took her about four years to raise the necessary money from the surrounding community. Frequently she was forced to rely on male representatives and spokesmen, so that people would not think women were originating such far-reaching plans. When the seminary opened in 1837, Miss Lyon inaugurated a curriculum as rigorous and academic as the one at Harvard. The students were carefully selected; they were expected to attend for three years, during which they took such courses as grammar, rhetoric, human physiology, algebra, natural philosophy, intellectual philosophy, astronomy, chemistry, ecclesiastical history, logic, and natural theology. They also performed domestic duties, of course, but as Eleanor Flexner has written, Mary Lyon helped to demonstrate "that women's minds were constituted, in bulk and cell structure and endowment, the same as those of their masculine counterparts. . . . "[30] What was required, as always, was opportunity to act on such capacities—opportunity at least more likely for the daughters of businessmen and ministers than for the children of the poor.

The atmosphere was restrictive at Mount Holyoke in spite of some of the liberating ideas. Emily Dickinson attended the seminary briefly in 1847 and found it too confining. Some time later she wrote a poem about respectability, which may in some sense incorporate part of her response:

> *What soft, cherubic creatures*
> *These gentlewomen are!*
> *One would as soon assault a plush*
> *Or violate a star.*
>
> *Such dimity convictions,*
> *A horror so refined*
> *Of freckled human nature,*
> *Of Deity ashamed,—*

It's such a common glory,
A fisherman's degree!
Redemption, brittle lady,
Be so ashamed of thee.[31]

Like many poems, this one means variously; among the possibilities it opens to the reader is an ironic view of the second sphere. The "gentlewomen," exposed to knowledge, equipped with what they believe to be "convictions," are the same conventional creatures Harriet Martineau described: people who did not have the "freedom of mind" required for deciding themselves what their duty was—for identifying a meaningful "redemption," one that was their own. Surely more was needed than an education in grammar and natural philosophy. It was possible for women to have minds equal to those of "their masculine counterparts" and, at once, to perpetuate a delicate, "dimity" conception of themselves. Only a few succeeded in emancipating themselves; only a few, in the mid-nineteenth century, transcended the "fisherman's degree."

It seemed to some that Oberlin College, founded in 1833 to serve both men and women and both whites and blacks, would overcome the traditional separation. It was a school founded in the spirit of abolitionism and reform, but in fact it reinforced the idea that educated women were to be helpmates, responsible for the mental health and moral balance of men doing evangelical work upon the frontier. Again, the old distinction was made: the attitude of the college was that, "women's highest calling was to be the mothers of the race, and that they should stay within that special sphere in order that future generations should not suffer from the want of devoted and undistracted mother care."[32] Women were segregated from men at the college, and they were required to do domestic work, including the laundry of their male fellow-students.

Lucy Stone and other feminists-to-be attended Oberlin in the early 1840s, but only on occasion did they break into such male fields as theology. Lucy Stone had already been a district school teacher and was older than many of the other students. She was active in peace and antislavery work on campus, and, when ready to graduate, she was selected to write a commencement oration. When she discovered that the oration would have to be read for her by a male student, she refused to accept the honor at all and went on, of course, to become a public speaker for the antislavery cause and for women's rights.

Lucy Stone was an exception—another exception. Most of the women at Oberlin acquiesced: they would live their lives as inferior and sustaining beings; they would accommodate to the "special sphere." But as the years went on and the country became more industrialized, more diverse, and more complex, increasing numbers of women became restive in the bonds of gentility and segregation. After the Civil War, more and more colleges opened for women, as high schools became available to girls.

There were Vassar, Smith, and (notably) Bryn Mawr. M. Carey Thomas, herself educated at Cornell, Johns Hopkins, and the University of Leipzig, was Dean and then President of Bryn Mawr. Like other women's colleges, Bryn Mawr created an island of intellectual commitment in a wilderness of acquisitiveness and exploitation, but M. Carey Thomas articulated, more boldly than many others, the necessity for loosening family ties and emancipating young women from traditional roles. The "Bryn Mawr type" was to effect a new equality in human relationships; Miss Thomas saw no reason why women should not enter all the technical and professional fields. "There is no reason to believe," she said, "that typhoid or scarlet fever or phthisis can be successfully treated by a woman physician in one way and by a man physician in another way. There is indeed every reason to believe that unless treated in the best way, the patient may die, the sex of the doctor affecting the result less even than the sex of the patient."[33]

Invigorating though these ideas surely were, successful though many Bryn Mawr graduates turned out to be, the separation between the spheres was not overcome. For educated, middle-class women, it was simply recast. For M. Carey Thomas (and she was in many ways exemplary), intellectual prowess and domesticity were irreconcilable; marriage and childbearing both were anathema to her, and she communicated some of this to her students. Ordinary sexuality seemed to her to be irrelevant; for the intellectual woman, friendships could and probably should take the place of the dependency required of the wife. Indeed, the majority of women college graduates in the late nineteenth century never married; the professional roles that most of them chose were nurturing roles, traditionally feminine roles: social worker, librarian, nurse, and teacher most of all. Because they chose in that fashion, it seems clear that their own internalized conflicts were seldom resolved. Few were so aggressively committed to the "intellectual renunciation" M. Carey Thomas prescribed. Most were afflicted by the ways in which social reality was interpreted by the people around, by the "official" definitions of women's powers and women's proper spheres. And, indeed, the schools—through the models they presented and in the absence of any effort at critique—could not but perpetuate what was taken for granted.

Novelists exposed it: women writers like Kate Chopin, Mary Austin, Mary Wilkins Freeman, and Edith Wharton, and certain male writers like Frank Norris, Theodore Dreiser, and Henry James.[34] In 1892, Henry James noted the "growing divorce between the American woman... and the male American immersed in the ferocity of business, with no time for any but the most sordid interests.... The divorce is rapidly becoming a gulf—an abyss of inequality, the like of which has never before been seen under the sun."[35]

But on all sides the separation of the sexes was encouraged by censors, pastors, and even by frightened women's groups who feared the loss of support. In a speech at a Baltimore meeting of the American Academy of Medicine in 1895, a Professor Ward Hutchinson said:

> The woman who works outside of the home or school pays a fearful penalty, either physical, mental, or moral, or often all three. She commits a biologic crime against herself and against the community, and woman labor ought to be forbidden for the same reason that child labor is. Any nation that works its women is damned, and belongs at heart to the Huron-Iroquois confederacy.[36]

And Dr. Hutchinson was only one of many. Henry Adams talked that way; scientific and educational writers emphasized the dangers implicit in making women learned; G. Stanley Hall at Johns Hopkins celebrated what he called the "madonna conception"[37] and called for monthly programs centered around the "Sabbath" of menstruation.

Faced with such a campaign of mystification, Jane Addams was undoubtedly not alone in being almost paralyzed early in her life by the conflicting claims of femininity and the desire to make a difference in the world.[38] She resolved the conflict when she discovered the existence of a British reform movement called "Christian Renaissance" and the possibility of becoming a kind of womanly saint through social reform. The establishment of Hull House turned out to be the solution. Her religious approach to education as the saving of souls and her involvement with early progressive thought led her to talk of "social control"[39] when she addressed the problem of inducting immigrant children into the society of the early twentieth century and even when she discussed the importance of pluralism or the recognition of cultural diversity. She resembled Lillian Wald, founder of the Henry Street Settlement, in considering teaching and social work to be her "natural" provinces; there is no question but that such women, displacing aspects of their femininity, played more sophisticated (and more knowledgeable) versions of the roles enacted by the "elevating and instructive" young women who first taught in the common schools.

For all the separateness of the spheres, however, and for all the tendency of women professionals to accede to the need for social control, some remarkable female educators appeared on the scene in the early part of the twentieth century—the century known to some as the "century of the child."[40] There was Ella Flagg Young, who worked with John Dewey in the Laboratory School he established at the University of Chicago and who later became the first woman superintendent of schools in Chicago. Not only did she work against the daily supervision that degraded so many teachers, she argued strongly for more women superintendents because she said (not surprisingly), "It is woman's natural field and she is no longer satisfied to do the greatest part of the work and yet be denied the leadership."[41]

There was Julia Richman, the first Jewish woman superintendent in New York City, who helped lay the foundations for testing by proposing that children be divided in terms of their ability into "the brightest material," "medium material," and the "poorest material."[42] In many respects, she was similar to Horace Mann in her righteous passion to improve, to Americanize, to tamp down incorrigibility, and to remedy through schooling the deprivation she found among the immigrants and the very poor.

And there were the great progressive innovators and educators: Margaret Naumburg, who founded what was to become the Walden School in 1915; Caroline Pratt, who opened the Play School (later, the City and Country School) in 1914; Marietta Johnson, who established an Organic School in Fairhope, Alabama, in 1907; Lucy Sprague Mitchell, who founded the Bureau of Educational Experiments (later, the Bank Street College of Education) in 1916, and others. With some exceptions, these women belonged to the stream of progressivism that carried with it interests in art, play, and therapeutic self-expression—what has been called the "romantic" dimension of progressive thought.

This was not, in their cases, because they were not well-educated or intellectual. All had had rich experiences in learning in the United States and abroad, and a number were well grounded in aesthetics and psychology. It has partly to do with the inherent appeal of the new freedom then associated with progressive ideas. Educators, particularly in the 1920s, selected out different aspects of the approach: some responded to the scientific component; others, to the implications for measurement; others, to the "life-adjustment" overtones; still others, to the concern for social control. The tendency of women educators to act on the possibilities of personal freedom in what *they* understood to be progressivism (and to reconceive the "child" each one was supposed to be) is an indication of their own awareness of constraints.

It was not nearly so simple for women to attain leadership positions in the public school systems, as it was not nearly so likely for women public school teachers to achieve autonomy. Diane Ravitch writes of the poorly trained women teachers in the early part of the century in New York:

> School officials preferred having female teachers, because they could save money by paying women less than men. Women were glad to have teaching jobs because it was one of the few respectable occupations open to them. And women were blatantly discriminated against by the school system. They were paid less than half of what men received for the same job.[43]

Until 1904, in fact, there was a bylaw in New York City that required the immediate dismissal of a female teacher who married. As late as 1932, the sociologist Willard Waller was commenting on the low social standing of the teacher, the paltry rewards, "the assimilation of the teacher to the female character ideal." In fact, he said, "It has been said that no woman and no Negro is ever fully admitted to the white man's world."[44] He wrote, as others had before him, of the teacher as child and of the negative status of the teacher being partly due to the extension of the child's perceptions of that teacher into his or her adult life.

Looking back, we may find it startling that so few women considered themselves or openly defined themselves as oppressed. Now and then in history there has been an expression of identification with the black person, slave or free, sometimes following the lead of Frederick Douglass, who made his sympathy with the women's rights movement so eloquently clear.

The Grimké sisters, Sarah and Angelina, are glowing examples. Not only did they, as slaveholders' daughters, perceive the full horror of slavery, they left the South on that account. Active in the antislavery movement, they were often barred—because they were women—from public platforms. Sarah Grimké wrote an essay on "The Equality of the Sexes," which makes clear the relation between the subordination of women and the plight of the slaves. She talked about women's "deficient education," the way in which they were treated as "pretty toys or mere instruments of pleasure," and the differential pay scales for men and women. "A man who is engaged in teaching can always, I believe, command a higher price for tuition than a woman—even when he teaches the same branches, and is not in any respect superior to the woman."[45] The same thing was true, she wrote, in tailoring, laundry work, and other fields where males and females worked side by side. And then she wrote:

> There is another class of women in this country, to whom I cannot refer, without feelings of the deepest shame and sorrow. I allude to our female slaves. Our southern cities are whelmed beneath a tide of pollution; the virtue of female slaves is wholly at the mercy of irresponsible tyrants.... Nor does the colored woman suffer alone: the moral purity of the white woman is deeply contaminated. In the daily habit of seeing the virtue of her enslaved sister sacrificed without hesitancy or remorse, she looks upon the crimes of seduction and illicit intercourse without horror, and although not personally involved in the guilt, she loses that value for innocence in her own, as well as the other sex, which is one of the strongest safeguards to virtue.[46]

At the end of the passage, she asks, "Can any American woman look at these scenes of shocking licentiousness and cruelty, and fold her hands in apathy, and say, 'I have nothing to do with slavery'? *She cannot and be guiltless.*" Clearly, Sarah Grimké saw the connection between one mode of subordination and another. More significantly, however, she appeared able to identify the connection between *personal* liberation and commitment to human liberation. And she made this clear in the context of a reasoned critique of what she ironically called woman's "appropriate sphere."

There were women, after the Civil War, who did not necessarily express themselves on the interrelationships among various modes of oppression, but who did voluntarily go South to teach the freed slaves. They went immediately after the fighting ended, when the campaign to maintain white supremacy was becoming vicious and violent. The schoolteachers who came from the North were treated as subversive, particularly when they tried to establish integrated or "mixed" schools. One teacher is quoted as saying, with reference to the freed slaves, "Oh what a privilege to be among them when their morning dawns, to see them personally coming forth from the land of Egypt and the house of bondage."[47] Henry Perkinson writes of the "schoolmarms" who even tried to teach Latin and Greek to their students and, most particularly, that blacks were the economic and social equals of whites. Teachers were flogged or tarred and feathered; frequently, their schools were burned. Thus far, we know relatively little[48] about the Yankee schoolteachers' feelings about themselves as women; it is reasonable to believe that however religious and traditional their motivation, on some level they could identify with those who had been in chains.

Some years later, at the start of the new century, Margaret Haley, an organizer for the Teachers' Federation in Chicago, was asking teachers to begin perceiving themselves as a white-collar proletariat.[49] An anonymous college-trained worker said, in answer to a survey in the 1890s, "The same work exactly, which I am engaged in, is done by men in the New York Department at double the pay. I find where women are employed and men are at the head, favoritism plays a very decided part in the matter of salaries. One reason for the inequality in women's wages, as compared with those paid men, is that women are patient in their willingness to earn something, be it ever so little. They *earn* it. They are not situated in life to apply the nerve required to demand what should be theirs justly...."[50] Managers and administrators in the school systems resisted self-assertion on the part of women workers and women teachers. The leaders in the school systems tried to utilize whatever socialization techniques they had available to keep their women employees docile, to make sure that they would never "apply the nerve required...."

On the surface, things have changed for women in education. There are no dual wage scales; there are few controls where, at least, traditional marriage is concerned. Women can, to some degree, attain leadership positions in organizations and unions. There are still relatively few female school administrators and college presidents, affirmative action legislation notwithstanding.[51] Work has only just begun to repair sexist practices in classrooms, to rewrite sexist literature, and to alter attitudes towards work and future expectations. Nevertheless, the existence of the "separate sphere" seems to me unquestionable, even today. There is little evidence of women identifying their subordination with the subordination of other groups in society. There is little explicit recognition of the need for critical consciousness—what Paulo Freire calls "conscientization"[52]—to overcome internalized oppression and perhaps to bring about (even within an inequitable system) a kind of equity.

There must be critique. There must be an ongoing demystification, as there must be an enlarging conversation among those who have the courage to identify themselves as subordinate, as oppressed. The connection between the kind of subordination imposed on women and the kind of subordination imposed on schoolchildren must finally be exposed. Illusions have to be eliminated, writes Carol Gould, the "illusions which bind us all to exploition." Only when we can develop the kind of critique that liberates us from such illusions will there be a possibility of freeing women "to discover and to *choose* what they want to become."[53]

That is indeed the next step for women in education, the step never taken in time past. The problem is to discover whether it *can* be taken apart from the kind of *praxis* that might transform both men's and women's common world.

Notes

1. R.S. Peters, *Ethics and Education* (Glenview, Ill.: Scott, Foresman and Co., 1967), p. 51.

2. William Boyd, ed., *The Emile of Jean-Jacques Rousseau* (New York: Bureau of Publications, Teachers College, Columbia University, 1960), pp. 134-35.

3. Benjamin Rush, *Thoughts upon Female Education* (Philadelphia: Prichard and Hall, 1887), p. 6.

4. Mrs. A.J. Graves, *Woman in America; Being an Examination into the Moral and Intellectual Condition of American Female Society* (New York: Harper and Brothers, 1841), p. 143.

5. Lawrence A. Cremin, ed., *The Republic and the School: Horace Mann on the Education of Free Men* (New York: Bureau of Publications, Teachers College, Columbia University, 1957), pp. 57, 90.

6. Catharine Beecher, "On the Peculiar Responsibility of American Women." In *Roots of Bitterness: Documents of the Social History of American Women*, edited by Nancy F. Cott (New York: E. P. Dutton, 1972), p. 171.

7. Alexis de Tocqueville, *Democracy in America*, vol. 2 (New York: Colonial Press, 1889), pp. 223-24.

8. Horace Mann, in Cremin, *The Republic and the School*, p. 58.

9. Ibid., p. 57.

10. Henry Barnard, "Gradation of Public Schools, with Special Reference to Cities and Large Villages," *American Journal of Education* 2 (December 1856): 461.

11. Horace Mann, "The Massachusetts System of Common Schools: Being an Enlarged and Revised Edition of the Tenth Annual Report of the First Secretary of the Massachusetts Board of Education" (Boston: Dutton and Wentworth, 1849), p. 86.

12. David B. Tyack, *The One Best System: A History of American Urban Education* (Cambridge, Mass.: Harvard University Press, 1974), p. 60.

13. See William Holmes McGuffey, *Newly Revised Eclectic Second Reader* (New York and Cincinnati: W.B. Smith and Co., 1848).

14. "Lucy Larcom's Factory Experience." In *Roots of Bitterness*, edited by Cott, p. 128.

15. Alice Felt Tyler, *Freedom's Ferment* (New York: Harper Torchbooks, 1962), p. 212.

16. Herman Melville, "The Paradise of Bachelors and the Tartarus of Maids." In *Selected Writings of Herman Melville* (New York: Modern Library, 1952), p. 210.

17. Ibid., p. 211.

18. Quoted in Eleanor Flexner, *Centuries of Struggle: The Woman's Rights Movement in the United States* (Cambridge, Mass.: Belknap Press of Harvard University Press, 1975), p. 58.

19. Catharine Beecher, "The Education of Female Teachers." In *The Educated Woman in America*, edited by Barbara M. Cross (New York: Teachers College Press, 1965), pp. 68-69.

20. Catharine Beecher, quoted in Flexner, *Centuries of Struggle*, pp. 30-31.

21. Catharine Beecher, "Ministry of Women." In *The Educated Woman in America*, edited by Cross, pp. 94-95.

22. "On the Peculiar Responsibility of American Women," In *Roots of Bitterness*, edited by Cott, p. 172.

23. Beecher, "The Education of Female Teachers." In *The Educated Woman in America*, edited by Cross, p. 70.

24. See Merle Curti, *The Social Ideas of American Educators* (Totowa, N.J.: Littlefield, Adams and Co., 1959), p. 181.

25. Tyler, *Freedom's Ferment*, pp. 206-211.

26. Harriet Martineau, *Society in America (1837)*, vol. 1 (New York: AMS Press, 1966), pp. 229-30.

27. Margaret Fuller, "Schoolteaching." In *The Educated Woman in America*, edited by Cross, pp. 109-11.

28. Barbara Cross, "Introduction." In *The Educated Woman in America*, pp. 17-30.

29. Curti, *The Social Ideas of American Educators*, p. 185.

30. Flexner, *Centuries of Struggle*, p. 36.

31. Emily Dickinson, "What soft, cherubic creatures..." in *Selected Poems and Letters of Emily Dickinson*, edited by Robert N. Linscott (Garden City, N.Y.: Doubleday-Anchor, 1959), p. 125.

32. Robert S. Fletcher, *History of Oberlin College to the Civil War* (Oberlin, Ohio: Oberlin College Press, 1943), p. 373.

33. M. Carey Thomas, "Education for Women and for Men." In *The Educated Woman in America*, edited by Cross, p. 147.

34. See Kate Chopin, *The Awakening* (New York: Capricorn, 1964); Mary Austin, *Earth Horizon* (Boston: Houghton Mifflin Co., 1932); Mary Wilkins Freeman, *Madelon* (New York: Harper and Brothers, 1896); Edith Wharton, *The House of Mirth* (New York: C. Scribner's Sons, 1905); Frank Norris, *The Pit* (New York: Doubleday, 1928); Theodore Dreiser, *Sister Carrie* (New York: Modern Library, 1947); Henry James, *A Portrait of a Lady* (New York: Washington Square Press, 1966).

35. Henry James, *The Notebooks*, edited by F.O. Matthiessen and Kenneth B. Murdock (New York: Oxford University Press, 1947), p. 129.

36. Quoted in Larzer Ziff, *The American 1890s: Life and Times of a Lost Generation* (New York: Viking Press, 1966), p. 280.

37. G. Stanley Hall, *The Psychology of Adolescence*, vol. 2 (New York: D. Appleton, 1905), p. 627.

38. See Allen F. Davis, *The Life and Legend of Jane Addams* (New York: Oxford University Press, 1963).

39. See Clarence Karier, Paul Violas, and Joel Spring, *Roots of Crisis: American Education in the Twentieth Century* (Chicago: Rand McNally and Co., 1973).

40. Lawrence A. Cremin, *The Transformation of the School* (New York: Alfred A. Knopf, 1961), p. 105.

41. John T. McManis, *Ella Flagg Young and a Half-Century of the Chicago Public Schools* (Chicago: A.C. McClurg, 1916), p. 144.

42. Tyack, *The One Best System*, p. 202.

43. Diane Ravitch, *The Great School Wars: New York City, 1805-1973* (New York: Basic Books, 1974), p. 103.

44. Willard Waller, *Sociology of Teaching* (New York: John Wiley, 1932), p. 50.

45. Sarah Grimké, "Letters on the Equality of the Sexes." In *Roots of Bitterness*, edited by Cott, p. 183.

46. Ibid., pp. 184-85.

47. Henry J. Perkinson, *The Imperfect Panacea: American Faith in Education, 1865-1965* (New York: Random House, 1968), p. 18.

48. See, for example, John Hope Franklin, *Reconstruction: After the Civil War* (Chicago: University of Chicago Press, 1961).

49. Margaret Haley, "Why Teachers Should Organize," *NEA Addresses and Proceedings*, 43rd Annual Meeting, St. Louis, 1904, p. 150.

50. "Testimony on Compensation for Educated Women at Work." In *Roots of Bitterness*, edited by Cott, pp. 336-37.

51. See, for example, Suzanne E. Estler, "Women as Leaders in Public Education." In *Signs: Journal of Women in Culture and Society* 1 (Winter 1975): 363-86.

52. Paulo Freire, *Pedagogy of the Oppressed* (New York: Herder and Herder, 1967).

53. Carol Gould, "Philosophy of Liberation and the Liberation of Philosophy." In *Women and Philosophy: Toward a Theory of Liberation*, edited by Carol C. Gould and Marx W. Wartofsky (New York: Putnam, 1976), p. 38.

3

Career and Life Satisfactions among Terman's Gifted Women

Pauline S. Sears and Ann H. Barbee

To define—and to live—a satisfying life is clearly the prime goal of most human beings, whether their IQ is 80 or 180. In the last few years we have seen an expansion of thinking with regard to women's options and choices in the pursuit of this goal. It is likely that women of differing ages, cultural backgrounds, talents, life experiences, and predispositions arrive at differing conclusions about what constitutes satisfaction in life-style for them at different points in time. This study utilizes data from the fifty-year longitudinal study initiated by Lewis M. Terman,[1] and attempts to

1. Melita Oden and Sheila Buckholtz, among others, have maintained the files over the years. Oden (1968) is the author of the publication preceding Sears (1977) and this one, and of course Lewis Terman conceived and directed the project until his death in 1956. With coauthors, he produced four volumes on the earlier development of his gifted "children" (Terman et al. 1925; Burks, Jensen, and Terman 1930; Terman and Oden 1947; Terman 1959). As in any study of this type,

Reprinted, by permission, from J. Stanley et al., eds., *The Gifted and Creative: A Fifty Year Perspective* (Baltimore: Johns Hopkins University Press, 1978), pp. 28-65.

isolate those factors contributing to satisfaction in gifted women following careers, variously and in combination, as income workers, wives, mothers, and homemakers.

DESCRIPTION OF THE SAMPLE

This research samples one cohort of women, born on the average about 1910, growing up during World War I, finishing high school just before the Great Depression, and living their early years in urban areas of California. They have most recently reported their current and retrospective life satisfactions in 1972, as they saw them at average age about sixty-two (Figure 3.1).[2]

The present sample consists of 430 California women, selected in the 1920s as falling in the upper 1 percent of the population according to tested intelligence. The subjects had a minimum IQ of 135. Field contacts were made with the subjects, their parents, and their teachers in 1921, 1927, 1939, and 1950. Mail surveys were carried out in 1936, 1945, 1955, 1960, and 1972, a total of nine contacts over the fifty years.

As of 1972, the 430 women responding to the questionnaire were classified as to their marital status, work pattern, and whether or not they had children. Percentages of the total sample falling into various groups are shown in Table 3.1. The large portion was currently married and living with a husband. This may not be a first husband—many divorces and second, third, and even fourth marriages have taken place in the group.

Another measure of marital status was used to separate those women who appeared to be independent or "on their own." In addition to the single women, all women who were either divorced or widowed and who had remained so since 1960 were classified as

---

much of the credit goes to the hundreds of subjects who have faithfully and conscientiously provided the information necessary to the success of this project. Robert Wolfe and Richard DeVeaux have acted as statistical consultants in the later stages of the data analysis presented here. Julian Stanley, Lee Cronbach, and Robert Sears have provided helpful criticisms of analysis and manuscript.

2. It would be of much interest to secure additional cohorts differing in age and/or geographical location to compare with this sample. Later we shall present such comparative data as are currently available for this purpose.

Figure 3.1   Age distribution of Terman women responding in 1972

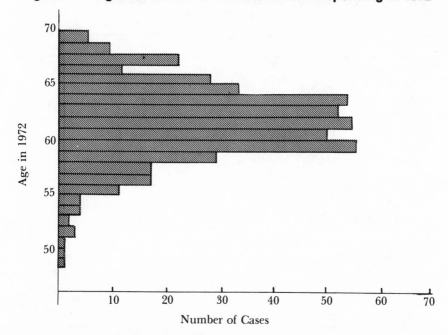

head-of-household (HH). For lack of any more appropriate term, the balance were called non-head-of-household (NHH).

The next section of Table 3.1 shows that 43 percent are income workers (IW), according to a rather stringent criterion—they must have had steady work for four out of six five-year periods, 1941-72. Subjects who worked fewer than four of these periods were designated homemakers (HM). Finally, 25 percent of the entire sample were childless; 75 percent had at least one child.

The percentage differences between the Terman figures and those of the 1970 U.S. Census are insignificant except in the following instances. Among the Terman women there are somewhat more currently divorced. More Terman women are employed on a full-time basis, and of the employed, more of the Terman sample are professional. The average number of children born to married women is 1.79, a little lower than the Census reports for women in this age group. In our group the total family income shows a median of $18,000 per year (not shown in Table 3.1). Sixty-eight percent reported a family income of $15,000 or better in 1971, whereas the

Table 3.1   Percentage Breakdown by Marital Status, Work Pattern, and Children

Category	Percent of Sample
Current marital status	
Always single	9
Divorced or separated	11
Widowed	15
Married	65
Head-of-household status	
Head-of-household	19
Single (9%)	
Divorced (6%)	
Widowed (4%)	
Non-head-of-household	81
Work pattern	
Income workers	43
Homemakers	57
Children	
Childless	25
Had children	75

1970 Census figures report 27 percent at or above that figure for the U.S. population of husband-wife families.

Attrition of Sample

In longitudinal studies, attrition is always an important variable. Of the 671 women in the original 1928 sample, 573 were believed to be living in 1972. Responses to the 1972 mailing sampled 75 percent of those women, or an N of 430.

Since twelve years had elapsed between follow-ups, we wondered whether our current sample was self-selecting in any significant way (for example, the most "successful" in marriage, income, career, and so on). Taking a base of response in 1960, we compared our 1972 respondents to nonrespondents on six variables: occupation, family income, marital status, health, general adjustment, and feelings of having lived up to intellectual ability. While there were some differences between those who responded and those who did not, these differences were minimal (from 1 to 5 percent as an average difference in any variable). What we did find was that generally those who had given us complete cooperation in the past continued to do so. Our fallout came largely from those subjects for whom data in 1960 were sketchy.

SATISFACTION MEASURES

Now, how do these women in different categories of marital status, occupation, and motherhood compare on the satisfactions they feel for their life-styles? (Cf. Andrews and Withey 1973.) From the 1972 returns, three measures of satisfaction with life-style were devised. One involved *work pattern*, whether the work done was income producing or not. Two other measures, broader in the sense of covering various aspects of the woman's activities, will be described later.

Work-Pattern Satisfaction

This measure was derived from a question which asked the women to consider their lives as falling into one of four possible patterns: (1) I have been primarily a homemaker; (2) I have pursued a career during most of my adult life; (3) I have pursued a career except during the period when I was raising a family; or (4) I have done considerable work for needed income, but would not call it a career.

Subjects checked their pattern under a column labeled "As it was." Then they were asked to indicate the pattern that fitted their plans in early adulthood. Finally, they checked the pattern they would prefer to have been in, as they looked back.

Our measure for work pattern satisfaction came from those subjects whose answers to the first "(a) As it was" and the third "(c) As I now would choose" were identical, whichever pattern it was. (Note that homemaking is considered work, as well as income-producing jobs.) Where there was agreement, satisfaction was called high. For any sort of disagreement, the subject was considered to have a moderate or low degree of satisfaction with her work pattern in comparing her actual style with that she would now choose. Childless women who checked "career during most of adult life" as "as it was," and then "career except when raising a family" as their preference now, were coded as high satisfaction; this was only eight cases. By these criteria, 68 percent of the total sample expressed high satisfaction with their work pattern.

Our naive theory predicted that women who were married, with children, having had income-producing work, and living on a higher-than-average income would report higher satisfaction than those in the reverse groups. As with many naive theories, most of these predictions proved false. Figure 3.2 gives the data for our head-of-household/non-head-of-household categories. The percentage figures in each of the cells are *not* the number of women in that category, but rather are the percentage of women in that category who report high work pattern satisfaction. Thus, of the head-of-household subjects, 80 percent show high satisfaction. Of the non-head-of-household group, 67 percent rate high—with a probability of .02 for the difference between these percentages.

Income workers gave an overall figure of 79 percent high satisfaction; homemakers rated 62 percent—a very significant difference (see the bottom of Figure 3.2). But note, within the cells, that those women who were head-of-household and income workers are 92 percent highly satisfied compared to 41 percent high satisfaction in those who are also head-of-household but homemakers.

Our most surprising finding concerns the fact of having children versus childlessness. In each pair of cells (except one with very small numbers), subjects with no children show a higher percentage of satisfaction than those with children. For "always single" childless women, the percent of high satisfaction is 89 percent. Is motherhood becoming an endangered species, as one of our developmental psychology colleagues observed?

Another surprise came when we looked at family income (not shown in Figure 3.2). Here the high satisfaction represents 66 percent of those below the median of $18,000 and 70 percent of those above the median, a nonsignificant difference. Since $18,000 is a pretty fair figure in itself, we separated out those in the lowest quartile of family income. Their high satisfaction figure was 67 percent—no different from those with larger incomes.

Possibly our naive theory stereotype of what life-style would prove most satisfying for the women born about 1910 neglected the fact that these subjects were responding as they felt in 1972. Whereas 41 percent of the women responded "primarily a homemaker" as their work pattern in the "As it was" column, only 29 percent "would now choose" that pattern (Table 3.2). Thirty percent placed

Figure 3.2 Percentages of high satisfaction with work pattern

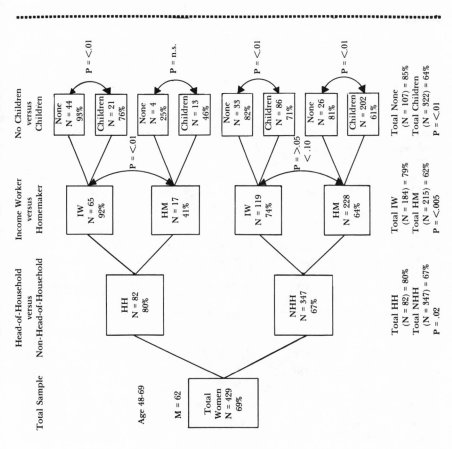

Total Sample	Head-of-Household versus Non-Head-of-Household	Income Worker versus Homemaker	No Children versus Children

N = number in subsample

% = percent of subsample *High* in Satisfaction (agreement between "At it was" and "As I would now choose.")

Head-of-Household, 1972
Always single, N = 38
Divorced, N = 26
Widowed, N = 18

Non-Head-of-Household, 1972
N =347 (living with husband for all or part of period, 1960-1972)

Income Worker
N = 184
Steady work for 4 out of 6 5-year periods, 1941-1972

Homemaker
N = 245
"Steady work" for less than 4 out of 6 5-year periods, 1941-1972

Children
None, N = 107
1 or more, N = 322

Total HH
(N = 82) = 80%
Total NHH
(N = 347) = 67%
P = .02

Total IW
(N = 184) = 79%
Total HM
(N = 215) = 62%
P = <.005

Total None
(N = 107) = 85%
Total Children
(N = 322) = 64%
P = <.01

Age 48-69

M = 62

Table 3.2   Cross-Tabulation of Number of Cases of "At It Was" Versus "As I Would Now Choose"

As it was	As I would now choose				
	Homemaker[a]	Career[b]	Career Except[c]	Income Worker[d]	Row Total
Homemaker[a]					
Married w/children	82	17	37	1	137
Married w/o children	7	2	1		10
Always single	1				1
Total	90	19	38	1	148
Career[b]					
Married w/children	2	38	6	1	47
Married w/o children	2	30	3		35
Always single	1	22	4		27
Total	5	90	13	1	109
Career except[c]					
Married w/children	2	6	34		42
Married w/o children		1			1
Always single			1		1
Total	2	7	35		44
Income worker[d]					
Married w/children	6	15	17	12	50
Married w/o children	2	3	2	3	10
Always single		2	1	1	4
Total	8	20	20	16	64
Column total	105	136	106	18	365[e]

[a]Full title of response category is: "I have been primarily a homemaker."

[b]Full title of response category is: "I have pursued a career through most of my adult life."

[c]Full title of response category is: "I have pursued a career except during the period when I was raising a family."

[d]Full title of response category is: "I have done considerable work for needed income, but would not call it a career."

[e]In addition to these 365 cases, 64 women responded with other answers to describe their specific work patterns.

themselves in the "career" category; 37 percent would now choose this option. The comparable figures for "career except when raising a family" are 12 percent and 29 percent; for the "income only" category, they are 18 percent and 5 percent. Many of these women thus would now choose a career or a career-except-when-raising-a-family rather than the homemaker or work-for-income-only work patterns.

The proportion of women in the United States who are in the "work" force (according to this definition, "work" does not include homemaking) has been steadily rising, and possibly some of the homemaker women felt that they had missed an interesting and challenging part of life. As shown in Table 3.1, 43 percent of the women were coded as income workers, according to the criterion of being employed four out of six five-year periods. However, the current (1972) status shows 65 percent as either employed or recently retired from employment (48 percent working, 17 percent retired).

Two Ways of Looking at Satisfaction with Life-Style

Satisfaction with life-style is described in two different approaches. One might be called the *demographic,* using such variables as work pattern, marital status, number of children, and income level to provide a subsample of the 430 women for a look at relative satisfaction (Figure 3.2). This we have just presented. The second approach is to look back at childhood and early adulthood variables to see whether these are associated *predictively* with (1) life-style, work pattern, and/or (2) satisfaction with that experienced style.

In these women now approaching ordinary retirement age, were there precursors or predictors in childhood and early adulthood of later satisfaction with their own life-styles and choices? This phase of the analysis depends upon the longitudinal design of the study and the enormous files of data meticulously kept over the years. We have looked at theoretically relevant possible predictors of later satisfaction such as: education and occupation of the subjects' parents; the girls' apparent identification with their mothers and with their fathers; attitudes of their mothers, fathers, and teachers toward them; the subjects' own attitudes toward themselves in terms of ambition, self-confidence, and the like; and goals and aspects of life giving them the most satisfaction at different points in their development. These possible predictors have been related to their actual careers as income workers, mothers, and homemakers at different points in time, and to the satisfaction they felt with them.

Hypotheses to be tested involved the following groups of variables:

1. Women coming from homes in which the father and mother were well-educated and in which the father (and perhaps the mother) followed a professional or higher business career would themselves be more likely to follow suit and show more satisfaction with their choice than those from homes in which the parents had lower levels of education and occupation.

2. Women coming from homes where parent-child relations were affectionately positive and parents' marriage a happy one would be more likely to show general satisfaction with their own lives, have happier marriages themselves, and enjoy their children more. No prediction was made with the work pattern the subject would follow in connection with this group of variables.

3. The subjects' early self-rating of self-confidence, lack of inferiority feelings, and presence of ambition should predict later feelings of satisfaction with the experiences actually encountered. More subjects with high self-ratings should fall in the income worker pattern than in the homemaker pattern.

4. As stated earlier, our naive theory predicted that for these women, marriage, number of children, and income level should be positively correlated with later satisfaction.

These hypotheses were tested for 149 variables taken from the files for 1922 and 1972. The next section and Table 3.3 give significant relations between variables and work pattern satisfaction. You will recall that high satisfaction came from the subjects' indicating at average age sixty-two agreement between the experience she had actually had ("As it was"), and the response to "As I would choose." Chi-square was used because work pattern is a discrete rather than a continuous variable. Some of the variables included are nonlinear. Note the parentheses following the name of the variable; this indicates the direction of the relationship. Thus, as we have already seen in Figure 3.2, the more satisfied women tend to be childless and hold income-producing jobs. However, they also are likely to value their family and cultural lives, as well as work and income.

Apparently, we must conclude that while rewarding, income-producing work and vocational advancement are facilitated by the absence of children, still it is part of women's lives (perhaps especially those of the Terman Study generation) to wish for and

Table 3.3   Work Pattern Satisfaction Related to Other Variables

Variable Description	Number of Categories	Date	Chi-square Significance (≤.05)
General satisfaction 5[a] (high)[b]	1.40-5.00	1972	.00
Joy in living satisfaction[a] (high)	5	1972	.00
Work pattern, income or homemaker (income)	2	1972	.00
S's occupation (professional-managerial-arts versus clerical-sales, housewife)	3	1950	.00
S's occupation (professional-managerial-arts versus clerical-sales, housewife)	3	1960	.00
Historical rating on general adjustment (satisfactory)	3	1960	.03
Health (very good)	5	1972	.00
Attainment: occupational success (high)[a]	5	1972	.00
Attainment: family life (high)	5	1972	.00
Attainiment: cultural life (high)	5	1972	.02
Satisfying aspects of life: work	3	1950	.00
Satisfying aspects of life: income	3	1950	.03
Satisfying aspects of life: children	3	1950	.00
Satisfying aspects of life: work	3	1960	.00
Satisfying aspects of life: children	3	1960	.00
Ambition for excellence in work since age 40 (high)	5	1960	.03
Number of children (none versus one to eight)	9	1972	.00

[a]This variable will be discussed later.

[b]Parentheses following name of variable indicate direction of relation to the criterion work pattern satisfaction. Work pattern satisfaction has two categories, high and moderate or low.

enjoy their children. Later we shall discuss findings from a nationwide sample of women (not gifted) in this regard.

Turning from this issue, observe that the variables related to work pattern satisfaction generally (but not exclusively) suggest reward from work, whatever it is, a bias in favor of income-producing rather than homemaking work, a professional occupation, and ambition for excellence and advancement in the occupation.

We do not see any relations to parent- or self-ratings on feelings of inferiority, persistence, self-confidence, helpfulness of parents, and the like. Those high on work pattern satisfaction do report that one of the satisfying aspects of life is income. Possibly, more women in the income-producing work pattern brought home enough to make a decent income (to them) and were pleased to have done so.

Parents' education and occupation do not show relationships to work pattern satisfaction, but the subject's occupation does. Evidently, the women working in teaching or other professions, the arts, or who are office or property managers are more likely to show high satisfaction on this measure than those who are sales clerks, in clerical jobs, or are housewives. But the actual income (total family) does not come out as a significant correlate of work pattern satisfaction.

General Satisfaction 5

A second and broader measure of life satisfaction came from another question in 1972: "How important was each of these goals in life in the plans you made for yourself in early adulthood?" Columns were labeled "occupational success," "family life," "friendships," "richness of cultural life," and "total service to society." Next, the subject was asked to rate her success in each of these respects. (Note that children/marriage surveyed in earlier questionnaires were not delineated in 1972 but lumped under one category labeled "family life.") There was also a sixth area, "joy in living," which is more global than the others. It was taken as a separate criterion to be discussed later. Following a suggestion of Sanford Dornbusch (personal communication), we have weighted the individual's judgment of her success in each area by her statement as to the importance of the area to her in early adulthood. Both ratings were retrospective judgments made when she was in her early sixties.

General satisfaction 5 is the quotient obtained by multiplying the planned goal (early adulthood) by the reported success in attaining that goal, adding the five of these multiplied areas, and dividing by the sum of the planned goals for each of the areas. These scores range from 0 through 5. They are continuous, not discrete. A high score means that in those areas she considered important for herself, her success was good. It also takes into account individual differences in the choice of important goals.

Table 3.4 summarizes the results reaching the .05 level of statistical significance obtained by a one-way-classification analysis

Table 3.4 General Satisfaction 5 (Five Areas) Related to Other Variables

Variable Description	Number of Categories	Date	ANOVA Probability. $F \leq .05$
Work pattern satisfaction (high)[a]	2	1972	.00
Joy in living satisfaction[b] (high)	5	1972	.01
Health (very good)	5	1972	.05
S's occupation (professional-managerial-arts versus clerical-sales, housewife)	3	1940	.05
Historical rating, general adjustment (satisfactory)	3	1960	.00
Percent time volunteer work, 1966-72 (high)	0-40	1972	.00
Feelings about present vocation (good)	5	1950	.01
Parent rating: self-confidence (high)	1-13	1928	.00
Parent rating: feelings of inferiority (low)	1-11	1940	.00
Parent/teacher rating: perseverance, desire to excel (high)	34	1928	.00
S rates: understanding with mother (high)	4	1950	.01
S rates: helpfulness of father (high)	4	1950	.01
S rates: vocational success of father (high)	4	1950	.00
S rates: admiration for mother (high)	4	1950	.04
Self-rating: feelings of inferiority (low)	1-11	1940	.00
Self-rating: persistence (high)	1-11	1950	.05
Education of spouse (AB or better)	3	1940	.00
Occupation of spouse (professional)	3	1940	.03
Satisfying aspects of life: marriage	3	1950	.00
Satisfying aspects of life: children	3	1950	.03
Satisfying aspects of life: community service	3	1950	.00
Satisfying aspects of life: marriage	3	1960	.00
Satisfying aspects of life: social contacts	3	1960	.02
Satisfying aspects of life: community service	3	1960	.03

[a]Parentheses following name of variable indicate direction of relation to the criterion general satisfaction 5. General satisfaction 5 is a continuous variable with scores from 1.40 to 5.00.

[b]This variable will be discussed later.

of variance for 158 variables.[3] Twenty variables, coming from reports made by subject and by parents in different years, appear to show positive prediction of general satisfaction in 1972. These fall into certain groups, as earlier hypothesized.

1. There are quite a number indicating positive relations with *parents* in earlier years. These come both from favorable ratings of the subject *by* parents and ratings of her father's and mother's qualities *by* the subject. Examples are the 1928 parents' rating of the child subject as high in self-confidence and low in feelings of inferiority. Subjects high in general satisfaction 5 in 1972 rated their parents favorably in 1950 on understanding and helpfulness. They showed admiration for their mothers.

2. As expected, favorable ratings of self qualities by the subject appear as early as 1940 and again later. These self-concept reports are rather highly correlated over the years.[4] It seems unlikely that the subjects could remember in 1972 how they responded in 1940 or 1950; thus a considerable stability in self-

---

3. A one-way classification analysis of variance of each of 158 independent variables was performed, using general satisfaction 5 scores as the dependent variable. For example, the question, "Please check to indicate your general health during 1970-1972" with five possible answers—very good, good, fair, poor, very poor—constitutes a five-level independent variable for the ANOVA. Variation among the means of responses "very good" versus "good" versus "fair" versus "poor" versus "very poor" is analyzed, as shown in Table 3.4. There, F with 4 and 412 degrees of freedom is statistically significant at the .05 level.

4. Self-rating correlations over different years of report give some indication of the consistency of rough reliability of these measures. For example:

Variable number	Description	N	Correlation with		
			2	3	4
1	Self-confidence (1940)	384	.56	-.49	-.46
2	Self-confidence (1950)	377		-.38	-.54
3	Feelings of inferiority (1940)	383			.55
4	Feelings of inferiority (1950)	375			

regard is indicated. These ratings were self-confidence, which was high, and feelings of inferiority, which were low.

3. Aspects of life reported as satisfying in earlier years (1950, 1960)—marriage, children, social contacts, community service—are associated with general satisfaction in 1972.

4. Good health and professional work appear as positive predictors of satisfaction, as do level of education and occupation of husband, and subject's opinion of vocational success of her father. Time devoted to volunteer work also comes out associated with general satisfaction 5, as does a staff rating on general adjustment.

It is unfortunate that those variables *not* predictive of satisfaction cannot be reported completely here.[5] Some, of course, came close to but did not quite meet the significance criteria. Among those which showed no relationship to satisfaction were number of children; 107 of the 430 women were childless but had nearly as high general satisfaction scores as those who had from one to eight children. Income and ambition for financial gain also do not show up in relation to general satisfaction. We have here in general satisfaction 5 several dimensions of life experiences which are not tapped by work pattern satisfaction.

Joy in Living Satisfaction

The simplest of our measures of satisfaction, Joy in Living Satisfaction, was derived from the subjects' answers in 1972 to the question of how successful they had been in pursuit of that goal. A five-point scale was used, ranging from "had excellent fortune in this respect" down to "found little satisfaction in this area." Predictors of this measure of satisfaction were found by use of chi squares instead of analysis of variance.

Joy in Living scores correlate .51 with general satisfaction 5 scores, and many of the same predictors appear in relation to both criteria (Table 3.5). Positive relations with parents and positive self-ratings are significantly related to both satisfaction measures.

---

5. Complete code books are available to qualified persons. Appendix 3.1 lists 149 of the variables entered into the analyses reported in Tables 3.3 through 3.9.

Table 3.5. Joy in Living Satisfaction Related to Other Variables

Variable Description	Number of Categories	Date	Chi-square Sigificance ≤.05
General satisfaction 5 (high)[a]	1.40-5.00	1972	.00
Work pattern satisfaction (high)	2	1972	.00
Work pattern, income or homemaker (income)	2	1972	.00
Health (very good)	5	1972	.00
Energy and vitality level (vigorous)	5	1972	.00
Historical rating, general adjustment (satisfactory)	3	1960	.00
Feelings about present vocation (good)	5	1950	.05
Teacher's rating of arithmetic (very superior)	6	1922	.00
Conflict w/father before S's marriage (none)	5	1940	.01
S rates understanding with mother (high)	5	1940	.01
S rates father's self-confidence (high)	5	1950	.00
S rates admiration for mother (high)	5	1950	.01
S rates rebellious feelings toward father (none)	5	1950	.05
S rates father's encouragement of independence (high)	5	1950	.04
Self-rating: feelings of inferiority (low)	1-10	1940	.00
Self-rating: feelings of inferiority (low)	1-11	1950	.03
Education of spouse (AB or better)	3	1940	.02
Satisfying aspects of life: community service	3	1950	.00
Satisfying aspects of life: marriage	3	1960	.00
Satisfying aspects of life: religion	3	1960	.02
Ambition for excellence in work, age 30-40 (high)	5	1960	.00
Ambition for excellence in work, since age 40 (high)	5	1960	.00

[a] Parentheses following name of variable indicate direction of relation to the criterion joy in living satisfaction. Joy in living satisfaction has five categories.

However, income workers, as contrasted with homemakers, score higher in joy, which was not the case on the broader measure of general satisfaction 5. Further, ambition for excellence in work, both in early and later adulthood (as recollected in 1960), is associated with joy. Of interest to those working with mathematically precocious children is the fact that teachers reported special ability in mathematics as early as 1922 for those subjects high in joy.

Reliability of Satisfaction Measures

These 1972 measures are a one-shot type of response. Additionally, they are based on combinations of separate responses. Conventional reliability is impossible to determine. We offer instead some indication of the consistency of certain measures of satisfaction repeated over a ten-year period as evidence that at least some satisfaction variables are not subject-quixotic but represent some moderately stable indication of the subjects' feelings at different points in their lives.

Self-ratings on self-confidence and feelings of inferiority, coming from 1940 and 1950, correlate .56 and .55, respectively. In 1950 and 1960, subjects were asked to rate certain aspects of life which were satisfying to them. Correlations between the two sets of responses showed the following: for work, .41; for marriage, .56; for children, .69; and for social contacts, .39.[6]

FACTOR ANALYSIS

For reduction in the huge number of variables contained in the reports over the fifty years 1922-72, certain variables were submitted to factor analyses. First, since the interest was in life-style satisfactions of these women, variables were selected which theoretically should relate to the three types of satisfaction measured in later life: (1) work-pattern satisfaction (including both income workers and homemakers); (2) general satisfaction 5, covering five areas of possible satisfactions; and (3) joy in living, another general type of satisfaction. The variables selected were thought to be possibly predictive of these satisfactions in later life: they included earlier attitudes toward homemaking and income-producing work, ambition, children, self-confidence, marriage, volunteer work, attachment to parents, and the like.[7]

---

6. The complete correlation matrix is given in Appendix 3.2.

7. In all, four factor analyses were done: (1) with 78 variables, using an orthogonal design with varimax rotation; (2) also with 78 variables, using oblique rotation, Δ = .3, the Rao factor; (3) fifty variables (leaving out those which appeared to duplicate one another), using PA2 factor with oblique rotation, Δ = .3; and (4) also fifty variables using oblique rotation, Δ = .3, and the Rao factor. All were done using SPSS programs. See *SPSS: Statistical Package for the Social Sciences* (Nie et al. 1975), pp. 468-86.

The first analysis resulted in ten meaningful factors; these will be reported here. The other three resulted in the following numbers of factors, respectively: 26, 19, and 19. Many of these incorporated only single variables and told little more than analysis of variance and the chi-squares with single variables and satisfaction scores.

Table 3.6 gives the chief variables in the ten factors, the percent of variance in the analysis accounted for by each factor, and the correlation of each factor with the three measures of satisfaction in 1972. These ten factors account for about 74 percent of the common variance expected from the correlation matrix of seventy-eight variables. Fifty-three of the seventy-eight variables correlated .35 or better with a factor. These are reported here.

It can be seen that one factor emphasizes income-producing work, and two factors (5 and 9) group variables involving marriage and children. These are not completely antithetical, as seen earlier in table 3.3, work-pattern satisfaction. Although number of children is lower in the income-worker group than in the homemaker, children appear to be one of the satisfying aspects of life (1950, 1960) as related to work-pattern satisfaction.

Factor 2 illustrates the clustering of positive self-ratings and is somewhat related to both general measures of satisfaction. These two measures of satisfaction are also self-rating but are reported at a time up to thirty years later than some of the self-confidence measures. If this clustering is due to response set, it is remarkably enduring over time. More likely, there is a true prediction: If a woman feels self-confident early in life, she is more likely to order her life in a way that promotes later satisfaction. Note that such women also consider themselves ambitious for vocational advancement.[8]

Factors 3 and 6 represent attachment to parents. Here the prediction to later satisfaction is not clear for attachment to mother, although there is some relation in the extent of positive regard for the father. Likewise, mother's occupation (factor 4) does not correlate highly with satisfaction.

---

8. In our search for approximations to consistency of response measures, several of these factors are illuminating, since they represent responses from many different years which cluster together in the factors.

Table 3.6 Factor Analysis of Seventy-Eight Variables[a]

Factor Number (% variance)	Description	General Satisfaction (five areas)	Work-Pattern Satisfaction	Joy in Living Satisfaction
1 (21.5%)	Income worker (1941-72),[b] occupation high level (1940), low time volunteer work—1960-65 (1972), work is rewarding (1950, 1960), ambitious for vocational advance—age 30-40 (1960)		+.26	
2 (17.1%)	Self-rating: self-confidence (1940, 1950), persistence (1950), ambitious for vocational advance—age 30-40 and since 40 (1960)	+.16		+.21
3 (11.8%)	Attachment to mother (1940, 1950)			
4 (10.1%)	Mother's occupation, high (1922, 1927, 1936, 1940)			
5 (9.2%)	Had children (1972), wanted them (1940), found them rewarding (1950, 1960), would do it again (1950)		-.19	
6 (7.0%)	Attachment to father (1940, 1950), parents' marriage happy (1940)	+.19		+.12
7 (6.7%)	S's education good (1940), husband's education and occupation high (1950)	+.17		
8 (5.9%)	Feels good about work (1972), good health (1972), not ambitious for excellence in work—age 30-40 (1960)	+.31	.+.17	+.45
9 (5.7%)	Married (1972), likes it (1950, 1960)	+.33	+.17	+.32
10 (4.9%)	S gets satisfaction from recognition of work (1950) and social contacts (1950, 1960)	+.13		

[a]This analysis used an orthogonal design with varimax rotation. Variables are not reported if correlation was less than .35 with the factor.

[b]Date is that of subject's response

Factor 8 presents the highest correlation with a satisfaction measure. This is more suspect with regard to response set, since two of the predictors came from the same year (1972) as the satisfaction measures.

Finally, factor 9, while contributing much less variance to the total than factor 1, shows that rewards from marriage constitute a fair prediction of general satisfaction later in life.

ANALYSIS OF SUBSAMPLES

A final analysis divides our sample into categories according to current marital status, work pattern, and presence of children. Table 3.7 gives percentages of the sample thus divided who reported *high* (favorable) ratings on a number of variables early and late in time. Since the categories for subsamples are those of 1972, many of the earlier responses were made *before* the woman was divorced or widowed. We shall look at the proportions of women in each category for suggestions as to dynamics or circumstances underlying their position in one or another category. Numbers in parentheses refer to variables listed in table 3.7.

Single Women

Not many in this group rated their parents' marriage as more happy than average (1) but more than in other groups reported that both father and mother encouraged independence in the child subject (2, 3). Few considered their mothers very self-confident (4). Their mothers were rarely in professional or managerial occupations (8). When we add in the fact that these single women were distinctly better educated than the other groups (9), a picture emerges of a woman without a strong maternal role model but encouraged to be independent by her parents and finding her own satisfactions in work for which she has been well prepared by education. These single women liked arithmetic very much as children (17) and were rated by their teachers as superior at it (18).

Married Women

This group showed a much higher percentage who felt their parents' marriage was very happy (1). The subjects' level of education is much lower than that of the single women (9), perhaps partly because marriage and/or children interrupted educational plans and goals, or perhaps because the women were willing to have them interrupted. A large proportion of these women take great satisfaction in marriage, family life, and children (10, 11, 12, 13). Interestingly, the percentage taking "great" satisfaction in children increased substantially from 1950 to 1960 (10, 11). Absence of older children from the home may make the heart grow fonder, and grandmothers are notorious for their love of children. In this group the husbands are well educated (15) and often hold professional or managerial jobs (14). The family income is high (16).

Divorced Women

To these women, their parents' marriage was seen as less happy (1), and the subjects believed that their fathers and mothers did not encourage independence in them to any great extent (2, 3). A relatively large number considered their mothers very self-confident (4), and many of their mothers had been employed in professional or managerial positions (8). Apparently, the subjects did not feel very close to either father or mother (6, 7). Obviously, very few felt great satisfaction with their marriages (12) and family life (13). Income is low for most (16). For these women, for whatever reason, the proportion who liked arithmetic very much as a child is small (17).

Widows

In this group, the parents' marriage was believed to be relatively happy (1); the proportion rating father and mother as encouraging independence is high (2, 3). In 1940, these women considered themselves to be close to both father and mother (6, 7). Their level of education was the least of all the groups (9) and their income in 1972 the least, on the average (16). It is provocative to observe a discrepancy for these women between their reports of health—the highest proportion of "excellent" responses of all the groups (20)— and a less favorable self-report of energy and vitality (19). These two variables correlate .70, so considerable correspondence is expected. Possibly the widowed women felt less energy, although health was good, because of the loss of their spouse and consequent sadness and depression. These women are not older than those of the other groups.

Table 3.7 Percentages of Subsamples Scoring High on Selected Variables, 1922-1972[a] (Top figure is number reporting; bottom is percent of that subsample high.)

Variable (year) % of Total	Current Marital Status				Work Pattern		Children	
Sample Reporting High:	Single	Mar.	Div.	Wid.	IW	HM	No	Yes
Work-pattern satisfaction	38	280	46	65	184	245	107	322
(1972) 69%	89%	68%	72%	63%	79%	62%	85%	64%
General satisfaction, five	35	274	44	64	180	237	102	315
areas (1972) 53%	43%	57%	39%	50%	51%	55%	52%	53%
(1) Rates parents' marriage	36	246	38	56	161	215	90	286
as happier than average	39%	60%	47%	54%	52%	59%	47%	58%
(1940) 56%								
(2) Father encouraged	33	229	35	52	149	200	86	263
independence (1950) 47%	58%	47%	29%	52%	50%	44%	50%	46%
(3) Mother encouraged	33	246	37	57	158	215	87	286
independence (1950) 51%	64%	50%	41%	53%	53%	50%	55%	50%
(4) Considers mother very	33	243	39	58	158	215	88	285
self-confident (1950) 13%	6%	13%	21%	16%	13%	14%	7%	15%
(5) Deep feeling of under-	33	234	36	54	153	204	86	271
standing w/father (1950) 14%	9%	15%	11%	19%	14%	15%	14%	14%
(6) Felt very close to father	33	230	35	51	147	202	81	268
(1940) 19%	24%	19%	11%	25%	16%	21%	16%	21%
(7) Felt very close to mother	35	241	35	55	158	208	84	282
(1940) 28%	26%	30%	20%	29%	22%	34%	29%	28%
(8)Mother employed as pro-	32	223	39	47	140	201	83	258
fessional or manager (1940)	3%	14%	31%	13%	14%	15%	14%	15%
15%								
(9) Education—AB or better	34	278	46	65	181	245	106	320
(1940) 67%	92%	64%	72%	62%	68%	66%	78%	63%
(10) Great satisfaction from	—	218	29	45	97	195	—	292
children (1950) 51%	—	51%	48%	53%	44%	54%	—	51%

[a]In order not to overburden this table, the *P* values for differences between percentages have not been given. The text reports differences which are generally greater than 10 percent. Some examples of comparisons involving small and large numbers in the subsamples are given in appendix 3.3 to help the reader estimate the probabilities of true differences.

Table 3.7. (Continued)

Variable (year) % of Total Sample Reporting High:	Current Marital Status				Work Pattern		Children	
	Single	Mar.	Div.	Wid.	IW	HM	No	Yes
(11) Great satisfaction from children (1960) 66%	— —	226 68%	27 63%	45 58%	100 60%	198 69%	— —	298 66%
(12) Great satisfaction from marriage (1960) 51%	— —	262 61%	41 12%	58 47%	172 37%	226 56%	63 51%	298 53%
(13) Highly satisfied with family life (1972) 45%	31 6%	273 56%	42 14%	65 38%	176 30%	235 56%	98 31%	313 50%
(14) Spouse employed as professional or manager (1960) 77%	— —	240 78%	14 71%	32 75%	92 64%	195 83%	42 81%	245 76%
(15) Spouse's education— AB or better (1950) 58%	— —	206 61%	34 50%	54 48%	107 44%	190 64%	40 48%	254 59%
(16) Family income greater than $18,000/year (1971) 52%	25 36%	233 66%	33 21%	53 15%	143 46%	201 56%	78 47%	266 54%
(17) Liked arithmetic very much (1922) 44%	28 54%	203 48%	35 29%	58 36%	141 48%	183 41%	83 47%	241 43%
(18) Superior rating by teacher in arithmetic (1922) 60%	18 67%	152 60%	27 56%	39 62%	94 66%	142 56%	55 65%	181 59%
(19) High energy level (1972) 37%	38 42%	280 35%	46 43%	66 38%	184 42%	246 33%	107 36%	323 37%
(20) General health excellent (1972) 44%	38 34%	279 43%	46 41%	65 57%	183 45%	245 43%	105 40%	323 46%
(21) Volunteer time 10%+ from 1960 to 1965 (1972) 23%	32 19%	256 26%	39 21%	61 16%	159 11%	229 32%	90 18%	298 26%
(22) Volunteer time 10%+ from 1966 to 1972 (1972) 24%	32 28%	250 26%	38 18%	60 18%	158 12%	222 34%	90 26%	290 24%

Income Workers Compared to Homemakers

Income workers are the group that has had rather steady employment during much of their lives. By marital status, we find the following percentages of income workers: 89 percent of the single women, 65 percent of the divorced, 45 percent of the widows, and only 32 percent of the married. Subtracting from 100 percent, we find the reverse percentages for the chiefly steady state of homemaker in each of the marital-status categories.

There are not early differences between the reports from these groups. The homemakers rate their parents' marriage as a little happier (1), and more of them felt close to their mother than did the income workers (7). Homemakers report more satisfaction from children, marriage, and family life (10, 11, 12, 13) than do income workers, as expected from the marital-status figures above. Their family income is generally higher (16). An interesting difference between the two groups is in energy level, on which the income workers rate themselves higher (19). On health, the two groups report no difference (20). The homemakers spent more of their time on volunteer work than did the income workers; but it is interesting to note that single women, and those without children, increased in proportion of time spent on this in the twelve years preceding the 1972 questionnaire (21, 22). They got older and some retired. Finally, on the child and teachers' view of arithmetic superiority, the income workers are a little higher (17, 18).

Childless Women Compared to Those with Children

Here again, the marital status intervenes in the figures. The childless group is composed of 100 percent of the single women, 30 percent of the divorced, 23 percent of the widows, and 14 percent of the married. The reverse figures from 100 percent indicate those who have one or more children. Of the childless, 72 percent are income workers and 28 percent are homemakers.

In this comparison, the women with children rate their parents' marriage as happier than those without children (1). Their mothers' self-confidence is rated higher (4). Husbands' occupation and education (14, 15) and family income are higher (16). Satisfaction with family is higher (13). Somewhat more volunteer time was spent in the early 1960s by those with children than by those without, but the two groups are essentially equal by the latter part of the decade (21, 22).

COMPARISON OF THE TERMAN SAMPLE WITH TWO NATIONWIDE PROBABILITY SAMPLES

Earlier, we presented some data comparing the Terman group with U.S. Census statistics. Unfortunately, the Census does not ask much about *satisfaction* in the life as it is lived, and that is our major concern here.

Campbell Study

At the Institute for Social Research at Michigan, Angus Campbell and coworkers *have* done just this. Their data, published by the Russell Sage Foundation in 1975, mesh in certain ways with the data of our Terman women.

Campbell used one of Michigan's Survey Research Center's representative samples of 2,164 adults over seventeen. There are breakdowns for men, women, age groups, marital status, children, employed, and the like. Since the Survey Research Center's methods of selecting a sample representative of the U.S. population are precise, we feel confident that we can compare our gifted women with their women at roughly comparable ages. Their publication, entitled *The Quality of American Life,* aims at "capturing the feelings of satisfaction or dissatisfaction that Americans draw from different parts of their lives and with how these specific experiences combine to produce satisfaction with life in general" (Campbell, Converse, and Rodgers 1975).

They obtained their data from a lengthy personal interview in 1971 with people of the selected representative sample, 1,249 women. Of these results, the older women (N=669) most comparable to our sample are used for comparison. The average age of these older women in Campbell's sample is less than that for the Terman women (the latter average age sixty-two in 1972), but most of this subgroup of Campbell's sample were over forty-five. The time of response is close, however: Campbell in 1971 and Terman in 1972. In both cases the number is large (Campbell 669; Terman 430), but the selection criteria are quite different.

Our question then becomes: How do the gifted women of the Terman sample resemble or differ from a representative sample of U.S. women of all IQ levels—somewhat younger, to be sure, but otherwise classified in ways that we can match with our sample? We shall first compare the dimensions of marital status, employment, and education. Second, we shall look at similarities and differences in the two samples as to the degree of satisfaction they feel with their lives.

Demographic Variables. Table 3.8 gives the comparison on the demographic dimensions. With regard to marital/children status, fewer of the Terman sample were currently widowed or divorced; more of the Terman group were currently married and had children. This may have resulted from more remarriages in our group, which on the average is somewhat older than Campbell's.

More of the Terman group were employed, whatever their marital status. A great many more had obtained a college degree: 67 percent of our sample as compared to 8 percent of Campbell's. However, the percentage of the two samples who were college graduates and also employed is very similar on the level of job held. In all probability, many of Campbell's 8 percent were as "gifted" in IQ as our sample.

Those subjects with some college short of obtaining a degree present an interesting comparison. In the Terman group, many more are at a higher level of employment (professional, managerial, arts, as compared to clerical, sales) than those in Campbell's group. Campbell's data suggest that his group having some college fare little better in level of employment than those with only a high school diploma.

The Terman data show the following percentages of professional, managerial jobs by groups having differing education: college graduate, 87 percent; some college, 67 percent; and high school graduate, 58 percent. Campbell's sample shows these figures: college graduate, 82 percent; some college, 16 percent; and high school graduate, 8 percent. The Terman data suffer from low numbers at the lower levels of education; the Campbell figures are based on low numbers at the higher education levels.

We are inclined to draw the speculative conclusion that the women of high IQ are able to prove themselves capable on the job, perhaps have higher vocational goals and aspirations because of their family background, and hence succeed in higher-level jobs and in more employment overall in the labor force than do the women in

Table 3.8 Percentages of Samples, Terman and Campbell Groups

	Terman N = 430), age ±62	Campbell (N = 669), age 30+
Current marital status		
Married, children, age ±62	56% (240/430)	
Married, younger child over 17, age 45+		33% (218/669)
Married, childless, age ±62	9% (40/430)	
Married, childless, age 45+		7% (50/669)
Always single, age ±62	9% (38/430)	
Always single, age 30+		8% (53/669)
Widowed, age ±62	15% (66/430)	
Widowed, age 55+		33% (220/669)
Divorced, separated, age ±62	11% (46/430)	
Divorced, separated, one-half under age 45		19% (128/669)
Current employment		
Housewives, homemakers	34% (147/430)	46% (450/974)
Total employed	66% (283/430)	54% (524/974)
Of employed: married	37% (158/430)	30% (293/974)
Of employed: single, widowed, divorced	29% (125/430)	24% (231/974)
Education		
College graduate	67% (284/424)	8% (58/737)
Of college graduates: homemakers	35% (98/284)	43% (25/58)
Of college graduates: employed	65% (186/284)	57% (33/58)
Of college graduates, employed:		
Professional, managerial	87% (162/186)	82% (27/33)
Clerical, sales	13% (24/186)	12% (4/33)
Some college	24% (101/424)	14% (101/737)
Of some college: homemakers	37% (37/101)	51% (52/101)
Of some college: employed	63% (64/101)	49% (49/101)
Of some college, employed:		
Professional, managerial	67% (43/64)	16% (8/49)
Clerical, sales	33% (21/64)	67% (33/49)
High school graduate	8% (35/424)	44% (329/737)
Of high school graduates: homemakers	26% (9/35)	59% (193/329)
Of high school graduates: employed	74% (26/35)	41% (136/329)
Of high school graduates employed:		
Professional, managerial	58% (15/26)	8% (11/136)
Clerical, sales	42% (11/26)	59% (80/136)

Campbell's representative sample. Also to be kept in mind is the fact that the Terman women are older than those of Campbell; the proportion of the Terman women employed has been increasing over the last twelve years, and no doubt the same will be true of his sample.

Satisfaction Variables. The Campbell satisfaction measure reported here was as follows: "We have talked about various aspects of your life, now I want to ask you about your life as a whole these days. Which number on the card comes closest to how satisfied or dissatisfied you are with your life as a whole?" A seven-point scale from "completely satisfied" to "completely dissatisfied" was used. High satisfaction was defined as points 1 and 2 at the completely satisfied end of the scale.

The three satisfaction measures for the Terman group have been described earlier. Work-pattern satisfaction and general satisfaction 5 correlate only .21 and, as we have seen, tap quite different aspects and correlates of satisfaction with life-style. General satisfaction 5 takes into account a broader spectrum of life satisfactions than does work-pattern satisfaction. As such, the general measure seems more comparable to Campbell's question on life as a whole. However, the percentages of high satisfaction are not meaningful in comparing the two Terman and one Campbell measures (Table 3.9).[9] Therefore, the most appropriate way to make the comparisons is on the rank order of the various groups of women *within* one measure and without attempting comparisons across columns of "high" satisfaction for different measures.

Marital Status and Satisfaction. Here we get fairly close correspondence between the two samples on Terman general satisfaction 5 and Campbell's results. Most satisfied with their lives are the married women, with or without children, followed by the widowed, then single, with divorced in the lowest position on satisfaction.

For our work-pattern satisfaction, the ordering of the Terman women is quite different. Single and then childless married women are most satisfied, followed by divorced, married with children, and widowed. All results so far show that absence of children contributes to satisfaction with work, at least in this group of sixty-year-old women. The strain of thinking and acting on children's development (even when the children are adults themselves?) apparently contributes to less wholehearted devotion to work and satisfaction in it. More single women have achieved better education and higher professional level of employment, which has been

---

9. Campbell had other measures, which are not reported here.

Table 3.9 Satisfaction in Life Style, Terman and Campbell Samples Compared

	Terman		Campbell
	Work-pattern satisfaction high[a]	General satisfaction high[b]	How satisfied with life these days?[c]
Current marital status			
Married, children, age ±62	64% (159/240)	54% (129/237)	
Married, youngest child over 17, age 45+			69% (148/215)
Married, childless, age ±62	85% (34/40)	65% (26/40)	
Married, childless, age 45+			69% (34/49)
Always single, age ±62	89% (34/38)	41% (15/37)	
Always single, age 30+			53% (28/53)
Widowed, age ±62	62% (40/65)	50% (32/64)	
Widowed, age 55+			56% (121/215)
Divorced, separated, age ±62	72% (33/46)	38% (17/45)	
Divorced, separated, one-half under age 45			33% (42/128)
Current employment			
Married, housewives	64% (78/121)	57% (69/121)	69% (311/450)
Married, employed	70% (110/158)	55% (86/156)	66% (195/293)
Single, widowed, divorced: employed	74% (92/125)	44% (54/123)	47% (107/231)
Total employed	71% (202/283)	50% (140/279)	58% (302/524)
Education			
College graduate	69% (197/284)	52% (147/284)	
Married, housewives	60% (48/81)	53% (43/81)	56% (14/25)
Married, employed	71% (68/96)	57% (55/96)	79% (26/33)
Total employed	76% (141/186)	53% (98/186)	77% (24/31)
Professional, managerial	77% (124/162)	52% (84/162)	81% (22/27)
Clerical, sales	71% (17/24)	58% (14/24)	50% (2/4)
Some college	68% (69/101)	54% (54/101)	
Married, housewives	81% (26/32)	72% (23/32)	69% (36/52)
Married, employed	66% (27/41)	56% (23/41)	69% (43/49)
Total employed	61% (39/64)	47% (30/64)	68% (28/41)
Professional, managerial	74% (32/43)	49% (21/43)	62% (5/8)
Clerical, sales	33% (7/21)	43% (9/21)	70% (23/33)
High school graduate	71% (25/35)	49% (17/35)	
Married, housewives	43% (3/7)	43% (3/7)	72% (139/193)
Married, employed	81% (13/16)	50% (8/16)	69% (94/136)
Total employed	77% (20/26)	46% (12/26)	71% (65/91)
Professional, managerial	73% (11/15)	33% (5/15)	55% (6/11)
Clerical, sales	82% (9/11)	64% (7/11)	74% (59/80)

[a] $N = 429$.
[b] $N = 423$.
[c] $N = 699$ age 30+. High satisfaction was determined by those subjects who answered with the two highest points on a seven-point scale to the question, "How satisfied are you with your life as a whole these days?"

shown to promote more satisfaction in work. Women with children may have come later, and with less preparation, to the jobs that might be rewarding to them personally.

Employment and Satisfaction. Here again, there is agreement between the Terman general satisfaction 5 and the normative Campbell sample. Married housewives (homemakers) are the most satisfied, while married employed and single/divorced/widowed women follow. The time released from job requirements no doubt permits the housewives to gain more satisfactions from other aspects of life: friendships, cultural activities, volunteer service to the community, and perhaps children and husbands. In regard to work-pattern satisfaction, the most satisfied are the employed women (whatever their marital status), with housewives lower.

Education and Satisfaction. Here are the most conspicuous differences between our gifted and the normative groups. Fortunately for the Terman group, 67 percent of its women were able to achieve college graduation, even in the days of the Great Depression. Eight percent of the Campbell sample did so, even though they were younger. On all three satisfaction measures, college-graduate housewives were lower on satisfaction than were employed married college graduates.

For those who had some college without graduation, the Campbell data show no difference in satisfaction between housewives and married employed women. Within the Terman group, housewives are more satisfied than the employed on both measures of satisfaction. Those employed in professional jobs report more satisfaction than those in clerical or sales work.

The high school graduates constitute only a small percentage of the Terman group, though nearly half of the Campbell sample. For the latter, the satisfaction for housewives and married employed women is very close. In the Terman sample, small numbers report the employed as more satisfied than the housewives on both measures of satisfaction.

Spreitzer Study

Another nationwide probability sample survey was carried out in 1973 by Spreitzer, Snyder, and Larson (1975). Questionnaire items tapping life satisfaction included the following: (1) "Taken all together, how would you say things are these days—would you say that you are very happy, pretty happy, or not too happy?"; (2) "In general, do you find life exciting, pretty routine, or dull?"; and (3) "Taking things all together, how would you describe your marriage? Would you say that your marriage is very happy, pretty happy, or not too happy?"

The respondents, 802 women, covered the age range eighteen to seventy-one plus, but most of the analyses of interest for comparison to the Terman group did not control for age. We have, however, figures on satisfaction by marital status and by employment, with education controlled for the whole range.

Marital Status. High perceived happiness (question 1) was reported most frequently by married women, followed by widowed and then single women, with divorced women distinctly lower. The Terman figures on general satisfaction 5 show the same ordering by status (Table 3.7), but the groups are much closer together, with divorced women not nearly so low. On our work-pattern satisfaction measure, the order is quite different: single women much the highest, divorced next, then married, and widowed as the lowest.

Employment Status. This was trichotomized into full-time work, part-time work, and full-time homemaking. No significant associations were found with the three indices of satisfaction. Nor did the introduction of marital status as a control variable produce significance.

However, level of education as a control variable resulted in interesting findings. Women with no college education engaged in full-time homemaking reported the most perceived happiness. Those with at least a year of college showed the highest percentage of perceived happiness associated with part-time work, and the college women were higher on perceived excitement in life, particularly in association with part-time work.

Summary of Comparison

These two surveys obviously leave much to be desired as comparative data to the Terman material. The Terman women are older, have much better education and more professional jobs when they are employed, have a higher rate of employment, and have higher family incomes (as compared to Census data); those married have husbands with more education and more professional occupations. This is in addition to IQ as a selection device. Finally, the measures of satisfaction are different.

In both normative studies, the effect of education as interacting with level of employment has been suggested as relating to life satisfaction. Education and IQ can be said to be correlated without saying that one or the other is causative. It is interesting to find this education variable cropping up in all three studies.

GENERAL DISCUSSION AND SUMMARY

The objectives of this study were (1) to delineate the current status of the 430 "gifted" women reporting in 1972 (these were selected for the study when they were children in 1922 and 1928 because of their having an IQ of 135 or higher), and (2) to investigate earlier variables in their life experiences and feelings that might predict satisfaction with their life-style and situation when in 1972 they averaged about sixty-two years of age.

Method

Material dating from 1922 to 1972—obtained from mail surveys at five periods and field contacts at four periods—was culled for variables theoretically relevant to life satisfaction as reported in 1972. Such satisfaction was measured in three ways, two rather global, tapping different areas of life experiences (general satisfaction 5—covering the five areas of occupational success, family life, friendships, richness of cultural life, and total service to society—and joy in living satisfaction), and one involving satisfaction in the pattern of work actually adopted or experienced earlier as homemaking, career, career except when raising a family, or working for needed income without career implications (work-pattern satisfaction). These three variables were used as criteria against which earlier experiences and feelings could be assessed for their predictive value.

The Sample

The demographic variables of current and historical status—marital, occupational, and production of children—showed no great differences from Census data or from two national surveys conducted on probability samples which did not use IQ as a selection device. At average age sixty-two, however, the Terman women showed a higher percentage employed as compared to full-time homemakers than did the normative samples, more of the married women in the Terman group were childless, more had relatively high incomes, and far more had better education and more professional levels of employment than did the other samples.

Comparative Results

Lopata (1973) suggested that the roles of wife and mother are seen as "basic and the only really important ones for adult women." This is not the case, he believed, for comparable male roles as viewed by men, for whom occupation is the major role. In contrast, Yockey (1975) proposed a model predicting a future reduction in family size as a result of contemporary role change, with increased female employment outside the home and increased sense of personal efficacy in employed women.

The Terman women were past child-rearing age in 1972, but they were not in 1941 when the records of employment used in a historically oriented classification of income worker versus homemaker begin. The normative samples cited here do not give clear breakdowns by age for employment, children, and satisfactions, which would permit direct comparison with the Terman group in late middle age or later maturity. And one must remember that if the Terman women had borne children, by 1972 nearly all of those children were grown and away from home.

Some things can be clearly compared: the situation of the women at average age sixty-two whom we have characterized as head-of-household (single, divorced, or widowed, and in that status for twelve years or more) is clearly more satisfying to them on work pattern than it is to the non-head-of-household group (those who have been married for all or some portion of the twelve-year period).

This is in distinct contrast to the normative samples, in which the divorced, widowed, and employed women come out lower on general happiness than do the married housewives. We suggest that for high-IQ women, the independence from an unhappy marriage or the challenge of making one's own life alone as a widow or single person activates over time feelings of competence rather than depression. The absence of children, with their needs for parental involvement, no doubt contributes to the ease with which this satisfaction is achieved. Good health and energy are also significant when care of children and concomitant outside employment are both involved.

In a number of recent studies of high school and college-age women, the distinction has been made between those "traditionally" oriented and those "nontraditionally" oriented. In one (O'Leary and Hammack 1975), traditional subjects generated more traditionally feminine characteristics on a self-rating scale than did the nontraditional in terms of femininity-masculinity, role activities they find acceptable for themselves as women, and career activities they consider more appropriate for men than for women.

Within the Terman group (which attended high school and college in the 1920s and 1930s), we may be seeing some of the same distinctions between traditional and nontraditional sex-role orientation.

Some of the ten factors produced by factor analysis on this group represent traditional or nontraditional views (and/or actions) on sex-role orientation. Consider factor 1 (Table 3.6). The following variables contribute to the factor: income worker (1941-1972), occupation high level (1940), low time volunteer work (1960-65), work is rewarding (1950, 1960) and ambitious for vocational advancement at age thirty to forty and since age forty (1960).

Women scoring high on this factor also generally showed high scores on work-pattern satisfaction; it should be remembered that in this context homemaking is considered "work" in the same sense as is work outside the home.

Another factor (number 5) also correlated fairly well in a negative direction with work-pattern satisfaction. Here are the variables for that factor: had children (1972), wanted them (1940), found them rewarding (1950, 1960), and would do it again (1950).

Factor 8 includes: feels good about work (1972), good health (1972), and not ambitious for excellence in work at age thirty to forty (1960). This factor has the highest relation of any of the ten factors to the criterion joy in living satisfaction. Factor 9 has the highest correlation with general satisfaction 5: married (1972), and likes it (1950, 1960).

It is clear that these gifted women achieved life-style satisfactions by different routes. Note that not all the variables reaching significance are contemporary as of 1972, nor retrospective from that date. Some are actual reports in 1940, when the women were on the average thirty years old. This is a longitudinal study of the same women over half a century.

Terman Results

Studying prediction of life-style satisfaction at average age sixty-two by reports made in early and middle adulthood was hypothesized to reveal certain characteristics and experiences contributing to the variance and others irrelevant to it. The following hypotheses were posed. The actual results follow.

1. Women coming from homes in which both father and mother were well educated and in which father (and perhaps mother) followed a professional or higher business career would themselves be more likely to follow suit and show more satisfaction with their choice than those from homes in which the parents had lower levels of education and occupation.

   The expectation was not confirmed, with the exception of a rating by the subjects made in 1950 of their opinions of the vocational success of their father (high), which was a significant predictor.

   On the contrary, rather than emphasizing parents' occupational achievements, the predictors reaching significance on the association with the three measures of satisfaction emphasize the subject's own level of education, occupation, health, and ambition. Education and occupation of the married women's husbands also reached statistical significance but not those of her parents.

   The foregoing results are correct for the total sample of 430 women, although when taking subsamples by marital status, some exceptions occur. Single and married childless Terman women rated their parents' marriage as less happy than did married women with children.

   Divorced women's mothers, significantly more than those of other groups, had been in professional and managerial positions, and more of the divorced subjects considered their mothers to be very self-confident. One may speculate that this example of the mother's occupational achievement stimulated these subjects to get out on their own rather than to remain in an unhappy marriage. We have seen earlier that divorced women from this sample appear to be more satisfied with life than those divorced women from the general population.

2. Women coming from homes where parent-child relations were affectionately positive and where the parents' marriage was happy were predicted to be more likely to show general satisfaction with their own lives, have happier marriages themselves, and enjoy their children more. No prediction was made as to the work pattern the subject would follow in connection with this group of variables.

No parent-child relations variable reached significance in the prediction of work-pattern satisfaction, but a great many did for general satisfaction 5 and for joy in living satisfaction. These included the subjects' ratings (most of them in 1950) of the understanding and helpfulness of parents, encouragement of subjects' independence by parents, and subjects' admiration for their parents. In addition, parents' ratings of their child subjects' feelings of self-confidence and lack of inferiority feelings were high (1922, 1928) in connection with general satisfaction, suggesting a child-rearing climate of mutual affection and admiration between parents and child.

Also in connection with high general satisfaction there occurs a larger proportion of married than not-married women, with marriage and children named as important aspects of life satisfaction. As has been stated earlier, subjects higher on general satisfaction 5 considered their parents' marriage to be happier.

3. The third prediction was as follows: the subject's early feelings of self-confidence, lack of inferiority feelings, and presence of ambition should predict 1972 feelings of satisfaction with the experiences actually encountered over the years. More subjects with high early self-ratings should fall in the income work pattern than in the homemaker.

The results: earlier ambition for excellence in work and vocational advancement from age forty on appear as predictors of all three measures of later satisfaction. For general satisfaction 5 and joy in living, high self-ratings on self-confidence, persistence, and low feelings of inferiority appear also as early as 1940. Not confirmed was the prediction that early-self-confident women would appear more frequently later as income workers than as homemakers.

4. Our first, naive theory predicted that marriage, children, and income level should be positively related to later satisfaction.

For general satisfaction 5 but not for the other two measures, married women came out higher than did the other groups. But on work-pattern satisfaction they were surpassed by both the single and the divorced women.

Total family income was high in the Terman sample (median $18,000 in 1971) as compared to the general population. The actual level of income did not relate significantly to any of the three satisfaction measures. However, it was mentioned as one of the satisfying aspects of life in connection with work-pattern satisfaction. So also were children, in spite of the preceding finding of greater satisfaction among the childless.

Summary

Finally, disregarding the specific hypotheses, what can we say about the factors that have contributed to the joy and well-being of these gifted women over the last half-century? Clearly, there is no single path to glory. There are many women with high satisfactions, both in the general sense and with respect to their work, who belong to each of the subgroups we have distinguished.

What does stand out is that happiness under various circumstances depends on one's earlier experiences. Married women with children are more likely to be happy if their own parents' marriage was a good one, and if there was an affectionate and warm relationship between them and their parents. But such a relationship does not guarantee happiness at average age sixty-two if the life-style followed by the gifted woman was one that led her into a single life or a childless married life. Or, to put the matter in the other direction, the conditions that led to a life-style producing single status simply did not include any reference to the family state of affairs in their own childhood. Indeed, with reference to life satisfaction, one comes inescapably to the conclusion that the degree of satisfaction, either in general or specifically with reference to work alone, is part and parcel of a total developing personality. The life-style which brings happiness to one woman with one kind of life experience does not necessarily bring it to another woman with a different experiential background.

The foregoing might be said about any woman growing up in the era under consideration. In the comparisons with a less gifted population of women, however, there are various suggestions that our gifted sample in many instances identified circumstances which would allow for the possibility of a happy life on their own without a husband, took advantage of these, and were able to cope comfortably with their lives thereafter. It may well be that the coping mechanisms which enable the gifted woman to adapt flexibly to a variety of conditions, and in whatever condition to find good satisfactions, are related to the intelligence they bring to their life situations.

REFERENCES

Andrews, F., and Withey, S.B. "Developing Measures of Perceived Life Quality: Results from Several National Surveys." Paper presented at the annual meeting of the American Sociological Association, New York, 1973.

Burks, Barbara S.; Jensen, Dortha W.; and Terman, Lewis M. *The Promise of Youth: Follow-up Studies of a Thousand Gifted Children, Genetic Studies of Genius,* vol. 3. Stanford, Calif.: Stanford University Press, 1930.

Campbell, Angus; Converse, Philip E.; and Rodgers, Willard L. *The Quality of American Life.* New York: Russell Sage Foundation, 1975.

Lopata, Helena Z. "Self-Identity in Marriage and Widowhood." *Sociological Quarterly* 14 (Summer 1973): 407-18.

Nie, Norma H.; Hull, C. Hadlai; Jenkins, J.G.; Steinbrenner, K.; and Bent, Dale H. *SPSS: Statistical Package for the Social Sciences,* 2d ed. New York: McGraw-Hill, 1975.

Oden, Melita H. "The Fulfillment of Promise: 40-Year Follow-up of the Terman Gifted Group." *Genetic Psychology Monographs* 77 (1968): 3-93.

O'Leary, Virginia E., and Hammack, Barbara. "Sex-Role Orientation and Achievement Context as Determinants of the Motive to Avoid Success." *Sex Roles* 1 (September 1975): 225-34.

Sears, Robert R. "Sources of Life Satisfactions of the Terman Gifted Men." *American Psychologist* 32 (February 1977): 119-28.

Spreitzer, Elmer; Snyder, Eldon E.; and Larson, David. "Age, Marital Status, and Labor Force Participation as Related to Life Satisfaction." *Sex Roles* 1 (September 1975): 235-47.

Terman, Lewis M. (assisted by B.T. Baldwin, E. Bronson, J.C. DeVoss, F. Fuller, F.L. Goodenough, T.L. Kelley, M. Lima, H. Marshall, A.H. Moore, A.S. Raubenheimer, G.M. Ruch, R.L. Willoughby, J.B. Wyman, and D.H. Yates). *Mental and Physical Traits of a Thousand Gifted Children, Genetic Studies of Genius,* vol. 1. Stanford, Calif.: Stanford University Press, 1925.

Terman, Lewis M., and Oden, Melita H. *The Gifted Child Grows Up, Genetic Studies of Genius,* vol. 4. Stanford, Calif.: Stanford University Press, 1947.

Terman, Lewis M. *The Gifted Group at Mid-Life, Genetic Studies of Genius,* vol. 5. Stanford, Calif.: Stanford University Press, 1959.

Yockey, Jamie M. "A Model of Contemporary Role Change and Family Size." *Sex Roles* 1 (March 1975): 69-81.

Appendix 3.1
Variables Used in Data Analyses

Variable Number	Description
003	Age at 1972 birthday
004*	Marital status at present (1972)
007*	Number of children born to subject, adopted, or stepchildren
010*	Classification of subject as income worker or homemaker (1972)
011*	Level of satisfaction with work pattern (1972)
019*	1972 occupational classification, simplified
029*	Feelings about work at present (1972)
041*	Total family income, 1971
043	Importance of goals planned: occupational success (1972)
044	Importance of goals planned: family life (1972)
045	Importance of goals planned: friendships (1972)
046	Importance of goals planned: richness of cultural life (1972)
047	Importance of goals planned: total service to society (1972)
048	Importance of goals planned: joy in living (1972)
049	Satisfaction with attainment: occupational success (1972)
050	Satisfaction with attainment: family life (1972)
051	Satisfaction with attainment: friendships (1972)
052	Satisfaction with attainment: richness of cultural life (1972)
053	Satisfaction with attainment: total service to society (1972)
054*	Satisfaction with attainment: joy in living (1972)
055*	Percent time spent in volunteer work: 1960-65 (1972)
056*	Percent time spent in volunteer work: 1966-72 (1972)
057*	Rating on general health, 1970-72
059*	Energy and vitality level (1972)
060	Subject's self-rating of interest in algebra (1922)
061	Subject's self-rating of interest in arithmetic (1922)
069*	Teacher's comparison with average in arithmetic (1922)
073*	Teacher rates math as best or worst subject (1924)
074	Becoming more like father or mother (1950)
075	Father's choice of vocation for subject (1950)
076	Mother's choice of vocation for subject (1950)
081*	Conflict with father regarding career choice (1950)
082	Conflict with mother regarding career choice (1950)
084*	Mother's occupation (1922)
085*	Mother's occupation (1927)
086*	Father's occupation (1936)
087*	Mother's occupation (1936)
088*	Parents' marital status (1936)
089*	Mother's occupation (1940)
090	Parents' opinion of best occupation (1936)
091	Favorite parent (1940)

Appendix 3.1 (continued)
Variables Used in Data Analyses

Variable Number	Description
092	Amount of conflict with father (1940)
093*	Amount of attachment to father (1940)
094*	Amount of conflict with mother (1940)
095*	Amount of attachment to mother (1940)
096*	Subject rates happiness of parents' marriage (1940)
098*	Subject's opinion on how often punished (1940)
101	Ever wished to be a member of the opposite sex? (1940)
109*	Did you want children? (1940)
114	Parents' report on amount of punishment used (1922)
118*	Subject's level of education (1940)
119*	Subject's occupation (1940)
120*	Combined quotient on Stanford Achievement Test (1922)
121*	Stanford Achievement Test: arithmetic quotient (1972)
122*	1922 Intellectual traits
123	1922 Volitional traits
124	1928 Intellectual traits
125	1928 Volitional traits
126*	Parent report on special ability in math (1922)
130	Father's occupation (1922)
131	Amount of schooling of father (1922)
132	Amount of schooling of mother (1922)
133	Parents' marital status (1922)
134	Father's occupation (1928)
135	Parents' marital status (1928)
136	Attitude toward present job (1940)
137	Was present work chosen or drifted into? (1940)
139*	Education level of spouse (1940)
140*	Occupation of spouse (1940)
142	Parents' rating of subject's traits: feelings of inferiority (1940)
143*	Parents' rating of subject's traits: persistence (1940)
144	Parents' rating of subject's traits: integration (1940)
145	Parents' marital status (1940)
146*	Self-rating on traits: self-confidence (1940)
147	Self-rating on traits: persistence (1940)
148	Self-rating on traits: integration (1940)
149*	Self-rating on traits: feelings of inferiority (1940)
163*	Extent of understanding with father (1950)
164*	Extent of understanding with mother (1950)
165	Subject's rating of father's self-confidence (1950)
166*	Subject's rating of mother's self-confidence (1950)

Appendix 3.1 (continued)
Variables Used in Data Analyses

Variable Number	Description
167	Subject's rating of father's helpfulness (1950)
168	Subject's rating of mother's helpfulness (1950)
169	Subject's rating of father's friendliness (1950)
170	Subject's rating of mother's friendliness (1950)
172	Opinion on vocational success of father (1950)
173*	Satisfying aspects of life: work (1950)
174*	Satisfying aspects of life: recognition (1950)
175*	Satisfying aspects of life: income (1950)
176*	Satisfying aspects of life: activities/hobbies (1950)
177*	Satisfying aspects of life: marriage (1950)
178*	Satisfying aspects of life: children (1950)
179*	Satisfying aspects of life: religion (1950)
180*	Satisfying aspects of life: social contacts (1950)
181*	Satisfying aspects of life: community service (1950)
182*	Self-rating aspects of life: other (1950)
183*	Self-rating on self-confidence (1950)
184*	Self-rating on persistence (1950)
185	Self-rating on integration (1950)
186*	Self-rating on feelings of inferiority (1950)
187*	Subject rates admiration for father (1950)
188*	Subject rates admiration for mother (1950)
189	Subject rates rebellious feelings toward father (1950)
190	Subject rates rebellious feelings toward mother (1950)
191*	Subject rates father's encouragement of independence (1950)
192*	Subject rates mother's encouragement of independence (1950)
193	Subject rates father's resistance of independence (1950)
194	Subject rates mother's resistance of independence (1950)
195	Subject rates father's rejection (1950)
196	Subject rates mother's rejection (1950)
197	Subject rates how solicitous was father (1950)
198	Subject rates how solicitous was mother (1950)
199*	Subject rates how domineering was father (1950)
200*	Subject rates how domineering was mother (1950)
201	Subject rates father's intelligence (1950)
202	Subject rates mother's intelligence (1950)
203*	Feelings about present vocation (1950)
204*	Subject's occupation (1950)
205*	Spouse's occupation (1950)
208*	Number of children same as planned? (1950)
210*	If life lived over, how many children? (1950)

Appendix 3.1 (continued)
Variables Used in Data Analyses

Variable Number	Description
223*	Prefer duties of housewife to other occupation? (1922)
224*	Subject's occupation (1960)
225*	Spouse's occupation (1960)
226*	Historical rating on general adjustment (1960)
229*	Subject's ambition: excellence in work, age 30-40 (1960)
230*	Subject's ambition: excellence in work, since 40 (1960)
231	Subject's ambition: recognition, age 30-40 (1960)
232	Subject's ambition: recognition, since 40 (1960)
233*	Subject's ambition: vocational advancement, age 30-40 (1960)
234*	Subject's ambition: vocational advancement, since 40 (1960)
235	Subject's ambition: financial gain, age 30-40 (1960)
236	Subject's ambition: financial gain, since 40 (1960)
237	Change in ambition for excellence in work (1960)
238	Change in ambition for recognition (1960)
239	Change in ambition for vocational advancement (1960)
240	Change in ambition for financial gain (1960)
241	Increase in responsibilities or work pressure (1960)
242*	Satisfying aspects of life: work (1960)
243	Satisfying aspects of life: recognition (1960)
244	Satisfying aspects of life: income (1960)
245	Satisfying aspects of life: activities/hobbies (1960)
246*	Satisfying aspects of life: marriage (1960)
247*	Satisfying aspects of life: children (1960)
248	Satisfying aspects of life: religion (1960)
249*	Satisfying aspects of life: social contacts (1960)
250	Satisfying aspects of life: community service (1960)
251	Satisfying aspects of life: other (1960)
252*	Satisfaction 5: measure of general satisfaction using variables 43-47 and 49-53 (1972)

Asterisk indicates variable used in factor analysis (table 3.6).

Appendix 3.2
Correlations Between Satisfying Aspects of Life—1950 and 1960

	1950 (N = 381)				1960 (N = 398)			
	Work	Mar- riage	Chil- dren	Social Contacts	Work	Mar- riage	Chil- dren	Social Contacts
1950								
Work		-.07	-.20	.12	.41	-.15	-.31	.13
Marriage			.47	.09	-.14	.56	.32	.01
Children				.11	-.17	.29	.69	.04
Social contacts					.06	-.03	-.03	.39
1960								
Work	.41	-.14	-.17	.06		-.12	-.15	.09
Marriage	-.15	.56	.29	-.03			.40	.00
Children	-.31	.32	.69	-.03				.00
Social contacts	.13	.01	.04	.39				

Appendix 3.3
Probabilities of Differences Between Subsamples in Table 3.7

Variable number	Description	Subsamples	Probability
1	Parents' marriage happy	Single vs. married	.02
1	Parents' marriage happy	No children vs. children	<.10 to >.05
2	Father encouraged independence	Single vs. divorced	.02
2	Father encouraged independence	Single vs. married	>.10
3	Mother encouraged independence	Single vs. divorced	.02
3	Mother encouraged independence	Single vs. married	>.10
4	Mother very self-confident	Single vs. divorced	<.10 to>.05
4	Mother very self-confident	Single vs. married	>.10
8	Mother professional	Single vs. divorced	<.01
8	Mother professional	Single vs. married	>.10
16	Family income over $18,000	IW vs. HM	<.10 to >.05
19	Energy level high	IW vs. HM	.05

4

Biology: Its Role in Gender-Related Educational Experiences

Lisa J. Crockett and Anne C. Petersen

Biological factors are often invoked as explanations for sex-related differences with cognitive, achievement, and educational variables. Although some biological correlates of these variables undoubtedly exist, assumptions about biological causation of sex differences in these variables are seldom based on objective research results. The fact that males and females differ biologically is taken ipso facto as evidence of other kinds of differences as well. Numerous differences do exist but not simply because of the biological differences. The only characteristics that *absolutely* differentiate males and females are genes on a single chromosome, form of external genitalia, and the possibility of the capacity for lactation. The only one of these with the potential for influencing sex differences in achievement-related variables is the gender difference; we shall discuss the evidence for this factor in this chapter. All other biological characteristics differentiating males and females involve *relative* differences. Therefore, explanations involving these characteristics must serve to define within-sex differences as well.

Although we do not intend to deny the potential importance of biological factors—indeed this entire chapter is devoted to an exploration of their significance—we feel strongly that it is important to place this pursuit in proper perspective. Interest in biological explanations has often been related historically to times of social change regarding the status of women. This certainly is one such time. Many beliefs regarding gender differences are currently being challenged, primarily by feminists. At the same time, others of opposing views have renewed efforts to reassert the primacy of the status quo related to gender. It is our goal to avoid polemical discussion. Nonetheless we want to recognize the importance polemical arguments have in the investigation of biological factors as explanations for gender differences. Unsubstantiated biological explanations may be polemical arguments in disguise.

The specific focus of this volume is the examination of equity versus equality as social goals. Equality presumes no inherent differences between males and females. This perspective would require that there be no biological factors giving either disadvantage or advantage to one gender or the other in terms of educational experiences. An equity perspective, on the other hand, assumes that there may be some inherent differences but that these should not become impediments to educational attainment. In this view, gender-related strengths or weaknesses important to educational attainment must be accommodated in any educational program. We will return to a discussion of these issues at the end of this chapter.

In this chapter, we review the biological sex differences that may be important to educational experiences. We then describe an integrated model that considers how educational programs might be structured to enhance the educational attainments of both boys and girls in our society.

Biological differences between the sexes potentially influence the educational experiences of girls and boys in two ways. First, biological differences may contribute directly to sex differences in cognitive performance. Since a child's level of performance is likely to affect both the nature of the learning experiences (including interactions with educators) and the ultimate level of achievement attained, a sex-related difference in cognition would be likely to result in somewhat different experiences for boys and girls. Second, biological factors are known to mediate physical characteristics such as height, which come to distinguish boys and girls, especially after puberty. Such physical markers are likely to affect interpersonal interaction and, consequently, relationships with teachers and peers. Thus, biological differences could indirectly promote sex differences in educational experience as well as differences within each sex. Of course, nonbiological factors also influence individual and situational factors in ways that promote different educational experiences for girls and boys. The focus of this chapter, however, will be on biological factors.

DIRECT BIOLOGICAL EFFECTS

Genes

Some researchers have theorized that individual differences in some cognitive abilities are genetically based. A genetic hypothesis could explain a sex difference in one of these abilities, however, only if boys and girls were not equally likely to inherit the gene(s) in question. Since the sexes differ genetically only in their sex chromosomes (females have two X chromosomes; males have one X and one Y), the gene would have to appear on one of these chromosomes. Thus, most genetic hypotheses attempting to account for sex differences in cognition posit the existence of a recessive gene carried on the X chromosome. Traits governed by X-linked recessive genes (like those for color blindness and hemophilia) are not evenly distributed in the population because recessive traits are expressed only when the gene is unopposed; this situation is more likely to occur in males than in females. The trait will always be expressed in a boy inheriting the recessive gene because there is no second X chromosome to carry an opposing gene. A girl, on the other hand, will manifest the trait only if she receives the recessive gene on *both* X chromosomes (that is, from both parents). Under these circumstances we would expect an X-linked trait to appear in about twice as many boys as girls. Analyzing the distributions of scores for males and females, then, is one way in which genetic hypotheses can be examined.

X-linked traits have another important property, however. If family members are scored on the trait being investigated, and these scores are then compared, a distinctive pattern of parent-to-children and sibling-to-sibling correlations emerges. The presence of this pattern, then, would be evidence in support of an X-linkage hypothesis. The pattern of correlations, however, is rarely observed in family studies of cognitive abilities. The main cognitive trait for which some evidence of X linkage has been reported is spatial visualizing ability—the ability to mentally rotate three-dimensional figures. Even here, the early evidence (Bock and Kolakowski 1973, Hartlage 1970, Stafford 1961) has not been confirmed in later studies (Boles 1980, Vandenberg and Kuse 1979); therefore the possibility of X linkage for cognitive abilities remains controversial.

Recently some investigators have speculated that mathematical aptitude is biologically based. This assertion rests on two sets of data. First is the frequent finding that beginning in adolescence, boys on the average obtain higher scores on mathematical achievement tests than do girls (Maccoby and Jacklin 1974). Second is the recent data of Benbow and Stanley (1980) addressing the issue of mathematical precocity. These researchers found that in a sample of mathematically gifted students, boys had higher average mathematics scores on the SAT than girls did, as early as seventh grade. Since elective courses in advanced mathematics are typically unavailable until high school, the sex difference in seventh-grade mathematics SAT scores could not be attributed to differential course taking. Having ruled out this experiential source of differences, Benbow and Stanley concluded that the boys and girls in their sample had similar mathematics preparation. They went on to suggest that the sex differences in test scores reflect a sex difference in mathematical ability that is in part genetically based and may be related to the sex difference in spatial ability.

There are several problems with this reasoning. First, according to its developers, the mathematics SAT is a test of mathematical reasoning skills, not of mathematical ability (Educational Testing Service 1980). Thus, if we were to accept the Benbow and Stanley finding that by the seventh-grade mathematically gifted boys tend to receive higher scores than mathematically gifted girls, we could conclude only that mathematics *achievement* appears to be greater in boys—the question of a gender difference in mathematical ability would remain unresolved. However, even the issue of greater mathematics achievement in seventh-grade boys has not been settled since the magnitude of the sex differences reported by Benbow and Stanley may be called into question. In their analyses of the same data, Fox and associates (1980) found that sampling bias in the identification of gifted youngsters contributed substantially to the sex difference in mathematics scores. Specifically, the sex difference was largest when students were recruited on a volunteer basis and nearly disappeared when recruitment was based on school testing. Since the Benbow and Stanley sample was a subsample of the larger Fox study, the possibility that the observed sex difference was due partly to sampling bias cannot be ignored.

Second, there is no direct evidence that genetic factors underlie mathematical ability. Few researchers have even attempted to address the issue, much less to use appropriate methods of genetic analysis. For example, Benbow and Stanley did not test any genetic or other biological hypothesis. The existing evidence, then, does not provide support for differential inheritability of mathematical precocity or aptitude.

Some previous investigators (for example, Guay and McDaniel 1977, Sherman 1967) have suggested that the sex difference in mathematical ability is in part a function of the sex difference in spatial ability. If this turned out to be true, evidence for X-linked inheritance of spatial ability could also support a genetic explanation of mathematical aptitude. As we stated earlier, however, the evidence for X-linked inheritance of spatial ability has not been confirmed in recent studies. Furthermore, correlations between mathematics achievement and performance on tests of spatial ability are not always high (for example, Fennema and Sherman 1977, Petersen 1982). Thus, at present, the relationship between mathematics and spatial ability remains ambiguous and offers little support for the genetic transmission of mathematical ability.

A third problem with the Benbow and Stanley (1980) conclusion is that ruling out the effect of differential course taking is not tantamount to ruling out the effects of all experiential factors on SAT mathematics scores. The experiences of girls and boys appear to differ substantially prior to seventh grade (see Lockheed, Chapter Five this volume), and such differential experience could contribute to the gender difference in mathematics scores. Pertinent to this argument, Fox and her colleagues (1980) observed important psychological differences between the boys and girls in their gifted sample. There were sex differences in attitudes toward the study of mathematics, in motivation to excel, and in confidence level. Such factors are likely to be at least partly based in experience, and any or all of them may have affected mathematics SAT scores. Benbow and Stanley (1980) admit that not all environmental explanations have been discounted, but they opt to favor an explanation involving genetic differences. In so doing, they discount the subtle but potent socializing influences that are continuously present in our society, influences that are likely to affect crucial performance variables such as motivation and confidence in one's ability.

Summary. Genetic explanations have frequently been invoked to account for individual and sex differences in cognitive performance, but the available genetic studies do not strongly favor the genetic hypothesis typically proposed. In some early studies, the pattern of intrafamilial correlations that indicate an X-linked trait was observed but only for one cognitive ability. More recent studies have not confirmed this finding. In general, then, evidence of X-linkage in the case of cognitive abilities is weak. Unless X-linkage is demonstrated, there would seem to be no basis for differential heritability of cognitive abilities in males and females. Since differential heritability is necessary to explain a sex difference (Wittig 1979), it seems unlikely that sex differences in cognitive abilities (including spatial ability and mathematical aptitude) could be accounted for on a genetic basis. While most cognitive abilities involve some genetic component, sex differences in cognition (and any effects such differences have on educational experience) must be explained in some other way.

Brain Organization

Brain organization is a second biological factor hypothesized to affect cognition. Although most complex mental tasks require the participation of both cerebral hemispheres, in many cognitive functions one hemisphere is involved to a greater degree than the other. For example, in most people, verbal tasks are processed primarily by the left hemisphere, while many nonverbal tasks preferentially engage the right. Brain organization, then, refers to the *degree to which* the two hemispheres are differentially engaged in the execution of various functions (that is, the degree to which functions are *lateralized* or organized asymmetrically).

Some findings from studies of brain-damaged individuals, from perceptual experiments, and from anatomical and physiological studies point to the existence of sex differences in cerebral asymmetry. For both spatial and verbal tasks, males appear to be more lateralized than females, particularly in adulthood (McGlone 1980, Springer and Deutsch 1981). In other words, cognitive functions are more likely to be processed by both hemispheres in females, while a single hemisphere predominates in males. Therefore, if greater lateralization (or specialization) is held to be more efficient, the greater degree of lateralization among males could account for their superior performance on spatial tasks. However, the hypothesis equating greater lateralization with greater efficiency is likely to be an oversimplification, since it would also predict a male superiority in verbal tasks; contrary to this expectation, females tend to outperform males in tests of verbal ability (Maccoby and Jacklin 1974). It should also be kept in mind that there is probably as much or more variation in brain organization *among* members of each sex as there is *between* the sexes, and that sex differences in laterality are not always observed (for example, Kail and Siegel 1978, Petersen 1981). Even when a sex difference is found, the magnitude is likely to be small. In many ways, then, the brain organizations of males and females are more similar than they are different.

An alternative hypothesis concerning sex differences in lateralization is based on the developmental finding that the cerebral hemispheres mature at different rates in males and females. According to perception studies, the right hemisphere matures earlier in boys than in girls (for example, Witelson 1976), while the left develops earlier in girls (Bryden 1970). Since in most people language functions are subserved primarily by the left hemisphere and nonverbal functions by the right, the different patterns of maturation should result in a relative advantage for girls on verbal tasks and for boys on spatial tasks. Consistent with this prediction is evidence that language develops earlier in girls (for example, Clarke-Stewart 1973) and that boys show superior performance on some spatial tasks as early as age six (Linn and Petersen, unpublished manuscript; Witelson 1976).

Yet, the assertion that boys excel in right-hemisphere functions while girls excel in left-hemisphere functions is also an oversimplification since girls are superior on only *some* tasks mediated by the left hemisphere, and boys are superior on only *some* right-hemisphere tasks. The complex pattern of sex-related differences in laterality and cognition has led some researchers to suggest that the important underlying factor may be the *mode of functioning* of each cerebral hemisphere rather than differences in the relationship between hemispheres. According to Levy (1980), there is a tendency for females to excel in tasks requiring a rapid encoding of information that is rich in contextual detail but which may not easily fit into an orderly logical framework. Males, on the other hand, tend to encode information according to formal or logical relationships and excel in tasks requiring the application of formal principles but not the recall of details. The retention of less structured information by females would increase their ability to take into account contextual features whose relationship cannot be clearly articulated. This type of ability may be particularly useful in interpersonal communication, where it would facilitate reading other people's emotional states or accurately recalling facial features and tone of voice. Males, on the other hand, might be more adept in areas like mathematics, where the relationships among components are purely formal and independent of contextual features. Levy (1980) goes on to argue that the within-hemisphere organization of females might facilitate bilateral (unlateralized) processing of information, while the formal systems of males would make interhemispheric integration difficult and force a more lateralized mode of processing. While intriguing, this line of reasoning is at present largely speculative.

The complicated pattern of sex differences in cognitive tasks intended to tap brain organization also attests to the fact that differences in performance depend heavily on the specific skills involved in each task. Calling a task "verbal" or "spatial" does not always allow one to predict whether boys or girls will obtain higher average scores. The complexity of the data may therefore reflect not a global effect of sex (for example, boys are better at spatial tasks and girls at verbal tasks) but a difference in the *strategies* boys and girls tend to apply to the same task (Bryden 1979). Boys may be more likely to apply a strategy that primarily engages the right hemisphere; girls may prefer a left-hemisphere strategy. Depending on the specific task, one or the other type of strategy will be more efficient, yielding a sex difference in performance. Although it is not yet clear why girls might preferentially engage one hemisphere and boys the other (perhaps the hemisphere that matures first comes to be preferred), the use of different strategies could account for sex differences in performance and perhaps for some of the findings on laterality. In any case, the role of brain organization in individual or sex differences in cognition remains a potentially important but poorly understood factor.

Some anatomical differences in the brains of human males and females have also been reported (Hier 1981). On the average, brains of adult males are larger than those of adult females, hardly a surprising finding since men are usually larger than women. There seems to be little evidence, however, for sex differences in human brain *structure;* although sex differences in neuronal circuitry and in nerve growth have been observed in some lower animals (Hier 1981), and a sex difference in the structure of hypothalamic nerve cells has been reported in macaque monkeys (Ayoub, Greenough, and Juraska 1983). Furthermore, the cerebral hemispheres seem to be largely similar in men and women. Preliminary data from a recent study of human brains, however, indicate a sex difference in the shape of the corpus callosum—the bundle of nerve fibers connecting the two hemispheres. The hind portion of this structure tends to be larger and rounder in females than it is in males (de Lacoste-Utamsing and Holloway 1982). Since this same area is known to play a role in the transfer of visual information between hemispheres, the authors speculate that the larger size of the area in females is related to the finding that females are more likely than males to process visual-spatial tasks bilaterally (that is, drawing equally on both hemispheres). However, the relationship between anatomical differences and sex-related differences in cognitive functioning has not been clearly established (McGlone 1980).

Summary. Although the sex difference in laterality seems fairly well established (McGlone 1980), the role of laterality in cognitive performance is not well understood. Simple explanations which assume that boys excel in right-hemisphere tasks while girls excel in left-hemisphere tasks cannot account for the complex patterns of sex differences in cognitive abilities. More complex hypotheses have been articulated but have not been adequately tested. Thus the proposed link between the sex difference in brain organization and that in cognitive performance has not been clearly established, and discussions dealing with the link remain highly speculative. The relationship between the few sex differences in human brain anatomy and sex-related differences in cognition is even less well understood than the laterality effects. At this time, then, the effects of sex-related differences in brain organization and anatomy on cognitive performance are unclear, and any influence on educational experience less certain yet.

Hormonal Factors

Hormonal differences have also been invoked to account for sex-related differences in cognition. The hormones thought to be involved are the sex hormones, or gonadal steroids (androgens, estrogens, and progestins), so called because characteristic concentrations of these hormones are strikingly different for males and females, particularly in adulthood. Although all of these hormones are present to some degree in both sexes, males have markedly higher androgen levels, while females have higher levels of estrogens and progestins. The sex difference in absolute levels of particular hormones is probably not as important in producing sexual dimorphism or cognitive sex differences as are differences in the *ratio* of androgenic to extrogenic steroids. Hormones have an effect only when they are taken up by tissues. Since sex hormones can compete for the available binding sites in the tissue, it is the amount of androgen relative to estrogen that is likely to determine which substance prevails at tissue sites and has the greater effect.

It is assumed that hormones influence cognition by affecting the brain. At least in lower mammals, it has been demonstrated that certain areas of the brain selectively take up (or utilize) these types of steroids (Goy and McEwen 1980). Presumably, then, the different amounts of each type of hormone typically reaching the brains of males versus females could contribute to sex differences in cognition. Unfortunately, the specific mechanisms by which hormones might operate to influence cognition have not been clearly articulated, much less precisely tested. Furthermore, it is not known when in the life-cycle hormones are most likely to exert their effects on brain functioning. Four types of hormonal effects have been suggested, however: those due to prenatal, pubertal, and postpubertal hormones, and those due to cyclic fluctuations in hormone levels.

Prenatal sex hormones (primarily androgens) govern the

development of the fetal reproductive system. Specifically, the presence of sufficient amounts of androgens causes the development of male reproductive structures, and the relative absence of this steroid results in the development of female structures. An extreme sex difference in androgen concentrations is known to exist during part of the prenatal period. Moreover, in the period just prior to and after birth, hormonal levels undergo a dramatic increase, temporarily reaching adult concentrations and producing an extreme sex difference in hormonal levels. Thus, there are at least two points during fetal development when hormones might be expected to affect the brains of males and females differentially. In lower mammals, where experimental manipulation of hormone levels is possible, some evidence suggests that prenatal hormones do affect behaviors that may be analogous to cognition (Reinisch 1981, see also Goy and McEwen 1980), but the role of prenatal hormones in human cognition has not yet been established. Research on humans progresses slowly, primarily because such research requires adequate numbers of individuals born with rare endocrine abnormalities. At least it is known that prenatal hormones affect some parts of the human brain (see Reinisch, Gandelman, and Spiegel 1979).

Sex hormone levels also show a dramatic increase at puberty, when they bring about the somatic and physiological changes characterizing boys and girls at this time. Two pathways by which the pubertal surge in hormones may affect cognition have been proposed: first, the high concentrations could exert a direct, disruptive influence on brain processes; second, hormones could affect brain functioning indirectly through their role in terminating physical growth.

The possible disruption of cognitive processes at puberty has been investigated in several studies (Carey 1981, Carey and Diamond 1980, Carey, Diamond, and Woods 1980). A decline in performance on some tests measuring the ability to rapidly encode and accurately recall faces and the ability to extract main figures from a distracting background (field independence) have been reported in girls during the pubertal years. Although the disruption hypothesis would predict a similar performance decrement in pubertal boys, boys have not yet been tested in these studies; there is, therefore, no evidence (either anecdotal or data based) of such a decrement. Furthermore, since it would apply to both sexes, the disruption hypothesis alone could not explain a sex-related difference in cognition. It is possible, of course, that for a variety of psychosocial reasons, boys but not girls recover their prior cognitive competence.

In our own studies involving the long-term assessment of young adolescents, we have found no evidence for a disruption in spatial ability, field independence, or any other cognitive variable during the early pubertal period (Kavrell and Petersen, forthcoming; Petersen, forthcoming). To the contrary we find a steady increase in performance on tests of ability. Grades, on the other hand, do decline for both boys and girls over the junior high school years.

Pubertal hormones could also affect cognition through the role they play in the adolescent's attainment of physical growth. It is well known that at puberty the high concentrations of sex steroids (primarily androgens) initiate the adolescent growth spurt. The long bones of the body grow at an accelerated pace and finally make connection with their terminal joints whereupon they fuse (again under the influence of androgen), preventing further growth. Pubertal hormones thus help terminate the growth process (Petersen and Taylor 1980).

It has been hypothesized (Waber 1976, 1977) that pubertal hormones have an analogous effect on important aspects of brain development. Specifically, Waber proposed that the upsurge in hormones at puberty curtails brain lateralization—the progressive specialization of the cerebral hemispheres for differing cognitive functions. Since boys on the average reach maturity two years later than girls, the lateralization process may continue that much longer, with the result that at maturity males would tend to be more lateralized than females. Waber's hypothesis fits the research finding of greater laterality or asymmetry of function in males. Moreover, Waber found that later maturers of both sexes tended to score higher on measures of spatial ability. If greater lateralization is assumed to improve efficiency and hence performance, Waber's data would support her contention that the timing of puberty affects both brain organization and cognition. The sex difference in performance on cognitive (at least spatial) tests could then be explained as a secondary effect of a sex-related difference in the typical age at which maturity is reached.

Some subsequent studies have replicated the association between later maturation and better spatial performance (Carey and Diamond 1980; Newcombe, Bandura, and Taylor 1983; Petersen and Gitelson, forthcoming), although other studies have failed to confirm it (Herbst and Petersen 1979, Petersen 1976). For the most part, the effect of timing on cognitive performance appears to be a weak one most likely observed when extreme groups (for example, very early versus very late developers) are compared. No study, however, has replicated Waber's second finding of an association between timing of maturation and degree of lateralization. Individuals who reach maturity relatively late do not seem to show more asymmetric functioning than those who mature early. Consequently, the mechanism by which timing of maturation might affect cognitive performance remains obscure. It may be that the development of laterality is not the key mediating factor at all. In fact, the issue of whether lateralization increases with age is at present highly controversial (Hiscock and Kinsbourne 1978, Kinsbourne and Hiscock 1977, Waber 1979).

Postpubertal or adult hormone levels could affect cognitive functioning, although research to date suggests that the relationship is quite modest. The main finding of this literature is that some forms of spatial ability (that is, spatial-visualization) are related to androgen levels. Presumably, androgens exert their effect on the same brain areas potentially affected by prenatal and pubertal hormones. It may be that a sensitivity to androgens in these areas is established prenatally and is subsequently maintained by adult hormone levels. Since males typically have higher androgen concentrations than females throughout the life cycle, any effect of androgens on cognition would be more pronounced in males, and this would create sex differences in cognitive performance.

The fact that males tend to out-perform females on tests of spatial ability and also tend to have higher androgen levels leads to the expectation that higher androgen levels would be associated with better spatial skills. Given this expectation, the findings with respect to postpubertal androgen levels are somewhat surprising. When men and women are arranged by androgen level along a single continuum, those individuals whose androgen levels are in the *intermediate* range tend to do best on spatial tasks (reviewed in Petersen 1979). Since women tend to have low androgen levels and men tend to have high levels, it is the women with high androgen levels relative to other women and men with low levels relative to other men who seem to do best. The same pattern emerged in a recent replication study (Berenbaum and Resnick 1982), although the finding did not reach statistical significance. A similar pattern was observed when androgen concentrations were directly measured in the blood, and, in this case, the curvilinear relationship reached statistical significance (Cantoni, Pellegrino, and Hubert 1981). Finally, the association was replicated when self-ratings of body shape were used to estimate hormone levels (Peterson and Gitelson, forthcoming). The fact that the pattern emerged with even this crude a measure indicates that the relationship is robust. In our own data, the strength of the association between androgen and spatial ability has been greater in males than in females, although it varies somewhat depending on the particular measures employed.

Alternatively, it has been hypothesized that in adults cognition is affected not so much by absolute hormone levels as by periodic fluctuations in the levels of these hormones. Such fluctuations are typical of the female menstrual cycle but also characterize some men (Doering, Kramer, Brodie, and Hamburg 1975). However, cyclic fluctuations in hormone levels have not been linked to consistent changes in cognitive performance (reviewed in Dan 1979), and even though some aspects of behavior may vary over the menstrual cycle (for example, activity level, sensory threshold, negative affect), these changes seem to have little effect on cognitive performance (Golub 1976). Thus it is unlikely that hormonal fluctuations could account for sex-related differences in cognition.

Summary. As with the biological factors previously discussed, the evidence for direct hormonal effects on cognitive performance is largely inconclusive. In some cases, research is simply too sparse to provide satisfactory evidence. The presence of differing prenatal levels of gonadal hormones provides a potential basis for individual and sex differences in cognition, but to date no strong causal link has been established, nor has the mechanism by which hormones exert an effect been articulated. In like fashion, a peripubertal decline in some cognitive skills has been reported, but there is no clear indication that the decline characterizes other important abilities or that it is hormonally induced. Parallel attempts to link pubertal maturation to cognitive performance via a hypothesized relation to degree of lateralization has been largely unsupported by the data. Although there is now evidence of a link between timing of maturation and some cognitive processes, the mechanisms underlying this relationship are largely unknown. A curvilinear association between androgen levels and spatial ability has been observed, but again the mechanism of hormonal action is unknown. Hormone levels may well affect cognitive functioning and educational experience, but at this point few effects have been demonstrated.

INDIRECT EFFECTS

Whether or not biological factors are found to have a direct effect on cognitive functioning, they enter into the educational experience of boys and girls in other, less obvious ways. Genes and hormones are the primary determinants of each individual's physical appearance, and certain physical attributes, particularly those related to size and gender, function as important social signals. In our culture and in many others, tallness seems to engender a response of awe or even fear; thus it lends a measure of prestige. Similarly, physical characteristics that signal the approach of reproductive maturity become symbols of soon-to-be-attained adult status that may affect both social expectations and self-perceptions. Both the responses or expectations of others and self-perceptions can affect behavior in important achievement domains. For example, it has been shown that adult (parental) expectations for achievement influence a child's achievement motivation (Parsons, Adler, and Kaczala 1982; Winterbottom 1958). Since in older children the effects of social expectations are likely to be mediated by perceptions of self, this second factor might also be assumed to influence achievement motivation and performance. Thus, biological factors may indirectly affect achievement variables relevant to the child's (and particularly to the adolescent's) educational experience.

Size

Height is probably the most salient aspect of size, although other skeletal dimensions such as the breadth of the shoulders and the deepness of the rib cage also contribute to overall body bulk. Skeletal dimensions are a function of bone length, which is governed primarily by genetic endowment. However, the size an individual ultimately attains depends not only on genetic factors but also on environmental factors, and in particular on nutrition. Thus, severely malnourished children are likely to be shorter than the maximum height provided for in their genetic blueprint. Furthermore, excessive exercise (more than five hours per day) during pubertal growth has been found to delay the rate of pubertal development leading ultimately to a taller individual because the prepubertal growth of the long bones is extended (Frisch, forthcoming). Additionally, a child's height at any given age depends in part on his or her developmental level: since children grow at different rates, height differences among children of similar age are partly attributable to differences in the proportion of adult height each has already attained. For this reason, boys and girls who are short relative to their peers in early childhood may "catch up" later on.

An individual's mature height (assuming optimal nutrition) may be genetically programmed, but the program is carried out partly through the influence of pubertal hormones. At puberty, the rise in gonadal hormones initiates a skeletal growth spurt in both boys and girls, but the same hormones ultimately curtail growth by causing the bones to fuse with their terminal joints. This fusing, called the closure of the epiphyses, prevents further bone growth. Adult height is thus partly a function of the timing of puberty: the later puberty arrives, the more time before hormone levels rise, and the longer the individual has before his or her growth is curtailed. The timing of puberty is a particularly important factor in the emergence of sex differences in stature. Before puberty, the average height of girls and boys is roughly the same. Girls and boys also grow approximately equal amounts during their pubertal growth spurts. Boys, however, reach puberty about two years later than girls and thus have two extra years in which to grow before their bones fuse. It is the extra years of prepubertal growth in boys more than differential height gain during the pubertal growth spurt that produces the adult sex difference in height (Petersen and Taylor 1980).

In our culture as well as in most others, tallness seems to be a symbol of status. Among adult males, height has been found to correlate with social class, the likelihood of being hired, starting salary, and occupational prestige (Freedman 1979). Thus, while height that far exceeds the normal range carries disadvantages because it may be perceived as abnormal, tallness generally gives men a social advantage. The reverse is also true: people in prestigious positions are often judged to be taller than they actually are (Brackbill and Nevill 1981). We do not know precisely why, but at some level tallness seems to be associated with power and competence. Perhaps we tend to construe height in terms of physical strength. In any case, tallness clearly affects social responses and expectations and therefore could easily play a role in dominance relations among both children and adults.

Height may affect educational experience since it seems to influence the achievement expectations adults have for children. In one experiment, taller children were assigned more difficult tasks than were shorter children of the same age, even when the tasks did not require physical strength (Brackbill and Nevill 1981). In other words, taller children were assumed to be cognitively superior. Furthermore, since high achievement motivation in children generally stems from parental pressure to achieve, a parent's judgment of her or his child's ability (erroneously based on the child's height) would be likely to influence the child's motivation to achieve. Thus, the child's height may influence parental expectations and pressure to achieve, which may in turn influence the child's actual achievement behavior. Extrapolating to the school situation, the expectations of parents and teachers may encourage high performance in taller students and discourage it in shorter students of the same age.

In the same way, differences in height may contribute to sex differences in school achievement. Brackbill and Nevill (1981) note that in elementary school, girls are slightly taller than boys and also receive better grades. In adolescence, boys surpass girls in height and begin to surpass them in high school subjects. In adulthood, men are often higher achievers than women academically and professionally. Unfortunately, these findings do not permit us to disentangle the effects of height from those of gender. If parents have higher achievement expectations for boys than for girls, they would on the average appear to have higher expectations for taller children, since after adolescence males are taller than females. In our estimation, a child's gender is at least as potent an organizer of adult expectations for him or her as is the child's height. Therefore, differential height is probably not the main factor leading to sex differences in achievement.

Size is likely to affect peer relations because children, like adults, might be expected to associate tallness with greater competence and power (Kohlberg 1966). Even infants exhibit a stronger fear reaction to tall strangers than to short ones (Freedman 1979). Furthermore, in childhood, the taller individuals are likely to be the stronger ones since other important aspects of strength such as muscle size do not substantially differentiate children until puberty. Thus taller children may be able to dominate their shorter peers.

Beginning at puberty, size differences become a function of both skeletal dimensions and muscle size. Consequently, both factors must be taken into account in estimating the interpersonal impact of an individual's physical appearance. A very tall basketball player such as Wilt Chamberlain is imposing, but so is a heavily muscled weight lifter such as Arnold Schwarzenegger. In this regard, it should be noted that musculature contributes at least as much to physical power as does height; thus to the extent that our response to a person's size is based on an assessment of overall strength and not on stature per se, musculature may be an important factor determining our reactions.

Muscle development occurs in conjunction with the adolescent spurt in height and is caused by the same pubertal hormones (Tanner 1972). Boys in particular show marked increases in muscle size and strength, and their greater gain relative to girls results in the adult sex differences in musculature and physical power. Of course, exercise also enhances muscle development, so women's increasing interest in exercise and body building could substantially reduce the male-female differences in muscle size and strength. At present, however, the sex differences are still marked and, together with the sex difference in height, probably play a role in power relations between the sexes.

Individual differences in muscle size also increase in adolescence due mainly to interindividual variation in hormonal activity. Of course, since children reach puberty at different ages, some differences in muscle development among adolescents of the same age are a function of differences in pubertal status and may be only temporary (Tanner 1972). Postpubertally, musculature reflects more enduring individual differences in physiology and hormonal activity.

Between the sexes, but also among individuals, size is likely to figure in dominance relations, although it is unlikely to be the sole determining factor. Dominance status may in turn affect access to and use of educational facilities, which may then create sex differences in behavior. At a recent conference, one of the authors overheard an anecdote that aptly illustrated this situation. Girls in one junior high school had been observed to use the computers less frequently than boys; on this basis it was assumed that the girls had less interest in computer work. On closer inspection, however, it was found that girls tried to use the computer but were frequently physically ousted by some of the boys. Once use was determined by sign-up rather than dominance, the sex difference in computer use disappeared. The dominance factor, then, contributed to the gender difference in computer use. While it might be assumed that dominance was based primarily on gender (boys having higher dominance status), this is not necessarily the case since it has been found that when size is controlled for, sex differences in dominance disappear (Lockheed 1982).

Size could also affect educational experience by its influence on classroom dynamics, especially when the teachers are female. The effect would be most likely to emerge in adolescence when boys and girls approach the size of adults. Again the sex difference in height is important—girls might reach the height of their female teachers but would rarely tower above them. Boys, on the other hand, tend to *surpass* their female teachers in height, and this could affect student-teacher interactions. Along these lines, some researchers have reported that boys who have reached puberty are more likely to attempt to dominate their parents in conversations than are prepubertal boys (Steinberg and Hill 1978).

Summary. Size is based primarily on biological factors, but it also acts as an important social stimulus. It is therefore likely to influence interaction among children and between teachers and pupils, although few studies have attempted to address this issue directly. Some evidence exists that children and adults associate greater height with greater competence and power. Thus, differences in size could influence dominance relations and expectations for academic performance, either of which would affect educational experiences.

Gender

Gender is a second biologically based attribute that strongly influences social responses and expectations. In terms of genetic endowment, the attribute of maleness or femaleness is a relatively minor feature of the human program: of the twenty-three pairs of chromosomes inherited from the parents, males and females are known to differ in only one. This final pair, aptly called the sex chromosomes, carries the genes in which the somatic and physiological differences between the sexes are encoded. As stated, females have two X chromosomes, and males have one X and one Y.

It is the addition of the Y chromosome that causes the development of male reproductive structures. If a Y chromosome is present, the fetus develops testes, which then produce potent androgens. These androgens cause the undifferentiated genital structures to develop as male. Females, because they have a second X chromosome instead of a Y, do not develop testes. In the absence of the large amounts of androgens secreted by testes, the genitalia of XX individuals develop as female (Money and Ehrhardt 1972).

The appearance of the external genitalia at birth is a biological fact. The classification as male or female and the significance ascribed to this classification, however, are sociocultural matters. In this culture, classification in terms of gender is one of the most fundamental distinctions made: gender is a central feature around which our perceptions of others and our expectations regarding their behavior are organized (Bem 1981).

The beliefs and expectations surrounding boys and girls are different from the start. For instance, adults perceive baby girls as softer, smaller, and more fragile than boy babies, regardless of how babies actually compare (Rubin, Provenzano, and Luria 1974). In other words, the appearance of the external genital structures is the distinguishing criterion to which are attached a host of cultural notions regarding "masculine" and "feminine" nature. Some of these notions may be based on social realities, others on cultural mythology, but in either case they influence the parents' perceptions of the child, their response to her or him, and their expectations regarding the child's future position in the social world.

Although there seems to be little evidence of overt differences in the early socialization of girls and boys, there is a strong indication of differential "shaping" of interest: parents tend to encourage "feminine" activities in girls and "masculine" activities in boys while discouraging their children (and particularly boys) from engaging in sex-inappropriate activities (Maccoby and Jacklin 1974). This means that a child's early experiences are weighted in one direction or the other, depending on assigned sex. From a very early age children know whether they are boys or girls. They also observe their parents and exhibit in play their developing conceptions of what males and females ("mommies and daddies") do (Brooks-Gunn and Matthews 1979). Since children learn that they will grow up to be "mommies and daddies," they are likely to incorporate these early conceptions of sex role into their emerging gender identities. Many times these identifications are highly stereotyped because the parents follow traditional male-female role behaviors. And throughout childhood this early sex-role learning is compounded by less subtle socialization pressures coming from the school, the peer group, and the media.

It seems likely, then, that a child's experience is tied to his or her gender label. While that label is based initially on the appearance of the genitalia, it comes to encompass much more as the child learns cultural beliefs and expectations attached to the label and realizes that these, also, apply to him or her. Sex-role expectations, then, guide behavior not only because they are the basis for differential reinforcement and punishment, but also because they are internalized in the older child as part of her or his self-concept. Of course, individuals have somewhat different experiences and therefore may incorporate different versions of sex roles, but some aspects of the cultural stereotypes are likely to be found in most of us. In any case, internalized beliefs about how members of one's own sex can and should behave are likely to influence behavior.

One area where cultural sex-role stereotypes may have a profound effect is on achievement. It is known that as early as the second grade, children readily sex-type achievement areas: social, artistic, and reading skills are seen as more feminine; arithmetic, spatial, and mechanical skills as more masculine (Stein and Smithells 1969). Interestingly, the early sex-typing of achievement areas does not seem to affect performance during the grade school years: the interests of boys and girls seem more similar than different. However, it has been suggested that despite the perception of skills as sex-appropriate or inappropriate, children of this age group (and girls more than boys) are permitted substantial flexibility in their achievement activities; achivement is encouraged in whatever form it takes. In other words, social pressures to act in conformity with sex-role stereotypes are not overly strong at this time (Brooks-Gunn and Matthews 1979). Sex-typing is learned but seems to be put on a back burner, as though it were perceived to be more relevant to future roles than to current behavior.

At puberty, however, the picture changes considerably. An increase in sex hormones brings about somatic changes that transform an essentially childlike body into that of an adult man or woman. Androgens promote genital development and an increase in shoulder breadth in boys as well as lowering the voice (Tanner 1972). Androgens also stimulate the growth of body hair (pubic and axillary) in both sexes and facial hair in boys. Estrogens are responsible for breast development and pelvic expansion in girls (Petersen and Taylor 1980).

The emergence of these secondary sex characteristics under the influence of pubertal hormones has several consequences. First, the somatic changes give adolescents an adultlike appearance and hence raise social expectations that they will act in accordance with adult roles. In this culture, adult roles are highly sex-typed. Second, they produce greater physical dimorphism, making gender differences in appearance more salient (Brooks-Gunn and Matthews 1979). The striking physical differences between the sexes may cause expectations for psychological and behavioral differences to be exaggerated, at least initially. A girl with a stereotypically "feminine" appearance is expected to *act* "feminine." Finally, the secondary characteristics signal the onset of reproductive maturity and heterosexual relationships. The complementarity of male and female heterosexual roles may be taken as the model for adolescent behavior: boys and girls may be expected to behave in complementary rather than similar ways in other domains as well.

For all these reasons, pubertal maturation is likely to increase the pressure from peers and adults to conform to cultural sex roles. In this climate of "gender intensification" (Hill and Lynch forthcoming), the well-ingrained male and female stereotypes acquired during childhood may be perceived by the adolescent as relevant sex-role prescriptions and proscriptions. The social message reaching adolescents is that sex roles are now to be taken seriously.

The somatic changes of puberty also affect the self-perceptions of the developing adolescent. Perceiving themselves as more adultlike, girls and boys may be eager to behave in ways that prove them ready to assume adult status. In a period marked by radical physical and cognitive changes, they are likely to fall back on sex-role stereotypes as a guide to acting like adults. Sex roles may thus provide a means of self-definition during a time of unstable identity. Moreover, adherence to sex-role stereotypes may yield a measure of consistency between physical appearance, perceptions of self as a young man or woman, and behavior (Kavrell and Petersen, forthcoming). Of course, the extent to which self-perceptions lead girls and boys to sex-role conformity depends on the degree to which their self-perceptions are sex-typed: a girl who sees herself as highly feminine may adhere more rigidly to stereotypic notions of sex role than a girl who sees herself as relatively androgynous (Nash 1979). In any case, some level of sex-role conformity is likely to be sought by most adolescents since they may feel that peer acceptance (especially from members of the opposite sex) depends on their displaying sex-appropriate behaviors. It is not surprising that traditional sex-role stereotypes are most strongly endorsed in adolescence (Benson and Vincent 1980).

It is during adolescence, then, that sex-typing of achievement areas is most likely to influence motivation and performance. Achievement in sex-inappropriate areas may have lesser attainment value, or an individual's standards for achievement may be lower in these areas. Moreover, internalized beliefs about one's abilities in sex-appropriate areas may affect confidence level, and expectations regarding one's future role may affect one's estimate of the usefulness of certain skills.

The effects of sex-typing on achievement have been most often studied in females. Females have higher attainment values in sex-appropriate areas, and this affects their performance (Stein and Bailey 1973). Moreover, girls have lower expectancies for success on "male" tasks, even when they actually perform well (Gitelson, Petersen, and Tobin-Richards 1982). Finally, they tend to see "male" academic areas as less relevant to their careers or, perceiving their future roles as marriage and motherhood, do not aspire to a career (Fox 1980).

On top of this, girls may anticipate rejection by peers if they pursue deviant (sex-inappropriate) interests. Clearly, sex-typing of achievement areas can affect achievement motivation, academic performance, and career choices, at least in girls. Obviously, these variables will affect academic preparation and hence future career opportunities. The future prospects of adolescents become, in this sense, self-fulfilling prophecies.

Given the likelihood that sex-typing of achievement domains influences performance during puberty, it is interesting that sex differences in some cognitive abilities first appear in early adolescence (Maccoby and Jacklin 1974). It is particularly interesting that the gender differences are in accordance with the sex-typing of those areas in this culture: girls show an advantage in the more "feminine" area of verbal skills, and boys excel in the "masculine" areas of spatial ability and mathematics.

Especially in the case of mathematics, it seems likely that adolescent sex-role conformity affects attitudes towards the subject in a way that contributes to sex differences in performance. Although high school boys and girls do not seem to differ in their enjoyment of mathematics, they both stereotype mathematics as a "male" domain. In girls, this perception appears to affect course selection and performance in mathematics (Fennema and Sherman 1977). Throughout high school, girls take fewer mathematics courses than do boys, and even when formal mathematics background is controlled for, girls tend to score slightly lower than boys on tests of mathematics achievement.

This persistent gender difference in mathematics performance is probably related to the differing attitudes boys and girls have towards the study of mathematics. In the Fennema and Sherman (1977) study of four high schools, the sex difference in mathematics achievement covaried with attitudes: that is, it appeared only in those schools where boys demonstrated significantly more positive attitudes than girls on most of the mathematics attitude scales employed. Furthermore, in the two schools where sex differences in mathematics did appear, the relationship disappeared when attitudes were statistically controlled for. Finally, scores on all of the attitude scales were significantly related to mathematics achievement scores, and these associations were especially strong for girls. Thus, it seems likely that attitudes towards mathematics and particularly the stereotyping of mathematics as a male domain profoundly affect achievement in this area, at least among adolescent females.

Similar findings emerged from a recent study of mathematically gifted young adolescents (Fox 1980). Researchers found that girls in their gifted sample were less likely to accelerate their mathematics training than were boys, despite similar talent. It was also found that the girls had more negative attitudes toward the subject, lower motivation to excel in mathematics, and less confidence in their abilities. Some of the girls even felt that participating in an accelerated mathematics program would hurt them socially. At the same time, girls were less likely than boys to aspire to careers in mathematics or mathematics-related fields; consequently, mathematics was less likely to be considered important to their future goals. Thus, it can be concluded that attitudes based on social concerns and on prospective adult roles (both of which are likely to be based on sex-role stereotypes) constitute an important factor limiting the entry of talented girls into traditionally masculine fields.

Since the choices regarding course selection made by adolescents shape their academic preparation, their apparent neglect of sex-inappropriate achievement areas in high school will limit their future career opportunities. As long as academic and professional fields are disproportionately populated by men or women, these fields will continue to be labeled as masculine or feminine, and females and males will be encouraged or discouraged from entering them because of this stereotyping. Thus, gender labels, deriving ultimately from biological differences between males and females, and sex-role stereotypes based on cultural tradition combine to limit the achievement domains of boys and girls, their educational preparation, and their career opportunities.

Summary. Gender is a biologically based social category. Because of its salience as a social stimulus, gender can affect educational experience by influencing social expectations concerning abilities and appropriate behavior and by influencing the child's own values and performance standards. From an early age, boys and girls sex-type academic domains and, especially in adolescence when pubertal changes increase the salience of gender, tend to pursue sex-appropriate activities. Sex-typing of academic areas can thus become a major force channeling the adolescent's achievement strivings and academic interests.

IMPLICATIONS FOR EQUALITY OR EQUITY

We cannot determine from the existing studies whether there are basic biological factors that influence differences in the educational outcomes of males and females. Biological potentials and culturally sex-related experiences become so confounded at an early age that we cannot differentiate their effects. It is possible, however, that there may be small biologically based differences on some characteristics that make males and females unequal. It would not matter if such characteristics were physical, cognitive, or motivational. If they influence educational outcomes, they are important.

Suppose there were even one such characteristic. Such a difference, alone, could render equality inappropriate as a goal. Assimilation, as described in the first chapter, would be unlikely. Given the risks involved in assuming equality of the sexes, we would do better to examine other ways to insure equity. Facilitating the best fit between talents and opportunities would seem to be a worthy goal. This could be accomplished by either of the pluralistic system models described in Chapter One. We need not assume that talents are distributed equally to insure that opportunities are available to those with the talents.

Applying such an "equal-opportunity" structure assumes, of course, that individuals will be motivated to seek the best fit between their talents and the available opportunities. We know that this does not occur. Both boys and girls will find a fit from among "sex-appropriate" opportunities. An active educational program, perhaps reinforced by a justice model, is necessary to change biases about sex-specificity of areas. Views can be changed, however, at least enough to recruit individuals into "cross-sex" courses or occupations.

The problems with insuring equal opportunity, however, go beyond stereotyping. The different social patterns of males and females can make participation in a "cross-sex" activity unrewarding. Why is it that many women in "cross-sex" fields such as mathematics were trained in single-sex institutions? If participation in an activity where one has talent also raises questions about one's identity, it can become impossible to pursue, particularly for adolescents. Efforts to produce enduring change will have to address these social problems, at least until there are sufficient numbers of the minority gender to reduce the impact of social isolation and negative labeling.

REFERENCES

Ayoub, David M.; Greenough, W.T.; and Juraska, J.M. "Sex Differences in Dendritic Structure in the Preoptic Area of the Juvenile Macaque Monkey Brain." *Science* 219 (14 January 1983): 197-98.

Bem, Sandra L. "Gender Schema Theory: A Cognitive Account of Sex Typing." *Psychological Review* 88 (July 1981): 354-64.

Benbow, Camilla, and Stanley, Julian C. "Sex Differences in Mathematical Ability: Fact or Artifact?" *Science* 210 (12 December 1980): 1262-64.

Benson, Peter L., and Vincent, Steven M. "Development and Validation of the Sexist Attitudes Toward Women Scale (SATWS)." *Psychology of Women Quarterly* 5 (Winter 1980): 276-91.

Berenbaum, Sheri, and Resnick, Susan. "Somatic Androgyny and Cognitive Abilities." *Developmental Psychology* 18 (May 1982): 418-23.

Bock, R. Darrell, and Kolakowski, Donald. "Further Evidence of Sex-Linked Major-Gene Influence on Human Spatial Visualizing Ability." *American Journal of Human Genetics* 25 (January 1973): 1-14.

Boles, David B. "X-Linkage of Spatial Ability: A Critical Review." *Child Development* 51 (September 1980): 625-35.

Brackbill, Yvonne, and Nevill, Dorothy D. "Parental Expectations of Achievement as Affected by Children's Height." *Merrill-Palmer Quarterly* 27 (October 1981): 429-41.

Brooks-Gunn, Jeanne, and Matthews, Wendy S. *He and She: How Children Develop Their Sex-Role Identity.* Englewood Cliffs, N.J.: Prentice-Hall, 1979.

Bryden, M.P. "Evidence for Sex-Related Differences in Cerebral Organization." In *Sex-Related Differences in Cognitive Functioning: Developmental Issues,* edited by Michele A. Wittig and Anne C. Petersen. New York: Academic Press, 1979.

Bryden, M.P. "Laterality Effects in Dichotic Listening: Relations with Handedness and Reading Ability in Children." *Neuropsycholgia* 8 (November 1970): 443-50.

Cantoni, V.J.; Pellegrino, J.W.; and Hubert, L.J. "The Relationship between Testosterone Levels and Human Spatial Abilities." Unpublished manuscript, 1981, available from V.J. Cantoni, School of Education, University of California at Santa Barbara.

Carey, Susan E. "Maturation and the Development of Spatial Ability in Children."

Paper presented at a conference on "Gender-Role Development: Conceptual and Methodological Issues," National Institutes of Health, Bethesda, Md., September 30-October 2, 1981.

Carey, Susan E., and Diamond, Rhea. "Maturational Determination of the Developmental Course of Face Encoding." In *Biological Studies of Mental Processes*, edited by David Caplan. Cambridge, Mass.: Massachusetts Institute of Technology Press, 1980.

Carey, Susan E.; Diamond, Rhea; and Woods, Bryan. "Development of Face Recognition—A Maturational Component?" *Developmental Psychology* 16 (July 1980): 257-69.

Clarke-Stewart, K. Alison. *Interactions between Mothers and Their Young Children: Charcteristics and Consequences.* In *Monographs of the Society for Research in Child Development*, Serial no. 153, 38 (December 1973): 1-109.

Dan, Alice J. "The Menstrual Cycle and Sex-Related Differences in Cognitive Variability." In *Sex-Related Differences in Cognitive Functioning: Developmental Issues*, edited by Michele A. Wittig and Anne C. Petersen. New York: Academic Press, 1979.

de Lacoste-Utamsing, Christine, and Holloway, Ralph L. "Sexual Dimorphism in the Human Corpus Callosum." *Science* 216 (25 June 1982): 1431-32.

Doering, Charles H.; Kramer, Helena C.: Brodie, H. Keith; and Hamburg, David A. "A Cycle of Plasma Testosterone in the Human Male." *Journal of Clinical Endocrinology and Metabolism* 40 (March 1975): 492-500.

Educational Testing Service. *Test Use and Validity: A Response to Charges in the Nader/Nairn Report on ETS.* Princeton, N.J.: Educational Testing Service, 1980.

Fennema, Elizabeth, and Sherman, Julia. "Sex-Related Differences in Mathematics Achievement, Spatial Visualization, and Affective Factors." *American Educational Research Journal* 14 (Winter 1977): 51-71.

Fox, Lynn H.; Brody, Linda; and Tobin, Dianne. *Women and the Mathematical Mystique.* Baltimore, Md.: Johns Hopkins University Press, 1980.

Freedman, Daniel G. *Human Sociobiology: A Holistic Approach.* New York: Free Press, 1979.

Frisch, R.E. "Fatness, Puberty, and Fertility: The Effects of Nutrition and Physical Training on Menarche and Ovulation." In *Girls at Puberty: Biological and Psychosocial Perspectives*, edited by Jeanne Brooks-Gunn and Anne C. Petersen. New York: Plenum Press, forthcoming.

Gitelson, Idy B.; Petersen, Anne C.; and Tobin-Richards, M. "Adolescents' Expectancies of Success, Self-Evaluations, and Attributions about Performance on Spatial and Verbal Tasks." *Sex Roles* 8 (April 1982): 411-19.

Golub, Sharon. "The Effect of Premenstrual Anxiety and Depression on Cognitive Functioning." *Journal of Personality and Social Psychology* 34 (July 1976): 99-104.

Goy, Robert W., and McEwen, Bruce S. *Sexual Differentiation of the Brain.* Cambridge, Mass.: Massachusetts Institute of Technology Press, 1980.

Guay, Roland B., and McDaniel, Ernest D. "The Relationship between Mathematics Achievement and Spatial Abilities among Elementary School Children." *Journal for Research in Mathematics Education* 8 (May 1977): 211-15.

Hartlage, Lawrence C. "Sex-Linked Inheritance of Spatial Ability." *Perceptual and Motor Skills* 31 (October 1970): 610.

Herbst, L., and Petersen, Anne C. "Timing of Maturation, Brain Lateralization and Cognitive Performance in Adolescent Females." Paper presented at the Fifth Annual Conference on Research on Women and Education, Cleveland, Ohio, 1979.

Hier, Daniel B. "Sex Differences in Brain Structure." In *Sex Differences in Dyslexia*, edited by Alice Ansara, Norman Geschwind, Albert Galaburda, Marilyn Albert, and Nanette Gartrell. Towson, Md.: Orton Dyslexia Society, 1981.

Hill, John P., and Lynch, M.E. "The Intensification of Gender-Related Role Expectations during Early Adolescence." In *Girls at Puberty: Biological and Psychosocial Perspectives*, edited by Jeanne Brooks-Gunn and Anne C. Petersen. New York: Plenum Press, forthcoming.

Hiscock, Merrill, and Kinsbourne, Marcel. "Ontogeny of Cerebral Dominance: Evidence from Time-Sharing Asymmetry in Children." *Developmental Psychology* 14 (July 1978): 321-29.

Kail, Robert V., Jr. and Siegel, Alexander W. "Sex and Hemispheric Differences in the Recall of Verbal and Spatial Information." *Cortex* 14 (December 1978): 557-63.

Kavrell, S.M., and Petersen, Anne C. "Patterns of Achievement in Early Adolescence." In *Women and Science*, edited by Marlin L. Maehr and M.W. Steinkamp. Greenwich, Conn.: JAI Press, forthcoming.

Kinsbourne, Marcel, and Hiscock, Merrill. "Does Cerebral Dominance Develop?" In *Language Development and Neurological Theory*, edited by Sydney J. Segalowitz and Frederick A. Gruber. New York: Academic Press, 1977.

Kohlberg, Lawrence. "A Cognitive-Developmental Analysis of Children's Sex-Role Concepts and Attitudes." In *The Development of Sex Differences*, edited by Eleanor E. Maccoby. Stanford, Calif.: Stanford University Press, 1966.

Levy, Jerre. "Cerebral Asymmetry and the Psychology of Man." In *The Brain and Psychology*, edited by Merlin C. Wittrock. New York: Academic Press, 1980.

Linn, M., and Petersen, Anne C. "Gender Differences in Spatial Ability: Emergence and Characterization." Unpublished manuscript.

Lockheed, Marlaine. Personal communication, June 1982.

Maccoby, Eleanor E., and Jacklin, Carol N. *The Psychology of Sex Differences.* Stanford, Calif.: Stanford University Press, 1974.

McGlone, Jeannette. "Sex Differences in Human Brain Asymmetry: A Critical Survey." *Behavioral and Brain Sciences* 3 (June 1980): 215-27.

Money, John, and Ehrhardt, Anke A. *Man and Woman, Boy and Girl: Differentiation and Dimorphism of Gender Identity from Conception to Maturity.* Baltimore, Md.: Johns Hopkins University Press, 1972.

Nash, Sharon C. "Sex Role as Mediator of Intellectual Functioning." In *Sex-Related Differences in Cognitive Functioning: Developmental Issues*, edited by Michele A. Wittig and Anne C. Petersen. New York: Academic Press, 1979.

Newcombe, Nora; Bandura, Mary M.; and Taylor, Dawn G. "Sex Differences in Spatial Ability and Spatial Activities." *Sex Roles* 9 (March 1983): 377-86.

Parsons, Jacquelynne E.; Adler, Terry F.; and Kaczala, Caroline M. "Socialization of Achievement Attitudes and Beliefs: Parental Influence." *Child Development* 53 (April 1982): 310-21.

Petersen, Anne C. "Physical Androgyny and Cognitive Functioning at Adolescence." *Developmental Psychology* 12 (November 1976): 524-33.

Petersen, Anne C. "Hormones and Cognitive Functioning in Normal Development." In *Sex-Related Differences in Cognitive Functioning: Developmental Issues*, edited by Michele Wittig and Anne C. Petersen. New York: Academic Press, 1979.

Petersen, Anne C. "Sex Differences in Performance on Spatial Tasks: Biopsychosocial Influences." In *Sex Differences in Dyslexia*, edited by Alice Ansara, Norman Geschwind, Albert Galaburda, Marilyn Albert, and Nanette Gartrell. Towson, Md.: Orton Dyslexia Society, 1981, pp. 41-54.

Petersen, Anne C. "Biological Correlates of Spatial Ability and Mathematical Performance." Paper presented at the annual meeting of the American Association for the Advancement of Science, Washington, D.C., January 1982.

Petersen, Anne C. "Pubertal Change and Cognition." In *Girls at Puberty: Biological and Psychosocial Perspectives*, edited by Jeanne Brooks-Gunn and Anne C. Petersen. New York: Plenum Press, forthcoming.

Petersen, Anne C., and Gitelson, Idy B. *Toward Understanding Sex-Related Differences in Cognitive Performance*. New York: Academic Press, forthcoming.

Petersen, Anne C., and Taylor, Brandon. "The Biological Approach to Adolescence: Biological Change and Psychological Adaptation." In *Handbook of Adolescent Psychology*, edited by Joseph Adelson. New York: Wiley, 1980.

Reinisch, June M. "Prenatal Environmental Contributions to the Development of Sex Differences." Paper presented at a conference on "Gender-Role Development: Conceptual Issues," National Institutes of Health. Bethesda, Md., September 30-October 2, 1981.

Reinisch, June M. "Prenatal Exposure to Synthetic Progestins Increases Potential for Aggression in Humans." *Science* 211 (13 March 1981): 1171-73.

Reinisch, June M.; Gandelman, Ronald; and Spiegel, Frances S. "Prenatal Influences in Cognitive Abilities." In *Sex-Related Differences in Cognitive Functioning: Developmental Issues*, edited by Michele A. Wittig and Anne C. Petersen. New York: Academic Press, 1979.

Rubin, Jeffrey Z.: Provenzano, Frank J.; and Luria, Zella. "The Eye of the Beholder: Parents' Views on Sex of Newborns." *American Journal of Orthopsychiatry* 44 (July 1974): 512-19.

Sherman, Julia A. "Problem of Sex Differences in Space Perception and Aspects of Intellectual Functioning." *Psychological Review* 74 (July 1967): 290-99.

Springer, Sally P., and Deutsch, Georg. *Left Brain, Right Brain*. San Francisco: W.H. Freeman, 1981.

Stafford, Richard E. "Sex Differences in Spatial Visualization as Evidence of Sex-linked Inheritance." *Perceptual and Motor Skills* 13 (December 1961): 428.

Stein, Aletha H., and Bailey, Margaret M. "The Socialization of Achievement Orientation in Females." *Psychological Bulletin* 80 (November 1973): 345-66.

Stein, Aletha H., and Smithells, Jancis. "Age and Sex Differences in Children's Sex-Role Standards about Achievement." *Developmental Psychology* 1 (May 1969): 252-59.

Steinberg, Lawrence D., and Hill, John P. "Patterns of Family Interaction as a Function of Age, Onset of Puberty, and Formal Thinking." *Developmental Psychology* 14 (November 1978): 683-84.

Tanner, James M. "Sequence, Tempo, and Individual Variation in Growth and Development of Boys and Girls Aged Twelve to Sixteen." In *Twelve to Sixteen: Early Adolescence,* edited by Jerome Kagan and Robert Coles. New York: Norton, 1972.

Vandenberg, Steven G., and Kuse, Allan R. "Spatial Ability: A Critical Review of the Sex-linked Major Gene Hypothesis." In *Sex-Related Differences in Cognitive Functioning: Developmental Issues,* edited by Michele A. Wittig and Anne C. Petersen. New York: Academic Press, 1979.

Waber, Deborah P. "Sex Differences in Cognition: A Function of Maturation Rate?" *Science* 192 (7 May 1976): 572-74.

Waber, Deborah P. "Sex Differences in Mental Abilities, Hemispheric Lateralization, and Rate of Physical Growth at Adolescence." *Developmental Psychology* 13 (January 1977): 29-38.

Waber, Deborah P. "Cognitive Abilities and Sex-Related Variations in the Maturation of Cerebral Cortical Functions." In *Sex-Related Differences in Cognitive Functioning: Developmental Issues,* edited by Michele A. Wittig and Anne C. Petersen. New York: Academic Press, 1979.

Winterbottom, M.R. "The Relation of Need for Achievement to Learning Experiences in Independence and Mastery." In *Motives in Fantasy, Action, and Society: A Method of Assessment and Study,* edited by John W. Atkinson. Princeton, N.J.: Van Nostrand, 1958.

Witelson, Sandra F. "Sex and the Single Hemisphere: Specialization of the Right Hemisphere for Spatial Processing." *Science* 193 (30 July 1976): 425-27.

Wittig, Michele A. "Genetic Influences on Sex-Related Differences in Intellectual Performance: Theoretical and Methodological Issues." In *Sex-Related Differences in Cognitive Functioning: Developmental Issues,* edited by Michele A. Wittig and Anne C. Petersen. New York: Academic Press, 1979.

5

Sex Segregation and Male Preeminence in Elementary Classrooms

Marlaine E. Lockheed

Two principal sex-related inequities are characteristic of coeducational elementary school classrooms: sex segregation and male preeminence. The presence of these inequities, which also characterize the adult labor force (Kahne and Kohen 1975), provides evidence for the statement that the structures of the larger society are reproduced in schools (Bourdieu and Passeron 1977). In this chapter these sex-related inequities are described, explanations for their presence are provided, and examples of how they may be overcome are given.

The dilemma exists today: if schools reproduce the larger culture in which they are embedded, how can schools be changed without first changing the larger society? Won't the larger society merely reassert its claim over the structure of the schools once limited efforts to effect change are instituted? Historical precedents indicate that without considerable and constant support, change is rarely maintained in schools or any organizations because of the institutional habits, norms, constraints, and supports that tend to create self-maintaining cultures. In addition, schools are by their very nature conservative; their initial purposes were to conserve knowledge and to pass it on to students through proven techniques. Fads in education may come and go, but schools continue to educate using traditional methods to impart the skills of reading, writing, and arithmetic. Because of their conservatism, schools lag behind social change by retaining norms already discarded by the larger society. Some school traditions, like white gloves for young ladies (Delamont 1980), are obviously out of step with society; others, like sex segregation, are not so clearly out-of-vogue. It appears, however, that while changes in demographics, the labor force, and the work place have steadily modified traditional patterns of sex segregation and male preeminence in the larger society, schools have been slow to adapt to these changes. Schools may now be at a point where changes in their structures could receive support from the larger society.

The initial task of this chapter is to review the evidence for the claim that the structure of elementary education is characterized by the sex-related inequities of sex segregation and male preeminence. These two characteristics are treated separately.

SEX SEGREGATION

Sex segregation in the classroom has been studied through sociometric, nomination, and observational studies. Each method has confirmed that sex segregation is highly characteristic of preschool and elementary classrooms.

Sociometric Studies

Sociometric studies typically ask children to evaluate all other members of their class on some criterion, such as "liking" or "willingness to work with." The resulting sociomatrices can be analyzed either to find symmetrical (clique) relationships or to compare within-group and cross-group ratings. These sociometric studies typically report extreme sex segregation. For example, Hallinan (1977) found "a total separation by sex" in the friendship cliques of fifty-one fifth- through eighth-grade classes. In eighteen fourth- through eighth-grade classes, over 75 percent of children identified as best friends were same-sex peers (Hallinan and Tuma, 1978). In another study, Lockheed and colleagues (Lockheed et al. 1981) asked students in twenty-nine fourth- and fifth-grade classrooms to rate their classmates with regard to his or her "willingness to work with," and they found same-sex sociometric ratings were twice as high as cross-sex ratings.

Nomination Studies

Nomination studies ask students to identify other students with whom they would like to study. Although teachers frequently use nomination procedures for composing classroom teams, such procedures are rarely used by researchers. One exception was a series of studies conducted by Lockheed. In her studies of fourth- and fifth-grade students conducted in New Jersey, California, and Connecticut between 1971 and 1981, the students were asked to "think of three people you would like to work with on a class project. Are they all girls, all boys, or both boys and girls?" In general, the majority of both boys and girls chose same-sex groups, although the extent of cross-sex choosing increased over time and differed between sites. The results of these studies are summarized in Figures 5.1 and 5.2.

Figure 5.1

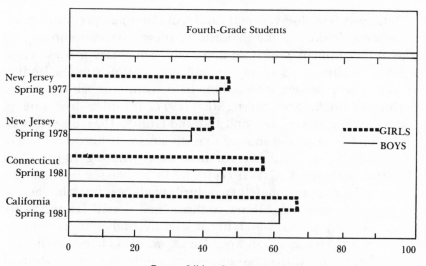

Percent Liking Cross-Sex Work Group

Figure 5.2

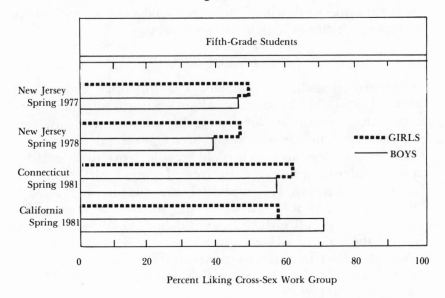

Percent Liking Cross-Sex Work Group

Observational Studies

Relatively few observational studies of classroom peer interaction have been conducted; the majority of these have concentrated on play interaction in preschool and early elementary grades. These studies confirm the sociometric and nomination studies, finding virtually no cross-sex interaction. In two nursery school classes, Serbin, Tonick, and Sternglanz (1977) found a low rate of cooperative cross-sex play, and Day and Hunt's (1974) observations of sixteen five-year-olds showed that students were biased in favor of interacting verbally with peers of the same sex. Among slightly older children, Berk and Lewis (1977) found that same-sex interchanges accounted for approximately two-thirds of all peer interchanges for four- to eight-year-old children in three "traditional" schools. Also, Grant (1982) reported observing a slightly higher proportion of same-sex interchanges than would be expected by chance in six first-grade classrooms, with cross-sex helping rarely observed. A study of one first-grade reading group also found a low rate of cross-sex interactions (Wilkinson and Subkoviak 1981).

Sex segregation has also been observed in upper elementary grades. For example, in an ethnographic study of one classroom of students aged eight to ten, Damico (1975) reported "no recorded incidence of spontaneous cross-sex academic helping behavior." In a large study of twenty-nine fourth- and fifth-grade classrooms, Lockheed and Harris (1982) found that cross-sex work groups accounted for only 7.9 percent of all observed work settings. Additionally, with older students in a study of seating patterns in a junior high school cafeteria, Schofield and Sagar (1977) found that "cross-sex adjacencies" were extremely rare.

Sex segregation is found among very young children and persists throughout elementary school. Boys and girls do not sit with one another, talk with one another, or help one another as frequently as they interact with same-sex peers.

MALE PREEMINENCE

To refer to male preeminence in elementary schools—where women constitute the majority of teachers and girls are believed to excel academically—may appear out of place. Yet many features of the elementary school, including its curriculum, its organizational structure, and its classroom interactions create and maintain a norm of male preeminence. Two of these features, the sex-related authority structure of the adult staff and the male-oriented curriculum, will be briefly discussed; a third, the preeminence of the male student, will be covered in greater detail.

From the child's eye view, the typical elementary school has three "bosses": the principal, the custodian, and the office secretary/receptionist. Each of these individuals has a separate source of power: the principal's power is based on his or her legitimate role as the ultimate authority in the school; the custodian's power is based on his or her control of resources (keys, sports equipment, and so on); and the receptionist's power is based on her or his delegated authority as the principal's representative to handle such matters as tardy slips, lunch money, telephone calls home, access to the principal, and so forth. Of these three powerful people in the school, one (the custodian) is nearly always male; another (the principal) is male in seven schools out of ten; and the third (the receptionist) is nearly always female. For most students, therefore, the norm of male preeminence is established early on by the staffing of the school. This topic is dealt with at length by others (see Stockard, Schmuck, Kempner, Williams, Edson, and Smith 1980).

The curriculum of elementary schools also stresses male preeminence: not only do male characters outnumber female characters in elementary readers and picture books (Scott and Schau, in press), but the subject matter of social studies stresses male leadership. In many classrooms, the pictures of the United States presidents are prominently displayed. While children should learn about the nation's history, the concentration of the elementary curriculum on military and political history in which men played leadership roles, instead of on social history in which both women and men had important roles, may be a major factor in creating a norm of male preeminence. These issues have been addressed by Women's History Week projects and by such curricula as *In Search of Our Past* (Groves 1983).

The principal aspect of male preeminence in the classroom addressed in this chapter is that of the preeminence of the male child. This preeminence is seen in three areas: leadership experiences of children, perception of male children as leaders by their peers, and greater salience of boys in the classroom.

Leadership Experiences

The leadership experiences of children have not been widely studied, perhaps because leadership has been considered an adult characteristic. When studied, however, the traits of successful leaders have been examined rather than the frequency with which children assume leadership roles (Stogdill 1974). When fourth- and fifth-graders were directly asked about having held specific leadership roles at school, sex differences in children's leadership experiences were found with boys reporting having held more leadership positions than did girls (Lockheed et al. 1981). Boys were also found to be more influential than girls in mixed-sex task groups of students from ongoing classrooms (Lockheed, Harris, and Finkelstein 1979). This latter finding of more male influence is characteristic of adult mixed-set task groups (Lockheed, 1983) and has often been described as the operation of sex as a status characteristic (Berger, Connor, and Fisek 1974, Lockheed and Hall 1976, Meeker and Weitzel-O'Neill 1977). However, direct laboratory tests have failed to confirm that sex functions precisely as a status characteristic among children (Lockheed, Harris, and Nemceff, in press).

Perceived Leadership

Not only do boys hold more leadership positions than girls do, they are also perceived to be leaders more frequently than are girls, even when girls are engaged in the same leaderlike behavior as boys. In a study of children's mixed-sex task groups, Lockheed, Harris, and Nemceff (in press) asked the members of four-person groups to identify the leader of their group. Even though no sex differences were found for either the amount or type of contribution made to the task or for the actual influence of the group members, the boys received 94 percent of the children's votes as leaders. Children's preference for identifying boys as leaders was also found in several other studies of mixed-sex groups (Lockheed, Harris, and Finkelstein 1979, Lockheed et al. 1981). Thus, from these studies of student perceptions, leadership appears to be clearly associated with males by the time of late elementary school. This association has been directly confirmed by studies of children's stereotypes of personality characteristics in which leadership ability was perceived as a male trait (Nash 1975).

Salience

Both teachers and other students behave as if boys were more important than girls in the classroom. Boys are more active than girls (Klein 1971), exhibit more disruptive behavior (Lockheed 1982), and therefore receive a greater proportion of the teacher's attention (Good 1982, Lockheed 1982). In interviews, teachers report that they find boys' answers and questions more interesting and informed than those of girls (Lockheed et al. 1981). This greater salience is also indicated by studies of teacher feedback to boys and girls: girls receive less praise for correct answers (Brophy and Good 1970); praise received by girls occurs for a random set of activities while boys are praised for academic performance (Delefes and Jackson 1972); girls receive more negative feedback in intellectual areas (Dweck, Davidson, Nelson, and Enna 1978); twice the proportion of criticism that girls receive is for "lack of knowledge or skill" (Spaulding 1963); teachers tend to encourage the intellectual development of boys by asking them more abstract questions (Sikes 1972), more product questions (Hillman and Davenport 1977), and more process questions (Good and Findley 1982); and teachers sex-stereotype academic fields by making more academic contacts with girls in reading and with boys in mathematics (Leinhardt, Seewald, and Engel 1979).

Male preeminence permeates the school setting, creating an environment in which the male students emerge as leaders receiving a disproportionate amount of teacher attention. Male students and their needs come to define the character of the elementary classroom; female students are substantially less salient in the classroom environment than are males.

ACCOUNTING FOR SEX INEQUITIES

Given that both segregation and male preeminence occur in elementary classrooms, to what should these inequities be attributed? That is, how do social forces affect the structure of the classroom? This is a difficult question to answer, but one possible answer is that parents, teachers, and school administrators tacitly agree that boys and girls are fundamentally different, so different, in fact, as to require segregated facilities, differentiated curricula, and differential treatment. Few Americans would agree to segregated facilities for the sexes (with the exception of segregated lavatory or dressing facilities), but many might agree to differentiated curricula in later school years. In fact, until only a decade ago, a differentiated high school curriculum was the norm in such subjects as cooking, sewing, woodworking, metalworking, or auto mechanics, to name a few. Differentiated curricula are still offered in vocational programs, with girls becoming beauticians and boys becoming plumbers. Yet for elementary school programs, because both boys and girls need the basic skills of literacy and numeracy, the curriculum has rarely been formally differentiated. Nevertheless, boys and girls are treated differently in elementary schools both by other students and by teachers. Why? One explanation is that they do, in fact, behave differently and hence deserve to be treated differently. Another explanation is that they are expected to behave differently and that these differences in behavior are permitted to the extent that they conform with the expected differences.

For example, the common expression of "boys will be boys" is interpreted to mean not that boys will not be girls but rather that boys will be rowdy or uncontrollable. Boys are, in fact, more disruptive than girls in school. A study of the behaviors of approximately 700 fourth- and fifth-grade target boys and girls found that the boys more frequently engaged in disruptive behavior than the girls (Lockheed 1982). Yet what is interesting about this study is not that the boys were "being boys"; what is interesting is that the teachers were doing nothing, or very little, to discourage the male disruption. The boys were acting as expected, and the teachers were accepting the expected behavior. In short, a societal norm exists that accepts male disruptive behavior, and teachers therefore also accept it. In explaining sex segregation and male preeminence, it is important to consider both the societal norms that permit sex segregation and male preeminence and societal expectations regarding male competence that may encourage inequities.

Societal Norms

As previously discussed, sex segregation and male preeminence are widely observed in elementary schools. This seems to be the societal norm for behavior. If students were asked, for example, why girls and boys do not group themselves together in mixed-sex groups, the response would probably be a blank stare followed by an explanation that it just is not done. That girls and boys should be separated appears to be a well-established belief. Moreover, the children have good reasons for this belief: they have observed sex-segregated scouts, soccer leagues, little leagues, professional sport teams, bowling teams, car pools, or religious orders. Children rarely observe sex-integrated groups of children or adults outside of the home.

Perhaps this situation will change because of Title IX. But, in the meantime, the culture of the classroom apparently requires sex segregation. The norm of sex segregation is taught to younger students by older students in the cafeteria and on the playground (Thorne 1979). That boys "own" certain parts of the playground and girls "own" other parts may be a residue of time past when playgrounds were physically divided by lines on the ground or other barriers. In one school a yellow line separated the boy's kickball fields from the girl's foursquare courts, jungle gyms, and hopscotch court. Even though playgrounds no longer have visible yellow lines separating one sex from the other, the children may still carry the boundary lines in their minds. Besides school areas, a sex-segregated social domain exists. For instance, one fifth-grade girl who had forgotten her homework called only the girls but none of the boys for the missing assignment. Why? "A girl couldn't call a boy." Clearly children's norms govern their behavior in this domain.

Male preeminence is also governed by norms, which are transmitted directly through elements of the school structure and the formal curriculum. Research on leadership in single-sex groups suggests that the strong association between males and leadership actually interferes with the emergence of a female leader in an all-female group (Lockheed 1977; Fennell, Barchas, Cohen, McMahon, and Hildebrand 1978). Girls apparently neither see themselves nor other girls as leaders because the norm of male leadership works against legitimizing leadership for females. Because sex segregation is so pervasive in elementary school, male leadership under mixed-sex settings rarely can be observed. Yet, in experimentally composed mixed-sex groups in elementary classroms, boys are generally viewed as the leaders (despite the absence of sex differences in behavior), suggesting the strong norm governing perceptions of leadership.

Expectations

Sex segregation and male preeminence may also be attributed to unconscious beliefs held by children regarding sex differences in competence. Competence expectations are associated with status differences (Berger et al. 1974), with sex long recognized as a status characteristic affecting interpersonal interactions (Lockheed and Hall 1976). In conceptualizing sex as a status characteristic, theorists have argued that women hold the less valued state (female) of the characteristic while men hold the higher valued state (male). Men, therefore, are expected to be more competent than women at a variety of tasks and will be more influential at collaborative tasks. Experiments designed to test the theory have found that adult males are indeed more influential than adult females at joint tasks (see Lockheed, in press, for a review of this literature). While such findings have not been confirmed for elementary school-aged groups (Lockheed, Harris, and Nemceff, in press), this does not mean that status characteristics do not influence behavior in mixed-sex groups of elementary children; it may mean that more than one status characteristic is operating.

One additional characteristic that might be operating may be perceived ability. For example, in elementary grades, girls have been typically characterized as better students than boys (Fennema and Koehler 1983); whether or not this view is justified by sex differences in academic performance is irrelevant. Since the operation of status characteristics on interpersonal interactions is affected by competence expectations (Berger et al. 1974), beliefs about greater female academic competence in elementary grades may be sufficient to offset general expectations for greater male competence. Thus, in task situations, girls may be equally as influential as boys because of the female's presumed greater academic ability. The effects of perceived academic ability on interpersonal interaction have been well documented (Tammivaara 1982, Morris 1977). Since sex differences in task influences have been found within high school groups (Lockheed and Hall 1976, Lockheed 1977), and high school girls are no longer perceived to be better students than boys, possibly the counterbalancing effects of views about superior female academic competence have worn off. What is seen in elementary school, perhaps, is just the balancing effect of male sex status and female academic status on influence in mixed-sex groups.

REDUCING SEX-RELATED INEQUITIES

One way to change the typical elementary classroom is to restructure it so as to facilitate greater cross-sex equal status interaction. The words *equal status* are stressed since many studies suggest that negative stereotypes are confirmed when interactions are not carefully designed. In this section, restructuring classrooms by means of cooperative small groups and leadership assignments is discussed as ways of reducing the sex-related inequities of sex segregation and male preeminence.

Cooperative Small Groups

A typical elementary classroom is structured as a single large group, with most interaction directed by and toward the teacher; cooperative small groups are rarely observed. For example,

Lockheed and Harris (1982) found that student groups were rarely used for instruction in twenty-nine fourth- and fifth-grade classrooms: 7 percent of the time in language arts, 10 percent of the time in mathematics, 11 percent of the time in social studies, 12 percent of the time in science, and 24 percent of the time in reading. Restructuring this organizational arrangement by composing small student work groups in which students are encouraged to interact with one another is a radical departure from the normal classroom arrangement. Nevertheless, it is a strategy that can have powerful effects on student achievement, attitudes, and behavior. It is a particularly powerful mechanism for changing stereotypical behavior, as studies of cross-racial groups have shown. Moreover, cooperation has been shown to improve student learning and promote educational excellence for all students (Slavin 1980). In cooperative settings, students can learn from one another, either as teachers or as learners, and can share knowledge with one another to gain a better understanding of the educational materials. As examples, different types of small group instructional methods have been shown to improve performance on standardized tests of student achievement (Sharan et al. 1982), to improve achievement in mathematics (Slavin, Madden, and Leavey 1982), and to enhance problem-solving abilities (Harris and Lockheed 1982).

Cooperation may also facilitate cognitive processes. Sharan has pointed out that cooperation requires students to evaluate information, exercise judgment, take initiative in using different sources of information, synthesize ideas contributed by different people in the group, understand the perspective of others regarding shared problems, frequently readjust one's perspective as a result of coordinating activities with other group members, critically evaluate one's work in light of feedback, make inferences about the task in light of others' comments, and analyze the statements and opinions of others (Sharan and Hertz-Lazarowitz 1980). In addition, cooperation has been shown to improve prosocial behaviors in nonacademic environments such as playgrounds and lunchrooms (Schofield and Sagar 1977, Weigel, Wiser, and Cook 1975). Berk and Lewis (1977) reported that cross-sex interaction, a minimal type of cooperative behavior, was more frequently observed in one school characterized as "progressive" than in three comparison schools. "Progressive" is a vague term that covers many different school types and provides little guidance to the educator who is seeking specific approaches to improve cross-sex interaction in the classroom. In the following paragraphs some specific effective approaches are described; several of these (identified by asterisks) are fully developed programs that are available from the authors.

Reinforcement of Cross-Sex Contacts. Teacher reinforcement of cross-sex play was found effective in increasing cross-sex interaction in a study involving two nursery school classes in which teachers praised, attended to, and publicly acknowledged naturally occurring cooperative cross-sex play (Serbin, Tonick, and Sternglanz 1977). Reinforcement increased rates of cooperative cross-sex play significantly in both classes, but removal of treatment resulted in a complete reversal to the original baseline rate of same-sex play.

*Group Investigation Method.** An experiment conducted by Sharan and his colleagues (Sharan et al. 1982) compared cooperation in small groups composed of students from thirty-three seventh-grade classrooms in three schools in Israel over a year's time. Classrooms were randomly assigned to one of three treatment conditions: the Group Investigative (GI) method (Sharan and Hertz-Lazarowitz 1980); Student-Teams Academic Divisions (STAD) method (Slavin 1980); and traditional whole-class (WC) instruction. Although both GI and STAD methods utilized forms of cooperative peer interaction in small groups, GI emphasized a shared academic task while STAD stressed peer tutoring and between-team competition. Raviv (1982) examined cross-sex cooperation at a standardized task and found statistically significant differences between the three methods. Specifically, students from GI classes demonstrated twice as much verbal and nonverbal cross-sex cooperation and one-third as much cross-sex competition as students from traditional whole-class instruction units; students in groups from STAD classes were similar to whole-class groups in verbal cooperation, similar to GI groups in competition, and in between GI and WC for nonverbal cooperation.

*Curriculum and Research for Equity (CARE).** Another study, quasi-experimental in nature, conducted in five fourth- and fifth-grade "units" in three New Jersey elementary schools over two years, examined both student willingness to participate in cross-sex groups and small-group interaction patterns resulting from either experimental or control conditions (Lockheed, Harris, and Finkelstein 1979). In the first year, teachers in the two experimental units received in-service CARE training regarding sex stereotypes, cross-sex interactions, and female leadership; they then developed related experimental curriculum materials that were used and evaluated in the second school year. Student pre- and posttests were administered, and small task groups composed of experimental and control "units" were videotaped and coded. Analyses showed that girls in the experimental units reported more interactions from experiences working in mixed-sex settings than girls did from similar settings in control units; however, no effect was found for boys in relation to their reported number of experiences in an experimental or control unit (Lockheed and Harris 1977). Analyses of behavior also indicated significant sex-by-grade-by-experimental-condition effects for verbal activity, actual influence, and perceived leadership indicating that experimental treatment reduced girls' status relative to boys' in the fourth grade but improved it in the fifth grade (Lockheed 1982).

Learning Center (Finding Out/Descrubrimiento). Although sex inequities in peer interaction have been observed in traditional classrooms, evidence exists that nontraditional classrooms may promote sex equity in peer interactions. One such nontraditional classroom organization is provided by learning centers designed to operate simultaneously with four or five children at each center. In nine such classrooms, in grades two to four, Cohen and Anthony (1982) observed target students working at such learning centers and found no sex-related differences on the observed rate of peer talking or working together.

Collaborative Groups. Lockheed and Harris's research on twenty-nine fourth- and fifth-grade classrooms in California and Connecticut adds to the information about the relationship between group work and cross-sex prosocial attitudes and behavior. Although few opportunities for cross-sex group work were typically provided in these classrooms, a comparison between the more and less collaborative classrooms showed that students from the more collaborative classrooms had a less male-biased perception of their classmates' competence (Lockheed and Harris 1982) and more productive cross-sex task groups (Harris and Lockheed 1982).

Direct Assignment of Leadership Opportunities

Student leadership in the elementary classroom includes formal leadership roles such as class president or team captain, student helping roles such as ball monitor or flag captain, "star" roles such as announcer at an assembly or lead in a student play, instructional roles such as peer tutor or project leader, as well as a variety of roles enabling the student to demonstrate competence. Although much is known about the conditions under which individuals come to assume such leadership roles, less is known about the consequences of student leadership roles. However, evidence exists indicating that students who have been assigned peer-tutor roles have higher achievement than control students (Allen 1976), and students who engage in relatively more student leadership roles have higher self-esteem, greater sense of efficacy, and fewer sex-role stereotypes regarding occupations (Lockheed, Harris, and Finkelstein 1979).

Still, research on student leadership in the classroom is virtually nonexistent, with little attention given to student leadership in mixed-sex classroom peer groups. Typical classrooms rarely provide students opportunities to be designated as leaders. For example, in the baseline year of Lockheed and Harris's study of twenty-nine fourth- and fifth-grade classrooms, fewer than 100 instances of student leadership out of a possible 24,000 were recorded by classroom observers, and individual students reported an average of fewer than three leadership experiences out of a possible fourteen during the course of the entire year. Furthermore, no studies have examined the effects of female leadership opportunities on reducing male preeminence in any but adult experimental settings.

SUMMARY

In this chapter, two characteristics that lead to sex-related inequities in elementary school are described, those being sex segregation and male preeminence. Ways in which the norms and structures of elementary classrooms might be changed to reduce these forms of inequities are also presented. In the larger society, sex segregation and male preeminence are viewed as major problems to be overcome. Normal human life requires interaction with many different types of people, and achievement in the larger society requires leadership experiences. Sex equity in the larger society begins with sex equity in the classroom.

REFERENCES

Allen, Vernon L., ed. *Children as Teachers: Theory and Research on Tutoring.* New York: Academic Press, 1976.

Berger, Joseph; Connor, Thomas L.; and Fisek, M. Hamit, eds. *Expectation States Theory: A Theoretical Research Program.* Cambridge, Mass.: Winthrop Publishers, 1974.

Berk, Laura E., and Lewis, Nancy G. "Sex Roles and Social Behavior in Four School Environments." *Elementary School Journal* 77 (January 1977): 204-17.

Bourdieu, Pierre, and Passeron, Jean-Claude. *Reproduction in Education, Society, and Culture.* London: Sage Publications, 1977.

Brophy, Jere E., and Good, Thomas L. "Teachers' Communication of Differential Expectations for Children's Classroom Performance: Some Behavioral Data." *Journal of Educational Psychology* 61 (October 1970): 365-74.

Cohen, Elizabeth G., and Anthony, Bobbie. "Expectation States Theory and Classroom Learning." Paper presented at the annual meeting of the American Educational Research Association, New York City, March 22, 1982.

Damico, Sandra B. "Sexual Differences in the Responses of Elementary Pupils to Their Classroom." *Psychology in the Schools* 12 (October 1975): 462-67.

Day, Barbara, and Hunt, Gilbert H. *Verbal Interaction across Age, Race, and Sex in a Variety of Learning Centers in an Open Classroom Setting, Final Report.* Chapel Hill, N.C.: Frank Porter Graham Center, University of North Carolina, 1974. ED 105 987.

Delamont, Sara. *Sex Roles and the School.* New York: Methuen and Co., 1980.

Delefes, Peter, and Jackson, Barry. "Teacher-Pupil Interaction as a Function of Location in the Classroom." *Psychology in the Schools* 9 (April 1972): 119-23.

Dweck, Carol S.; Davidson, William; Nelson, Sharon; and Enna, Bradley. "Sex Differences in Learned Helplessness: II. The Contingencies of Evaluative Feedback in the Classroom and III. An Experimental Analysis." *Developmental Psychology* 14 (May 1978): 268-73.

Fennell, Mary L.; Barchas, Patricia R.; Cohen, Elizabeth, G.; McMahon, Anne M.; and Hildebrand, Polly. "An Alternative Perspective on Sex Differences in Organizational Settings: The Process of Legitimation." *Sex Roles* 4 (August 1978): 589-604.

Fennema, Elizabeth, and Koehler, Mary S. "Expectations and Feelings about Females' and Males' Achievement in Mathematics." In *Research on Relationship of Spatial Visualization and Confidence to Male/Female Achievement in Grades 6-8*, edited by Elizabeth Fennema. Final Report, National Science Foundation (SED78-17350), August 1983.

Good, Thomas L., and Findley, M.J. "Sex Role Expectations and Achievement." Unpublished manuscript, 1982.

Grant, Linda. "Sex Roles and Statuses in Peer Interactions in Elementary Schools."

Paper prepared for the American Educational Research Association meeting, New York, March 1982.

Groves, S. *In Search of Our Past: Units in Women's History.* Newton, Mass.: Women's Educational Equity Act Publishing Center, 1983.

Hallinan, Maureen T. *The Evolution of Children's Friendship Cliques.* Chicago: Spencer Foundation, 1977. ED 161 556.

Hallinan, Maureen T., and Tuma, Nancy B. "Classroom Effects on Change in Children's Friendships." *Sociology of Education* 51 (October 1978): 270-82.

Harris, Abigail M., and Lockheed, Marlaine E. "Individual and Group Scientific Problem Solving Performance for Boys and Girls." Paper presented at the annual meeting of the American Educational Research Association, New York, 1982.

Hillman, Stephen, and Davenport, G. Gregory. "Teacher Behavior in Desegregated Schools." Paper presented at the annual meeting of the American Educational Research Association, New York, 1977. ED 138 670.

Kahne, Hilda, and Kohen, Andrew I. "Economic Perspectives on the Roles of Women in the American Economy." *Journal of Economic Literature* 13 (December 1975): 1249-92.

Klein, Susan S. "Student Influence on Teacher Behavior." *American Educational Research Journal* 8 (May 1971): 403-21.

Leinhardt, Gaea; Seewald, Andrea M.; Engel, Mary. "Learning What's Taught: Sex Differences in Instruction." *Journal of Educational Psychology* 71 (August 1979): 432-39.

Lockheed, Marlaine E. "Cognitive Style Effects on Sex Status in Student Work Groups." *Journal of Educational Psychology* 69 (April 1977): 158-65.

Lockheed, Marlaine E. "Sex Equity in Classroom Interaction Research: An Analysis of Behavior Chains." Paper presented at the annual meeting of the American Educational Research Association, New York, March 1982.

Lockheed, Marlaine E. "Sex and Social Influence: A Meta-analysis Guided by Theory." In *Status, Attributions, and Rewards,* edited by J. Berger and M. Zelditch. San Francisco: Jossey-Bass, in press.

Lockheed, Marlaine E.; Amarel, Marianne; Finkelstein, Karen J.; Harris, Abigail M.; Flores, V.M.; Holland, Paul W.; McDonald, Frederick J.; Nemceff, William P.; and Stone, Meredith K. *Year One Report: Classroom Interaction, Student Cooperation, and Leadership.* Princeton, N.J.: Educational Testing Service, 1981.

Lockheed, Marlaine E., and Hall, Katherine P. "Conceptualizing Sex as a Status Characteristic: Applications to Leadership Training Strategies." *Journal of Social Issues* 32, no. 3 (1976): 111-24.

Lockheed, Marlaine E., and Harris, Abigail M. "Modifying Status Orders in Mixed Sex Groups of Fourth- and Fifth-Grade Children: An Application of Expectation States Theory." Paper presented at the annual meeting of the American Sociological Association, Chicago, September 1977.

Lockheed, Marlaine E., and Harris, Abigail M. "Classroom Interaction and Opportunities for Cross-Sex Peer Learning in Science." *Journal of Early Adolescence* 2, no. 2 (1982): 135-43.

Lockheed, Marlaine E.; Harris, Abigail M.; and Finkelstein, Karen J. *Curriculum and Research for Equity: A Training Manual for Promoting Sex Equity in the Classroom.* Princeton, N.J.: Educational Testing Service, 1979.

Lockheed, Marlaine E.; Harris, Abigail M.; and Nemceff, William P. "Sex and Social Influence: Does Sex Function as a Status Characteristic in Mixed-Sex Groups of Children?" *Journal of Educational Psychology* 75 (December 1983): 877-78.

Meeker, B.F., and Weitzel-O'Neill, P.A. "Sex Roles and Interpersonal Behavior in Task-Oriented Groups." *American Sociological Review* 42 (February 1977): 91-105.

Morris, Richard A. "A Normative Intervention to Equalize Participation in Task-Oriented Groups." Doctoral dissertation, Stanford University, 1977.

Nash, Sharon C. "The Relationship among Sex-Role Stereotyping, Sex-Role Preference, and the Sex Difference in Spatial Visualization." *Sex Roles* 1 (March 1975): 15-32.

Raviv, S. "The Effect of Three Teaching Methods on the Cooperative and the Competitive Behavior of Pupils in Ethnically Desegregated Junior High School Classrooms." Doctoral dissertation, Tel Aviv University, 1982.

Schofield, Janet W., and Sagar, H. Andrew. "Peer Interaction Patterns in an Integrated Middle School." *Sociometry* 40 (June 1977): 130-38.

Scott, K.P., and Schau, C.G. "Sex Equity and Sex Bias in Instructional Materials." In *Achieving Sex Equity Through Education,* edited by S. Klein. Baltimore, Md.: Johns Hopkins University Press, in press.

Serbin, Lisa A; Tonick, Illene J.; and Sternglanz, Sara H. "Shaping Cooperative Cross-Sex Play." *Child Development* 48 (September 1977): 924-29.

Sharan, Shlomo, and Hertz-Lazarowitz, Rachel. "A Group Investigation Method of Cooperative Learning in the Classroom." In *Cooperation in Education,* edited by Shlomo Sharan, Paul Hare, Clark D. Webb, and Rachel Hertz-Lazarowitz. Provo, Utah: Brigham Young University Press, 1980, pp. 14-46.

Sharan, Shlomo; Kussell, P.; Sharan, Yael; Bejerano, Y.; Raviv, S.; Hertz-Lazarowitz, Rachel; Brosh, T.; and Peleg, R. *Cooperative Learning, Whole-Class Instruction and the Academic Achievement and Social Relations of Pupils in Ethnically-Mixed Junior High Schools in Israel.* Final report to the Ford Foundation: The Israel Ministry of Education and Culture, 1982.

Sikes, Joseph N. "Differential Behavior of Male and Female Teachers with Male and Female Students." *Dissertation Abstracts International* 33 (July 1972): 217A.

Slavin, Robert E. "Cooperative Learning." *Review of Educational Research* 50 (Summer 1980): 315-42.

Slavin, Robert E.; Madden, Nancy A.; and Leavey, Marshall. "Combining Cooperative Learning and Individualized Instruction: Effects on the Social Acceptance, Achievement, and Behavior of Mainstreamed Students." Paper presented at the annual meeting of the American Educational Research Association, New York City, 1982.

Spaulding, Robert L. *Achievement, Creativity, and Self-Concept Correlates of Teacher-Pupil Transactions in Elementary Schools* (Cooperative Research Project No. 1352). Washington, D.C.: Office of Education, U.S. Department of Health, Education, and Welfare, 1963.

Stockard, Jean; Schmuck, Patricia A.; Kempner, Ken; Williams, Peg; Edson, Sakre K.; and Smith, Mary A. *Sex Equity in Education* New York: Academic Press, 1980.

Stogdill, R.M. *Handbook of Leadership: A Survey of Theory and Research.* New York: Free Press, 1974.

Tammivaara, Julie S. "The Effects of Task Structure on Beliefs about Competence and Participation in Small Groups." *Sociology of Education* 55 (October 1982): 212-22.

Thorne, B. "Claiming Verbal Space: Women Speech's and Language in College Classrooms." Paper presented at the Research Conference on Educational Environments and the Undergraduate Women, Wellesley College, September 1979.

Weigel, Russell H.; Wiser, Patricia L.; and Cook, Stuart W. "The Impact of Cooperative Learning Experiences on Cross-ethnic Relations and Attitudes." *Journal of Social Issues* 31, no. 1 (1975): 219-44.

Wilkinson, L.C., and Subkoviak, M. "Sex Differences in Classroom Communication." Paper presented at the International Interdisciplinary Congress on Women, Haifa, Israel, 1981.

6

Girls, Women, and Mathematics

Elizabeth Fennema

A few years ago, a new coin was put into circulation in the United States. The coin was worth one dollar and had on it a likeness of Susan B. Anthony, an early leader in the suffrage movement for women in the United States. She was the first real woman to be featured on any United States currency. Before the coin was issued, the following comments appeared in a national newsletter.

> Like women generally, the coin could be said to represent cheap labor. The Treasury regarded it as a less expensive substitute for the paper dollar, which is less durable.
>
> It is smaller than the traditional silver dollar.
>
> It is less esteemed. It is described as "cuprous-clad" rather than silver.
>
> It is service oriented. One edge is a raised eleven-sided ridge to aid the blind.
>
> Its employment is seen by banks and merchants as a problem (WEAL, 1979).

The coin was not generally accepted by the business and working world and is currently infrequently used.

While this is a humorous metaphor relating the acceptance of women to that of a coin (and humorous ideas about the role of women in society are hard to find), it contains a kernel of truth. Women and their work outside the home in particular are less esteemed and more service oriented; their employment is seen as a problem, and they are seldom found in the higher status and/or well paid jobs. The reasons for this are many, varied, deeply rooted in the mores of society, and far beyond what can be addressed here. However, if one is committed to the belief that women should have the same opportunity as men to participate in all aspects of society, then the issue of sex-related differences in mathematics specifically becomes vital.

Lucy Sells, an American sociologist, expressed the situation well when she said that "mathematics is a critical filter." Without adequate preparation in mathematics, people are effectively filtered out of most postsecondary education options and an increasing number of jobs and professions. The option of career advancement or change in adulthood is also severely handicapped by a lack of mathematical training. While inadequate training in mathematics hampers everyone, many more females than males fail to achieve their full potential in mathematics. This is one of the most serious inequities that currently exists in education. Without mathematical knowledge and skills, women will never be able to achieve equity in society.

Before sex-related differences in mathematics can be eliminated, it is necessary to know precisely where they exist and something about what factors influence their development. Identifying where differences exist is a comparatively simple job; understanding why they exist is much more difficult.

SEX-RELATED DIFFERENCES IN MATHEMATICS

There are two major facets of sex-related differences in mathematics: (1) the opportunity and/or election to study mathematics in secondary school, and (2) achievement in mathematics.

Differences in Enrollment

There have been strong sex-related differences in the percentage of females and males who are enrolled in mathematics classes in secondary schools. In 1964, Husén reported that in the twelve countries studied in the International Study of Achievement, the ratio of males to females enrolled in mathematics at the end of secondary education ranged from 1.73 to 7.13 with an average ratio of 3:7 (Husén 1967, vol. 2, p. 234). Basically, these data are similar to those reported by Fennema and Sherman in the United States for the 1974-75 school year, (Fennema and Sherman 1977). The third National Mathematics Assessment reports results from a national sample on enrollment in high school mathematics courses by sex (Table 6.1) for two years. It should be noted that the male-female differential is not large at any time, but it is largest in the most advanced classes.

Table 6.1   Changes in Percentages of Males and Females Taking Mathematics Courses, Age Seventeen

Course	Percentages of Seventeen-year-olds Who Have Taken at Least a Half Year	
	Males	Females
Algebra 1		
1978	70.7	73.6
1982	69.4	72.2
Geometry		
1978	51.1	50.5
1982	51.8	51.8
Algebra 2		
1978	37.8	36.1
1982	38.9	38.0
Trigonometry		
1978	14.7	11.1
1982	15.0	12.7
Precalculus/Calculus		
1978	4.7	3.1
1982	4.7	3.6
Computer		
1978	5.9	4.1
1982	11.1	8.6

Source: National Assessment of Educational Progress. The Third National Mathematics Assessment: Results, Trends, and Issues. Report No. 13-MA-01. Education Commission of the States, Denver, Colorado, 1983.

While differences in enrollment patterns continue between girls and boys, adult differences in mathematics-related careers cannot be totally traced to differences in course taking. It is known, for example, that enrollment patterns differ widely by school, with some schools reporting more females than males enrolled in advanced courses while many more schools report just the opposite. Can discrepancy in adult use of mathematics be explained by sex-related differences in achievement or the learning of mathematics?

Differences in Achievement

Mathematics educators have used sex as a variable in research concerned with mathematics achievement for a number of years, and many summaries have been published that include information about comparative mathematics learning by females and males. Basically, all reviews published before 1974 concluded that while there might not have been a sex-related difference in mathematics achievement in young children, male superiority was always evident by the time learners reached upper elementary or junior high school.

Before 1974, most studies that reported male superiority in mathematics learning (Fennema 1978) used random samples of females and males enrolled in secondary schools. Since traditionally females have not chosen to study mathematics as often as have males in advanced secondary school classes, a population of males who had spent more time studying mathematics was being compared to a population of females who had studied less mathematics. As the single most important influence on learning mathematics is studying mathematics, it would indeed be strange if males had not scored higher on mathematics achievement than did females.

During the 1974-78 years, there were a number of studies published which indicated that sex differences in achievement in favor of males were not as strong as had been previously believed. The Fennema-Sherman studies (Fennema and Sherman 1977, 1978) indicated that when females elected to study mathematics as much as did males, differences were small and nonexistent in many cases. Schonberger (1978) reviewed problem-solving literature and concluded that better male performance was rarely found and when it was present, it was usually limited to students of higher ability and related to certain types of problems. Wise (1978) reanalyzed extant data that had previously indicated strong differences in favor of males. He found that when he controlled for number of mathematics courses studied, the sex differences in favor of males were eliminated.

I hypothesized at about this time that sex differences in mathematics might be eliminated if schools would somehow ensure that girls elect to study mathematics as often as boys did. However, within the last two to three years, a number of studies have been reported that have made me at least partially reject the hypothesis. These studies have carefully controlled the number of mathematics courses studied by both girls and boys and have also used items of differing cognitive complexity to assess learning.

The California State Assessment of Mathematics was done in 1978 (Student Achievement in California Schools 1978). Students in grades six and twelve (twelve- and eighteen-year-olds) who reported studying the same number of mathematics courses were tested on a variety of content areas with items of differing cognitive levels. A committee was named to evaluate the results and concluded that girls scored higher in computational or lower cognitive level tasks while boys tended to score higher on higher cognitive level tasks. Armstrong (1980) collected data from a sample of students from the entire United States and concluded, "Twelfth grade males scored significantly higher then females on the problem-solving subtest. Thirteen-year-old females scored significantly higher on the lower level mathematical skill of computation." The Mathematics Assessment of the Second National Assessment of Educational Progress indicated also that females were somewhat better in computational tasks than were males, while males achieved higher than females in higher-level cognitive tasks (Fennema and Carpenter 1981). The Third National Mathematics Assessment reports approximately the same thing (National Assessment of Educational Progress 1983). A totally different result was reported by Smith where no sex-related differences on the New York State Regents High School mathematics examinations in ninth, tenth, or eleventh grade were found (Smith 1980).

One can only conclude from a variety of sources that while sex-related differences in achievement are not always found, when they are found, they indicate that boys perform better than girls in high-level cognitive tasks. The other major conclusion is that differences in both election and achievement are very school specific. In some schools no differences are found, while in others differences are consistently found.

WHY DIFFERENCES EXIST

What is the cause of these sex-related differences in mathematics, both election to study and achievement? Involved is the cognitive acquisition of mathematics by females, as well as the attitudes or affective beliefs held by females, male peers, parents, and educators toward females as learners of mathematics. The cognitive and affective components are so intertwined that it is difficult if not impossible to separate them. Not only are they intertwined, but they are developed over a period of years in a complex social matrix that involves home, community, and school. Therefore, in seeking to understand why inequity exists in mathematics, one must study the cognitive and affective components affecting the acquisition of mathematical skills and knowledge in the social environment where they are developed.

Although intellectually pleasing to discuss, at the present time it is impossible to study the totality of causative behavior. However, it has been possible, and indeed profitable, to select variables that exert major influence and to study the development, interrelationships, and effects of these variables on mathematics learning.

The Cognitive Variables

"Mathematics is essentially cognitive in nature; and the principal, distinguishing goals or objectives of mathematics instruction are (and should be) cognitive ones" (Weaver 1971, p. 263). Since mathematics is a cognitive endeavor, the logical place to begin looking for explanatory variables of sex-related differences in mathematics is in the cognitive area. It is well accepted that the cognitive variables of general intelligence and verbal abilities are highly important in the learning of mathematics. However, these two variables are not helpful as possible explanations of sex-related differences in mathematics. No differences exist between males and females in general intelligence. While there appears to be some female superiority in certain verbal skills in children (Maccoby and Jacklin 1974), by the time learners reach the secondary school, males and females possess approximately equivalent skills in the verbal areas that are related to the learning of mathematics (Fennema and Sherman 1978). Therefore, general intelligence and verbal skills are not helpful variables in understanding differences in mathematics between females and males.

One cognitive variable that many believe may help to explain sex-related differences in mathematics performance is spatial visualization, a particular subset of spatial skills. Even though the existence of many sex-related differences is being challenged, the evidence is still persuasive that in many cultures, male superiority on tasks that require spatial visualization is evident beginning during adolescence (Fennema 1975, Maccoby and Jacklin 1974). Spatial visualization involves visual imagery of objects, movement of the objects, or changes in their properties. In other words, objects or their properties must be manipulated in one's "mind's eye," or mentally. The relationship between mathematics and spatial visualization is logically evident. In mathematical terms, spatial visualization requires rotation, reflection, or translation of rigid figures. These are important ideas in geometry. Many mathematicians believe that all of mathematical thought involves geometrical ideas (Bronowski 1947). Therefore, if spatial visualization items are geometrical in character and if mathematical thought involves geometrical ideas, spatial visualization and mathematics are inseparably intertwined.

Not only are spatial visualization skills related to ideas within the structure of mathematics, but spatial representations are being increasingly included in the teaching of mathematics. For example, the Piagetian conservation tasks, which are becoming part of many school programs, involve focusing on correct spatial attributes before quantity, length, and volume are conserved. Most concrete and pictorial representations of arithmetical, geometrical, and algebraic ideas appear to be heavily reliant on spatial attributes. The number line, which is used extensively to represent whole numbers and operations on them, is a spatial representation. Illustrating the commutativity of multiplication by turning an array 90 degrees involves a direct spatial visualization skill.

Although the relation between the content of mathematics, instruction in mathematics, and spatial visualization skills appears logical, results from empirical studies that have explored the relationship are not consistent. Some investigators have definitely concluded that spatial skills and mathematics learning are not related, while other authors feel that data indicate a positive relationship (Fennema 1975). Even less is known about the effect that differential spatial visualization skills have on the mathematical learning of females and males. One indication that spatial visualization is an important consideration is the concurrent development of sex-related differences in favor of males in mathematics achievement and spatial visualization skills. However, the Fennema-Sherman studies specifically investigated the relationship between mathematics achievement and spatial visualization skills, and these data do not support the idea that spatial visualization is helpful in explaining sex-related differences in mathematics achievement. In these studies of females and males enrolled in mathematics courses, grades six through twelve, few sex-related differences in either mathematics achievement or spatial visualization skills were found. The two were related similarly ($r \sim$ 0.5) for both sexes, and spatial visualization appeared to influence both females and males equally to continue studying mathematics (Fennema and Sherman 1978).

How do spatial visualization skills influence the learning of mathematics? It appears evident that tasks which measure spatial visualization skills have components that can be mathematically analyzed or described. From such an examination, one could hypothesize a direct relationship between mathematics and spatial visualization. An item from the space relations portion of the Differential Aptitude Test (Bennett et al. 1973) requires that a two-dimensional figure be folded mentally into a three-dimensional figure (Figure 6.1). The spatial visualization test called the Form Boards Test (French, Ekstrom, and Price 1969) requires that rigid figures be rotated and translated to a specified location. The Cubes Test (French, Ekstrom, and Price 1969) requires rotation of a three-dimensional shape, a cube. The activities required by these items can be described as mathematical operations. Yet this set of operations is only a minute subset of mathematical ideas that must be learned, and, indeed, one could learn a great deal of mathematics without these specific ideas.

The hypothesis that currently appears valid is that the critical relationship between mathematics and spatial visualization is not direct but quite indirect. This relationship involves the translation

Figure 6.1   Spatial visualization task

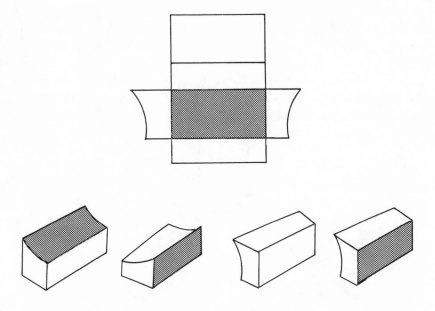

of words and/or mathematical symbols into a form where spatial
visualization skills can be utilized. Consider the following problem:

> A pole 12 meters long has been erected near the bank of a lake. Two and a half
> meters of the pole have been hammered down into the bottom of the lake; one
> half meter is above the surface of the water. How deep is the lake? (Werdelin 1961)

For children of eleven to twelve years of age, this is a moderately
difficult problem because of keeping track of the steps and
sequencing them accurately. One must add the lengths of two pieces
of the post and then subtract that length from the total length: that
is, 2-1/2 + 1/2 = 3 and 12 – 3 = 9. Consider the problem from a spatial
visualization perspective. If one can visualize in one's mind what is
involved, a picture like the one shown in Figure 6.2 might be seen.
The solution of the problem then becomes simpler. One has an
image that enables movement of the pieces above and below the
water together; then that length can be subtracted from the total
length in order to get the correct answer. Once the problem can be
visualized, spatial visualization skills can be a major aid in arriving
at a solution.

Figure 6.2   Lake problem representation

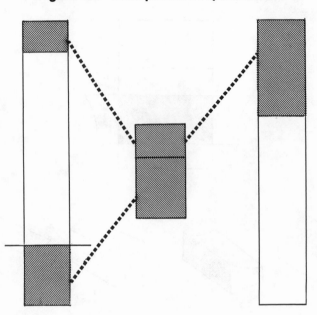

Consider a symbolic problem met by children of the same age: 1/2 + 1/3. While it can be solved with symbols, many children—because of their developmental level—have trouble really understanding the symbolic process involved. Now consider the problem represented pictorially much as it could be visualized in the mind (Figure 6.3). Once it is visualized in the mind, spatial visualization skills can be used and finding the answer is easier.

It is true that females tend to score lower on spatial visualization tests than males. What is not known is whether females differ from males in their ability to visualize mathematics, that is, in the translation of mathematical ideas and problems into pictures. The sex-related differences found in a three-year logitudinal study just completed (Fennema and Tartre 1983) does give some credibility to the belief that sex-related differnces in solving problems of this type may be due to how girls and boys use their spatial visualization skills. Boys and girls with equivalent spatial visualization skills did not solve the same number of problems, nor did they use the same processes in solving those problems. It also appeared that a low level of spatial visualization skills was more debilitating for girls than for boys.

Figure 6.3   1/2 + 1/3

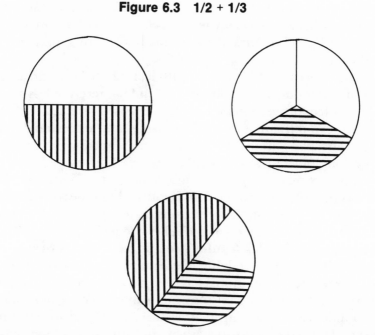

It increasingly seems that there is no direct causal relationship between spatial visualization skills and mathematics learning in a broad, general sense. In American schools, classrooms do not appear to use mathematical representations that either encourage or require the use of spatial visualization skills. While some primary mathematics programs encourage the use of concrete and pictorial representations of mathematical ideas, by the time children are ten to eleven years old, symbolic representations are used almost exclusively. Perhaps boys more than girls use concrete representations during primary years and thus develop higher skills in using spatial visualization in learning mathematics.

Whatever influence spatial visualization skills have on the learning of mathematics is subtle, to say the least. This provides an interesting area of investigation and discussion, but an emphasis on the development of spatial visualization skills will probably not do very much to eliminate sex-related differences in mathematics.

Affective Variables

If sex-related differences in mathematics can't be explained by cognitive variables, are there other variables that will help explain?

Several variables that can be labeled as affective variables provide important insight into why females elect not to study mathematics beyond minimal requirements and are not learning mathematics as well as males.

Affective variables have to do with feelings, beliefs, and attitudes. The affective domain is complicated and has received less attention than the cognitive domain, partly because variables within this domain are difficult to define, measure, and understand. All too often, affective variables have all been lumped together into one large conglomerate and labeled attitudes. This type of combining often masks many important things, however. There has been an increasing amount of literature published that deals with specific affective variables and their relationship to sex-related differences in mathematics study (Fox et al. 1979, Fennema 1978, Reyes 1980). Two well-defined variables (confidence and perceptions of usefulness) are closely related to studying mathematics, and one other complex variable (causal attributions) has been hypothesized as an important determinant of electing to study mathematics (Wolleat et al. 1980).

Confidence in learning mathematics is related to general self-esteem. High confidence in mathematics appears to be located at one end of a continuum and anxiety toward learning mathematics at the other end. Confidence in mathematics is a belief that one has the ability to learn new mathematics and to perform well on mathematical tasks. It often is measured by Likert-type scales that include items such as: I am sure that I can learn mathematics; I can get good grades in math; or I'm no good in math.

The literature strongly supports the fact that there are sex-related differences in the confidence-anxiety dimension. It appears reasonable to believe that lesser confidence or greater anxiety on the part of females is an important variable which helps explain sex-related differences in mathematics studying. In the Fennema-Sherman study (Fennema and Sherman 1978), at each grade level from six through eleven, boys were more confident in their abilities to deal with mathematics than were girls (see Figure 6.4). In most instances, this happened when there were no significant sex-related differences in mathematics achievement. In addition, confidence in learning mathematics and achievement were more highly correlated than any other affective variable and achievement ($r \sim 0.40$). Confidence was almost as highly related to achievement as were cognitive variables of verbal ability and spatial visualization.

Figure 6.4   Confidence in learning mathematics

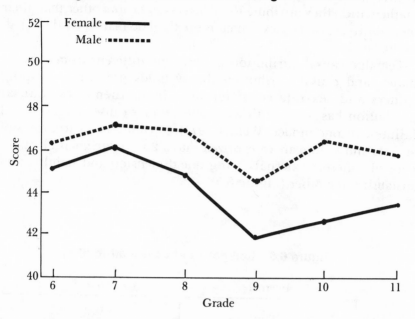

While abundant evidence exists that there are sex-related differences in this confidence-anxiety dimension related to mathematics, much is unknown about its true effect or how such feelings are developed. The relationship between spatial-visual processes and the confidence-anxiety dimension has not been explored. What effect do feelings of confidence have on cognitive processes involved in learning mathematics and in solving mathematical problems and vice versa? Are feelings of confidence stable within individuals across time and across a variety of mathematics activities? Does lessening anxiety increase either learning or the willingness to elect to study mathematics? Do low levels of confidence affect females differently than they do males? Are there really sex differences in confidence toward mathematics; or, as many have hypothesized (Nash 1979), are females just more willing to admit their feelings than males are?

Currently, many studies are underway that will help answer these questions. Until available though, one must just accept the evidence that females, across a wide age range, do report more anxiety and less confidence toward mathematics than males do. Certainly no one knows why many females develop a lack of confidence in their own ability to do mathematics. Even when females succeed in mathematics, they attribute their success to factors other than their own ability, such as luck, much more than do males (Wolleat et al. 1980).

Females' causal attribution patterns are different from those of males, and causal attribution theory holds promise in helping understand sex-related differences in mathematics. Causal attribution has to do with what one believes causes successes and failures. In one model (Weiner 1974), attributions as to causes of success and failure are categorized into a 2 x 2 matrix with locus of control (internal-external) being one dimension and stability and instability the other (Figure 6.5).

Figure 6.5   Categories of causal attribution

	Internal	External
Stable	Ability	Task
Unstable	Effort	Luck or environment

One can believe that success or failure occurs in mathematics because one is smart or dumb (ability), one tried or did not try (effort), the mathematics one is doing is easy or difficult (task), or one has or does not have a good teacher (luck or environment). It is best to examine some items from a scale designed to measure causal attribution to understand this idea (Fennema et al. 1979). In this scale, students are presented with an event. They are asked to respond to possible causes of that event in a five-point scale that ranges from strongly agree to strongly disagree.

Patterns of causal attributions affect persistence in achievement-oriented behavior. In a somewhat simplistic summary, if one attributes success to an internal, stable dimension (ability), then one expects success in the future and will continue to strive in that area. If one attributes success to an unstable or an external cause (for example, the teacher), then one will not be as confident of success in the future and will be less apt to strive or persist. A somewhat different situation is true of failure attributions. If one attributes failure to unstable causes such as effort, one might work harder the next time and failure could be avoided. With this situation the tendency to approach or persist at tasks will be encouraged. Attribution of failure to a stable cause, on the other hand, will lead one to believe that failure can not be avoided.

While we must be careful of overgeneralizing data and concluding that all males behave one way and all females another way, many studies have reported that females and males tend to exhibit different attributional patterns (Deaux 1976, Bar-Tal and Frieze 1977). Males tend to attribute successes to internal causes and failures to external or unstable causes. Females tend to attribute successes to external or unstable causes and failures to internal causes. This attributional pattern has been observed in mathematics (Wolleat et al. 1980) as well as in other areas and probably affects both long-term persistence (election of courses) and short-term persistence (sticking with a hard problem).

This particular combination of attributions (success attributed externally and failure attributed internally) has been hypothesized to strongly affect academic achievement, particularly females' achievement. Bar-Tal (1978, p. 267) states that "females and individuals with certain causal perceptions may perform in a classroom below their abilities because of their maladaptive patterns of attributions."

Another affective variable that helps explain why females do not elect to take mathematics is the perceived usefulness to them of mathematics (Fox 1977, Fennema 1978). Mathematics is a difficult subject and not particularly enjoyable for many learners. Why should one study it if it is of no future use? Females in secondary schools, as a group, indicate that they do not feel they will use mathematics in the future. Females, more than males, respond negatively to such items as: I'll need mathematics for my future work, or Mathematics is a worthwhile and useful subject. Males, as a group, are much more apt to report that mathematics is essential for whatever career they plan. As early as sixth grade, these sex differences appear (Figure 6.6). If females do not see mathematics-related careers as possibilities, they will also not see mathematics as useful.

In addition to indicating more negative beliefs than do males on these specific affective variables, females also report they perceive that parents, teachers, and counselors are not positive toward them as mathematics learners. In addition, males more than females, starting at least as early as grade six (twelve years of age), stereotype mathematics as a male domain at much higher levels than do females (Figure 6.7).

Society's stereotyping of math as a male domain is at least a partial cause of females' less positive attitudes toward mathematics. While females deny that math is a male domain, everything else in society is at variance with this denial. Of course, the main users and teachers of mathematics are male. Males, much more than females, say that mathematics is a male domain. Evidence also exists in abundance (Fox 1977) that parents, teachers, and counselors believe that mathematics is a more appropriate activity for males than it is for females. These beliefs are undoubtedly communicated to girls in a variety of subtle and not so subtle ways. Mathematics is perceived to be inappropriate for girls. It seems logical to believe that when young girls feel mathematics is inappropriate, they will feel anxious about succeeding in it and have more negative attitudes because they must, at least partially, deny their femininity in order to achieve in mathematics.

Perceived sex role is a mediator of cognitive performance (see Nash 1979 for a thorough discussion). Sex-role identity is important to everyone. A portion of that sex-role identity is achievement in domains seen as appropriate for one's sex. Mathematics is not seen as an appropriate domain for females. Therefore, achievement by a female in the mathematical domain results in her not fulfilling her sex-role identity adequately. She perceives that teachers and peers have lowered expectations of her mathematical success because she is a girl. She also perceives that others see her as somewhat less feminine when she achieves in mathematics, and she becomes increasingly uncomfortable with her achievement. Success is not valued because she thinks others have negative feelings about her success.

Educational Variables

While the entire social milieu influences how well one learns as well as how one feels about mathematics, the most important influences occur within the classroom where mathematics is taught.

Figure 6.6   Usefulness of mathematics

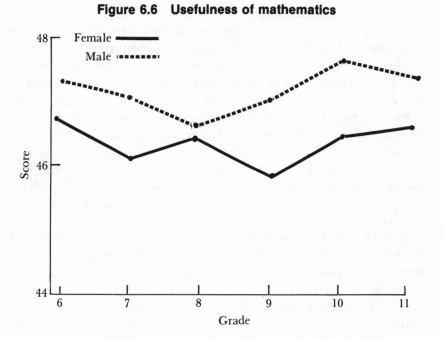

Figure 6.7   Mathematics as a male domain

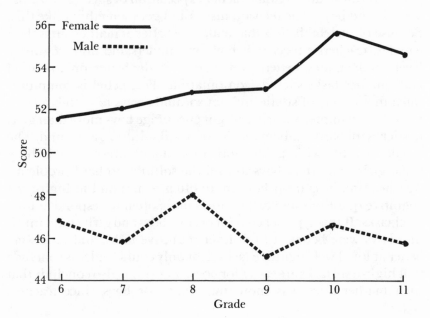

Learning environments for girls and boys within classrooms, while appearing to be the same, differ a great deal. The most important component of the learning environment is the teacher. Part of the teacher's influence is in the learner's development of sex-role standards, which include definitions of acceptable achievement in the various subjects. The differential standards for mathematics achievement are communicated to boys and girls through differential treatment as well as differential expectations of success. To start with, teachers interact more with boys than they do with girls. Boys generally receive more criticism for their behavior than do girls, and boys also receive more praise and positive feedback than do girls. Boys just seem to be more salient than girls in the teacher's view.

Boys who are high in confidence interact more with mathematics teachers than any other group of students (Fennema et al. 1980). Interestingly enough, girls who are high in confidence interact with teachers less than any other group. It was also found that in sixth-grade classrooms, many girls do not interact with their teacher about mathematics at all on many days. Why this differential teacher-boy and teacher-girl interaction pattern occurs is unclear.

Many people feel that differential treatment of girls and boys is a partial result of differential teacher expectation of success or failure by girls and boys. The relevant discussion goes something like this. Because of societal beliefs that males are better at mathematics than females, teachers expect that boys will understand high cognitive level mathematics better, and girls will do better on low-level mathematics tasks such as computation. This belief is communicated in a variety of subtle and not so subtle ways to both boys and girls. For example, a teacher might encourage boys more than girls to stick with hard mathematical tasks until solutions are found. The teacher might, with good motivation about preventing failure, assist girls more than boys to find the solution to hard problems. Teachers might call on boys more often to respond to high-level cognitive questions and call on girls more often to respond to low-level tasks. If this type of behavior occurs, boys and girls could intuit that boys were better at high-level cognitive tasks, and girls were better at low-level cognitive tasks. Not only could students conclude that high-level tasks are easier for boys, they could also conclude that such mathematics was more important for boys since teachers encouraged boys more than girls to succeed in such tasks. In addition to these subtle messages, boys would actually be practicing high-level cognitive tasks more than girls would. Since students learn what they practice, boys would learn problem-solving activities better than girls.

The hypothesis of differential teacher expectation is intuitively logical. Indeed, Brophy and Good (1974) report that teachers' expectancies are related to the way they interact with students. An interesting study by Becker (1979), which was done in tenth-grade geometry classes, confirms this. Becker hypothesizes that the sex-related differences she found in teacher-student interactions were strongly related to differential teacher expectancies. One other study designed explicitly to examine teacher expectancies reports no differences in expectancy of success in mathematics by teachers for girls and boys (Parsons et al. 1979). Another study states that in the sixth grade, students report that teachers have higher expectancies of success for girls than for boys but by eighth grade, both girls and boys report diminishing expectancies for girls by teachers and peers (Fennema and Koehler, in preparation). Once again, no clear-cut conclusion about teacher expectancies of girls and boys in learning mathematics can be reached. There appears to be little doubt, however, that teachers as a group treat boys and girls (as groups) differently. In other words, the average number of times a group of teachers interact in specific ways with girls and boys differs. However, just like the danger of overgeneralizing about individuals and the learning of mathematics, one must also be very cautious about believing how all teachers interact with girls and boys. For example, Reyes (1981) found tremendous variation in the behavior of twelve seventh-grade teachers. Some teachers asked many more high-level questions of boys than they did of girls. Other teachers asked about equivalent numbers.

The problem of differential treatment of male and female students by teachers is well documented, and no doubt it strongly influences learning. It is easy to conclude that, but the longer the problem is studied, the more complex it becomes. Most overt behavior by teachers appears to be nonsexist and fair to most students. In many cases, teachers interact more with boys because they feel they must to maintain control. Many negative interactions occur between boys and teachers. On the surface, teachers' interactions with girls are more positive and what have been considered to be good educational practice. However, the end result appears to be negative. At least a partial result is that females, more so than males, are not reaching one of the important goals of mathematics education, that of becoming thinkers who are independent problem solvers and who do well in high-level cognitive tasks. Girls, much more than boys, fail to become autonomous in mathematics. This is indicated by girls' more negative attitudes related to their ability to perform high-level cognitive tasks, specifically, confidence in learning mathematics and attributional patterns that indicate lack of control in mathematics outcomes as well as lowered performance in problem-solving tasks. In order to become increasingly autonomous, one must develop confidence in one's ability to do difficult learning tasks and also believe that one is in control of the outcomes of achievement striving.

Little is known about how one becomes an autonomous learner. It is believed that dependent-independent behaviors are developed by the socialization process, mainly within social interactions. Young girls, more so than boys, are encouraged to be dependent. Girls receive more protection and less pressure for establishing themselves as individuals separate from parents. Girls are less likely to engage in independent exploration of their worlds (Hoffman 1975). Because of the sex-typed social reinforcement of dependent-independent behaviors, children enter school with girls tending to be more dependent on others and boys tending to be more self-reliant. What appears to happen is that schools merely reinforce and further develop in girls and boys the dependent-independent behaviors they bring to school. This set of behaviors is particularly apparent in mathematics.

What prohibits girls, more than boys, from becoming autonomous learners of mathematics? It would be nice if an answer to this question could be written that would be both accurate and easily understood, but that is not possible. The factors that cause behavior are many and varied, and interact in a complex way. Indeed, there probably are as many combinations of causative factors as there are individuals. Many influences on development of behaviors are subtle and difficult to identify. However, I firmly believe that a large component of developing autonomous learning behaviors in mathematics takes place in mathematics classrooms.

CHANGING SCHOOLS

Can schools be changed so that females learn and elect to study mathematics better? All too often, comments imply that schools cannot do much. The argument goes like this: because mathematics is stereotyped male, and because stereotyping of sex roles is so deeply embedded in society, schools are powerless to improve females' studying of mathematics until society changes. Let me state as emphatically as possible that this argument is fallacious. Schools can indeed increase females' studying and learning of mathematics. Evidence strongly shows that schools can be effective, specifically from two intervention programs that have been intensively evaluated. The first program, called *Multiplying Options and Subtracting Bias*, is aimed specifically at increasing females' belief of the usefulness of mathematics (Fennema et al. 1981). The rationale behind this program is that merely telling high school females about the importance of mathematics is insufficient. Forces that influence these girls to make their decisions are complex and deeply embedded in societal beliefs about the roles of males and females. Asking adolescent girls to change their behavior without changing the forces operating upon them would place a heavy burden on their shoulders. It is necessary, rather, to change the educational environment of these females so that they can recognize the importance of mathematics. This environment is composed of several significant groups of people: mathematics teachers, counselors, parents, male students, and the female students themselves. *Multiplying Options and Subtracting Bias* was designed to change these significant groups' beliefs about women and mathematics as well as to change each group's behavior.

Multiplying Options and Subtracting Bias is composed of four workshops: one each for students, teachers, counselors, and parents. Each of the four workshops is built around a unique version of a videotape designed explicitly for the target audience. Narrated by Marlo Thomas, an American television star, the tapes use a variety of formats, candid interviews, dramatic vignettes, and expert testimony to describe the problem of mathematics avoidance and some possible solutions. The videotapes and accompanying workshop activities make the target audiences aware of the stereotyping of mathematics as a male domain and of females' feelings of confidence toward mathematics, the usefulness of mathematics for all people, and differential treatment of females as learners of mathematics. Discussed specifically are plans for action by each group. The workshops, each of which is about two hours long, are designed to influence the total school environment.

Nine midwestern high schools from urban, suburban, and rural-suburban areas were selected for the field testing of the videotape series. Two or more ninth-grade classes of algebra students and two or more tenth-grade classes of geometry students from each of the sample schools participated in the collection of baseline data during the spring of 1978.

During the 1978 fall term, five schools were randomly assigned to be experimental schools, and the four target audiences were shown the videotape series as part of a standardized workshop. The workshop formats developed for the testing of the videotapes' effectiveness added little content in addition to that on the tapes. They consisted of a standardized introduction; showing the videotape; a 10-minute, structured discussion period; and a standardized conclusion. Each workshop fit into the 45-to-55-minute class period found in the schools. Three trained *Multiplying Options and Subtracting Bias* staff members presented all of the workshops.

The four schools not assigned to be experimental schools served as control schools. Approximately three weeks after the video workshops were presented in the experimental schools, both experimental and control school students were given a battery of instruments or questions similar to those completed during the spring term.

The data that had been collected during the 1978 spring semester formed the baseline from which the amount of change effected by the video intervention was measured. The control schools permitted a comparison of the amount of change in the experimental group to that arising from naturally occurring factors during the two semesters of the investigation. More than 700 students, 64 teachers, 39 counselors, and 28 parents participated in the validation study.

Data were collected on cognitive, affective, and behavior variables. These data showed that changes did occur in the experimental group. Female students in the experimental group significantly increased their plans to study mathematics both in high school and after high school. Their amount of information about sex-related differences in mathematics increased. Their perception of the usefulness of mathematics for their futures increased significantly more than did the females in the control group. A trend in the direction of lowered attributions of their failures to a lack of ability was also found.

Male students who were members of the experimental groups also increased their plans to study mathematics during and after high school. The extent to which males perceived mathematics as a "male domain" dropped. Because the attitudes of male students undoubtedly affect the election of mathematics by female students, this drop in stereotyping mathematics by males was important.

Not only did we assess what students said they were going to do but also their actual enrollment in mathematics. Schoolwide mathematics preenrollment statistics indicated that the proportion of all junior- and senior-year mathematics courses *increased* in the experimental schools while it *decreased* slightly in the control schools. The increase was greatest among junior-year females. The higher the percentage of the school's population involved in the study, the greater the change.

This increase in enrollment and positive attitudes was not obtained by only working with students. The *Teacher* tape was shown to all the mathematics teachers and the *Counselor* tape was shown to all the counselors in each of the five experimental schools. It is doubtful if having only the students view their videotape would have been as effective as reaching all of the target audiences. It can safely be concluded that exposure to the *Multiplying Options and Subtracting Bias* series can substantially influence students' attitudes about mathematics, the stereotyping of mathematics, and their willingness to take more mathematics courses.

The other intervention program is one developed, planned, and implemented by the San Francisco Bay Area Network for Women in Science (now called the Math/Science Network). The network is a unique cooperative effort undertaken by scientists, mathematicians, technicians, and educators from twenty colleges and universities, fifteen school districts, and a number of corporations, government agencies, and foundations. The goal of the network is to increase young women's participation in mathematical studies and to motivate them to enter careers in science and technology. While the evaluation was much more extensive than is reported here, the evaluation of seven conferences that took place in the spring of 1977 and 1978 (Perl and Cronkite 1979) is significant. Supported by the Women's Educational Equity Act of the federal government, these conferences were designed to increase the entry of women into mathematics- or science-oriented careers.

These one-day conferences involved bringing junior and senior high school girls together in a central location. They attended a general session with a panel or main speaker, one or two hands-on science-mathematics workshops, and one or more career workshops that provided opportunities for interaction with women working in mathematics or science-related fields. Subjects of this evaluation were 2,215 females who volunteered to attend the conferences. Pre- and postconference questionnaires were administered and responses analyzed. The evaluators concluded that the conference (1) increased participants' exposure to women in a variety of technical and scientific fields, (2) increased participants' awareness of the importance of taking mathematics and science-related courses, and (3) increased participants' plans to take more than two years of high school mathematics.

The two intervention programs described indicate quite clearly that it is possible to change females' mathematics behavior and to do so in relatively short periods of time.

CONCLUSION

What, then, can be concluded about women and mathematics learning?

1. Sex-related differences still exist in electing to study mathematics in high school. While not as dramatic as was once suggested, females tend not to study, as much as do males, the most advanced mathematics courses and courses peripheral to math, such as computer science, statistics, and physics. It appears that the size of the differences varies tremendously by school and by region of country. At the post high-school levels, differences are still large.

2. Even when amount of mathematics studied is controlled, females appear not to be learning math as well as males in some

instances. This trend should concern us all. When females excel, it is in lower-level cognitive tasks. Even when females and males report they have been enrolled in the same mathematics courses, males perform better on more difficult and complex tasks.

3. Affective variables may help us in understanding sex-related differences. Females as a group, more than males as a group, have less confidence in learning mathematics, perceive mathematics to be less useful to them, and attribute successes and failures in mathematics differently.

4. The classroom learning environments are different for females and males in a variety of ways.

5. Males perform better than females on tests of spatial visualization, although the impact of spatial visualization on the learning of mathematics is largely unknown.

6. The causation of sex-related differences in mathematics rests within the schools.

I would like to conclude on this last note. While laying the blame for sex-related differences on schools seems unduly harsh to many people, it is the most positive thing that has been said. If schools cause the problem, this means they can solve the problem. Educators have the power to effect change. When they do so, they will go a long way in ensuring that equity for females in mathematics education is achieved.

REFERENCES

Armstrong, Jane M. *Achievement and Participation of Women in Mathematics: An Overview*. Denver, Colo.: Education Commission of the States, 1980.

Bar-Tal, Daniel. "Attributional Analysis of Achievement-Related Behavior." *Review of Educational Research* 48 (Spring 1978): 267.

Bar-Tal, Daniel, and Frieze, Irene H. "Achievement Motivation for Males and Females as a Determinant of Attributions for Success and Failure." *Sex Roles* 3 (June 1977): 301-13.

Becker, Joanne. "A Study of Differential Treatment of Females and Males in Mathematics Classes." Doctoral dissertation, University of Maryland, 1979.

Bennett, George K.; Seashore, Harold G.; and Wesman, Alexander G. *Differential Aptitude Tests, Forms S & T*, 4th ed. New York: Psychological Corp., 1973.

Bronowski, Jacob. "Mathematics." In *The Quality of Education*, edited by Denys Thompson and James Reeves. London: Muller, 1947.

Brophy, Jere E., and Good, Thomas L. *Teacher-Student Relationships: Causes and Consequences.* New York: Holt, Rinehart & Winston, 1974.

Deaux, Kay. "Sex: A Perspective on the Attributional Process." In *New Directions in Attribution Research,* vol. 1, edited by John H. Harvey, William Ickes, and Robert F. Kidd. Hillsdale, N.J.: Lawrence Erlbaum Associates, 1976.

Fennema, Elizabeth. "Spatial Ability, Mathematics, and the Sexes." In *Mathematics Learning: What Research Says about Sex Differences,* edited by Elizabeth Fennema. Columbus, Ohio: ERIC Information Analysis Center for Science, Mathematics, and Environmental Education, 1975.

Fennema, Elizabeth. "Sex-Related Differences in Mathematics Achievement: Where and Why?" In *Perspectives on Women and Mathematics,* edited by Judith E. Jacobs. Columbus, Ohio: ERIC Information Analysis Center for Science, Mathematics, and Environmental Education, 1978.

Fennema, Elizabeth, and Carpenter, Thomas. "The Second National Assessment and Sex-Related Differences in Mathematics." *Mathematics Teacher* 74 (October 1981): 554-59.

Fennema, Elizabeth, and Koehler, Mary S. "Expectations and Feelings about Females' and Males' Achievement in Mathematics," in preparation.

Fennema, Elizabeth; Reyes, Laurie H.; Perl, Teri H.; and Konsin, Mary Ann. "Cognitive and Affective Influences on the Development of Sex-Related Differences in Mathematics." Paper presented at the annual meeting of the American Educational Research Association, Boston, April 1980.

Fennema, Elizabeth, and Sherman, Julia A. "Sex-Related Differences in Mathematics Achievement, Spatial Visualization, and Affective Factors." *American Educational Research Journal* 14 (Winter 1977): 51-72.

Fennema, Elizabeth, and Sherman, Julia A. "Sex-Related Differences in Mathematics Achievement and Related Factors: A Further Study." *Journal for Research in Mathematics Education* 9 (May 1978): 189-203.

Fennema, Elizabeth, and Tartre, Lindsay A. "The Use of Spatial Skills in Mathematics by Girls and Boys," in preparation.

Fennema, Elizabeth, and Tartre, Lindsay A. "The Use of Spatial Skills in Mathematics by Girls and Boys: A Longitudinal Study." In *Research on Relationship of Spatial Visualization and Confidence to Male/Female Achievement in Grades 6-8,* edited by Elizabeth Fennema. Final Report, National Science Foundation, SED78-17350, August 1983.

Fennema, Elizabeth; Wolleat, Patricia L.; and Pedro, Joan D. "Mathematics Attribution Scale." *Journal Supplemental Abstract Serrvice,* May 1979.

Fennema, Elizabeth; Wolleat, Patricia L.; Pedro, Joan D.; and Becker, Ann D. "Increasing Women's Participation in Mathematics: An Intervention Study." *Journal for Research in Mathematics Education* 12 (January 1981): 3-14.

Fox, Lynn H. "The Effects of Sex-Role Socialization on Mathematics Participation and Achievement." In *Women and Mathematics: Research Perspectives for Change,* NIE Papers in Education and Work, no. 8. Washington, D.C.: National Institute of Education, 1977.

Fox, Lynn H.; Tobin, Diane; and Brody, Linda. "Sex-Role Socialization and Achievement in Mathematics." In *Sex-Related Differences in Cognitive*

Functioning: Developmental Issues, edited by Michele A. Wittig and Anne C. Peterson. New York: Academic Press, 1979.

French, J.W.; Ekstrom, R.B.; and Price, L.A. *Kit of Reference Tests for Cognitive Factors,* rev. 1963. Princeton, N.J.: Educational Testing Service, 1969.

Hoffman, Lois W. "Early Childhood Experiences and Women's Achievement Motives." In *Women and Achievement,* edited by Martha T. Mednick, Sandra S. Tangri, and Lois W. Hoffman. New York: John Wiley, 1975.

Husén, Torsten, ed. *International Study of Achievement in Mathematics: A Comparison of Twelve Countries,* 2 vols. New York: John Wiley, 1967.

Maccoby, Eleanor E., and Jacklin, Carol N. *The Psychology of Sex Differences.* Stanford, Calif.: Stanford University Press, 1974.

Nash, Sharon C. "Sex Role as a Mediator of Intellectual Functioning." In *Sex-Related Differences in Cognitive Functioning: Developmental Issues,* edited by Michele A. Wittig and Anne C. Petersen. New York: Academic Press, 1979.

National Assessment of Educational Progress. *The Third National Mathematics Assessment: Results, Trends, and Issues,* Report No. 13-MA-01. Denver, Colo.: Education Commission of the States, 1983.

Parsons, Jacquelynne E.; Heller, K.A.; Meece, Judith L.; and Kaczala, Carol. "The Effects of Teachers' Expectancies and Attributions on Students' Expectancies for Success in Mathematics." Paper presented at the annual meeting of the American Educational Research Association, San Francisco, April 1979.

Perl, Teri H., and Cronkite, R. "Evaluating the Impact of an Intervention Program: Math-Science Career Conference for Young Women." Unpublished manuscript, 1979. (Available from Dr. Teri Hoch Perl, 525 Lincoln, Palo Alto, Calif. 94301.)

Reyes, Laurie H. "Attitudes and Mathematics." In *Selected Issues in Mathematics Education,* edited by Mary M. Lindquist. Berkeley, Calif.: McCutchan Publishing, 1980.

Reyes, Laurie H. "Classroom Processes, Sex of Student, and Confidence in Learning Mathematics." Doctoral Dissertation, University of Wisconsin–Madison, 1981.

Schonberger, Ann K. "Are Mathematics Problems a Problem for Women and Girls?" In *Perspectives on Women and Mathematics,* edited by Judith E. Jacobs. Columbus, Ohio: ERIC Information Analysis Center for Science, Mathematics, and Environmental Education, 1978.

Smith, S.E. "Enrollment and Achievement by Sex in Mathematics and Science for Five 1978 Regents Samples." Paper presented at Northeast Educational Research Association Convention, Ellenville, N.Y., October, 1980.

Student Achievement in California Schools: 1977-78 Annual Report. Sacramento, Calif.: California Assessment Program, 1978.

Weaver, J. Fred. "Seductive Shibboleths." *Arithmetic Teacher* 18 (April 1971): 263-64.

Weiner, Bernard. *Achievement Motivation and Attribution Theory.* Morristown, N.J.: General Learning Press, 1974.

Werdelin, Ingvar. *Geometrical Ability and the Space Factor in Boys and Girls.* Lund, Sweden: C.W.K. Gleerup, 1961.

Wise, Lauress L. "The Role of Mathematics in Women's Career Development."
    Paper presented at the Annual Convention of the American Psychological
    Association, Toronto, Canada, 1978.
Wolleat, Patricia L.; Pedro, Joan D.; Becker, Ann D.; and Fennema, Elizabeth. "Sex
    Differences in High School Students' Causal Attributions of Performance in
    Mathematics." *Journal for Research in Mathematics Education* 11 (November
    1980): 356-66.
Women's Equity Action League. *WEAL Washington Report*, August 1979.

7

Women's Studies at the Secondary School Level

Shirley Jane Kaub

The growth of women's studies courses at the high school level began in the early 1970s, receiving impetus from the women's studies movement in higher education. Given the greater support for program development in higher education and the continuing difficulties in gaining academic acceptance, it is not surprising that women's studies at the secondary level is not so developed or accepted as standard offerings. There is less of a supportive network, and the political structure is different. There is also less freedom to offer innovative courses at the secondary level because of prescribed state standards and requirements for graduation from high schools. An ERIC search in May 1983 specifying secondary-level women's studies programs or courses resulted in the identification of only a very few items. Thus, we have little information available describing either the extent or content of curricular offerings, and we do not know how many school districts or even states offer such instruction.

This essay describes the development of women's studies courses in a large urban high school located in a community considered to be liberal and socially avant-garde. Considerations unique to a secondary public school will be reviewed and content recommendations offered. The stated goals are general and reflect a context similar to the humanities and social studies, but the content is revisionist in the same way that women's studies in higher education has often become revisionist. This is to say, instruction in general social studies, history, or language arts at the secondary level has not, heretofore, reflected an analysis of the role and condition of women, nor has the academic content been couched in words and illustrations that would have meaning for adolescent girls and boys (Ahlum and Fralley 1976). In describing the nature and structure of high school women's studies courses, philosophical questions are posed that serve to stimulate considerations for structure, content, and refinement of programs. For example, the yearly *Women's Week* as described herein was an outgrowth of the classroom instructional program and served to involve the entire school in attending to matters that at first glance appeared to be of concern and interest only to women, but which on closer examination involved boys and young men in a thoughtful analysis of their values, attitudes, and roles vis-à-vis women.

ORGANIZATION AND STRUCTURE

In most secondary schools, women's studies is not institutionalized but depends instead upon the commitment of a few interested teachers. If these individuals leave the staff or are given different assignments, the courses or program offerings are often dropped. When queried about their involvement in program development, teachers will reply: "I initiated this course because I was asked to teach what I wanted to. . . . I was also pursuing my own questions about women's roles" or "I initiated this course out of wanting to teach something I was excited about." The replies do not reflect a more formal, official stance of the school district where a school administrator or a school board might have dictated the development of such programs. Instead, program development seems to depend on the initiative and interest of individual teachers.

Partially because of this, and also because too few offerings exist to constitute a formal department, high school women's studies courses are found under the aegis of various departments. Most often they are in English or social studies with occasional interdisciplinary arrangements.

In many schools courses are optional or elective and without departmental affiliation, a distinct disadvantage in building enrollments. This tenuous status also indicates the fragility and vulnerability of many women's studies courses, and it is important to formalize the status of women's studies courses by gaining administrative support and credibility from the teachers involved in the school system and the community at large. Because courses include a survey of stereotypic sex roles, such study may be perceived as a challenge to community mores or, perhaps legitimately, as a version of values clarification, an approach that has been under heavy criticism in various parts of the country by conservative parent groups.

Although in a broad sense women's studies may be identified as part of many classes throughout school, formal courses are most commonly found in grades ten to twelve, with a few at the junior high school level. The credibility of women's studies courses may be challenged by departments that are traditionally staffed by male teachers, such as social studies. The issue is sometimes raised of whether the course should carry graduation credit only and not credit satisfying departmental requirements. Pragmatically, it may be necessary to add the phrase "emphasis on women" to a standing course description in order to resolve the issue of credits earned.

PURPOSES AND GOALS AT THE SECONDARY LEVEL

The purpose of women's studies at the secondary level is not to prepare students to continue such studies at the postsecondary level, as is often the case in other academic areas, but rather to begin developing an understanding of feminism. It is important for teachers of such courses to key materials and experiences to the student's current level of self-awareness and self-understanding; to be able to capture for the students the historical antecedents for attitudes, practices, and behaviors; and to appreciate the political and economic results of such attitudes, practices, and behaviors. Course content should reflect both affective and cognitive learning, but whatever the substantive approach used the basic goals should include the following:

—to arouse or increase awareness of students about sex stereotyping in schools and society, its causes and effects;

—to remedy the omissions of history, to emphasize the contributions of women in various realms such as politics and economics, and to explore the culture of women;

—to encourage an understanding of the ways in which social values and attitudes influence behavior vis-à-vis the position of women;

—to enhance the understanding that human beings of all times and cultures are more alike than different through a cross-cultural comparison of the roles of women;

—to provide a supportive, nonthreatening atmosphere in which students may explore their own feelings, behaviors, and expectations about themselves as women or men;

—to enhance self-awareness and self-esteem among high school women, attributes which have been shown to be especially poorly developed in high school women;

—to inform students about outstanding women and their lives, and also to explore day-to-day reality and identify ways to deal with problems and situations confronting women;

—to expand career options and encourage students to rethink their career plans in light of new understandings of their own and societal expectations.

The major portion of a high school course may be devoted to understanding female-male roles in our society, in which case the course may be considered sociology, social psychology, or human sexuality. This emphasis might also be combined with a study of women in American history using historical events for illustration. Commonly the topic of sexual stereotyping is either an introduction or is integrated with content in history, comparative cultures, or literature. Learning specific skills and understandings within a discipline can be accomplished by using data and information specific to women. For example, skill development in social studies might include using a time line to record major events affecting women in the United States, or reading and interpreting graphs and tables might incorporate a study of the average annual income of women and men at various periods in time and in differing occupations.

Historical concepts are enhanced by a study of women including class and race as key factors in history and the influence of these factors on behavior. Other historical concepts brought in include:

—the impact of the industrial revolution by analyzing the resulting change in women's role and status;

—the lag in social values and attitudes in comparison with increased social legislation by studying such relationships as the Civil Rights Act of 1964 and the current status of women;

—an analysis of the constancy of change in history recognizing that change is cyclical rather than lineal through a study of the status of women in the United States from the colonial period to the present;

—the role of religion in influencing social, economic, and political behavior by studying the effect on women of religion at various times and in various cultures;

—the importance of the labor movement in the United States by studying the contributions of women to labor.

In addition to general historical understandings, several concepts are peculiarly pertinent and vital to women's studies, including sexual division of labor, status of women in traditional (precolonial) societies, and women and power. Students should be helped to understand that in some cultures tasks are or were assigned by sex without according higher status to those performed by the male or by the female (Matthiasson 1974). By comparing this situation to career status in contemporary society, it can be illustrated that occupations and professions typically dominated by men involve higher rewards in money and/or prestige than do those commonly entered by women. While this point might appear to be elementary, it is often new information for high school students.

In considering women and power, students should be helped to understand that in some traditional societies, such as Ghanian, women enjoyed an autonomy in the social and economic spheres that they were not to know after the imposition of European mores by colonial rulers (Smock 1977). It is a novel and possibly disturbing idea to many young persons that Western culture does not necessarily mean progress in all respects.

Women's studies at the secondary school level presents what is perhaps the first opportunity to address issues not commonly included within the traditional content areas of study. It is important that adolescent girls and boys become aware of the meaning and importance of power, in the sense of possession of and ability to use control over the actions of self and others.

Psychoanalysts and sociologists have written extensively about the difficulties women have in acquiring and using power; through high school women's studies adolescent females are introduced to the concept through analysis of social, political, and economic power possessed by women at different times and in different cultures. Questions posed might include:

—Did (does) the representative woman of the period or culture have control over her own body, over decisions involving her children and personal life-style?

—Did (does) she have suffrage and the right to hold office, a right implying meaningful influence on community decisions?

—Did (does) she have the opportunity for training in the work of her real choice without limiting socialization or access to employment or business without discrimination, and the right to use her economic rewards as *she* sees fit?

Emphasizing the typical woman and not the few unrepresentative ones who are outstanding and well known serves to highlight the variety and richness of the roles of women and to clarify options for role modeling. Illustrating adaptability to change can be accomplished by studying contrasts between women in rural and city settings in the same culture and or the conditions of women over time within any one culture.

Through the study of literature, teachers can emphasize consciousness raising through analysis of sex-role stereotyping in literary works by studying the relatively small number of women protagonists and by highlighting women authors who are frequently omitted in traditional literature courses. The materials may include the Bible, classical literature, medieval tales, novels, dramas, short stories from all periods, and representations in advertising, music, radio, and television.

In addition to strengthening critical interpretation and developing an ability to use literary techniques, the students develop an increased awareness that Western literature includes works of excellence by female as well as male authors, and they also gain an understanding of the role of media in socialization. Affective goals in such courses include developing student confidence and encouraging women to write creatively.

THE PEDAGOGY OF WOMEN'S STUDIES AT THE SECONDARY LEVEL

It is a sound general pedagogical principal to illustrate and model in teaching a course the attitudes that are included in the affective goals. In secondary school women's studies courses, it is crucial to have an atmosphere that is nonthreatening with an emphasis on self-expression. At this point in the development of young adolescents, they must be taught to experience self-exploration and self-expression, to question their own attitudes and behaviors as well as others', and to dare to explore nontraditional, nonstereo-typed information. In order to understand the concepts of socialization and to internalize an acceptance of self, the students must be facilitated to share experiences, opinions, and feelings about sex roles without fear of criticism. Female students have to be taught to be assertive in expressing their ideas, and they should receive reinforcement at every step, particularly as they strive to achieve nonstereotypic goals in careers, life-styles, and school-related activities. Males have to learn to share feelings more openly and to accept their expression by others. They have to be helped to see females as individuals with interests, values, aptitudes, and career aspirations as varied and valid as their own. Males, too, need to be helped to feel free to express interest in nonstereotypic ideas and activities.

In classes of mostly female students, the atmosphere becomes more one of consciousness raising. If both sexes are represented the dynamics are different; in some respects there may be a better balance of viewpoints, but in either case an atmosphere of trust is essential in order to encourage a broadened repertoire of behaviors. No one is faulted for any opinion, and the students must be assured that confidentiality outside the classroom will be maintained. It is important for the instructors as role models to express opinions, identified as such, with the understanding that students will accept such statements as opinions. Continued reinforcement of this attitude is effective in assisting students to integrate personal experiences with broad issues and with cognitive learning.

In modeling psychologically androgynous attitudes, a team teaching approach is ideal. In addition to the primary teacher, another adult such as a guidance counselor, social worker, or other support staff person may be involved. Student teachers also present another point of view, and this mix of adults has the additional benefit of displaying a natural expression of friendship between adults.

As a beginning exercise to develop a supportive classroom climate, it is helpful to divide students into dyads for various activities such as introducing each other to the class and interviewing each other. To illustrate how deeply this type of exercise can touch feelings the following anonymous note was handed in on the day of such introductions:

Ms.—

I wish you would read this to our second hour class.

A lot of you people are liars and fakes. Things you wrote are crap. You say you like people for what they are—you lie. All of you stay in your little groups. *No one gets in*. Always—constantly you talk about people behind their backs. If our world was filled up with people like you we would all soon die. Your kind are worth nothing. Grow up and keep secrets and feelings to yourself. Expressing them really hurt (sic) people sometimes. Sometimes people aren't as bad as you think they are.

Classes such as women's studies with an emphasis on judging people by their true natures and not by appearances help students who are hurting as much as this writer feel free to test themselves in other relationships.

Another valuable exercise for use early in a course, whether in social studies, literature, or an interdisciplinary offering, is asking students to report on personal expectations. This requires each student to interview a familiar adult—mother, grandmother, teacher, friend—asking questions such as the expectations the person had in high school about marriage or relationships, the type of work (career and/or homemaker) pursued, use of leisure time, and factors related to children within the lives of each adult. The expectations expressed are compared with current reality, with an explanation of what the interviewee thinks caused her to be doing something different from what she had hoped or what she perceives as having enabled her to reach her goals. This activity helps portray life situations that do not materialize as anticipated, emphasizing the importance of options and flexible planning. The adults interviewed are sometimes so interested that they send messages back to the class such as "When I was in high school I thought I would work for a short time and then get married and have someone to take care of me. Now I am divorced and working to support a family. I'd like to tell girls to be realistic when they are deciding what courses to take in school."

Consciousness raising is enhanced by introductory discussions focusing on a student's past experiences: whom and what I played with when I was little; what I was punished for; what sports I participated in; ways in which teachers treat boys and girls differently; how I would answer these questions if I were my brother or sister. Current television presentations, soap operas, movies, and songs can be analyzed for character profiles and subtle comments about sex roles. The perceptions of social conditioning students gain through such activities are useful in understanding the roles of men and women in literature or in other cultures. For example, in discussing the differences between the relatively expanded rights of the Egyptian woman in the economic and political spheres and her restricted rights in the private sphere, students are asked to analyze and compare this with perceptions of their own life-styles.

AS A STEP IN CONSCIOUSNESS RAISING

It is apparent that a major effect of women's studies courses at the secondary level is that of consciousness raising. In accomplishing this, teachers use areas of study as the vehicles for exploring the status of women in contemporary society. Within any of the disciplines, a variety of teaching methods and techniques have proven effective with adolescent girls and boys, but because of the fledgling state of women's studies at the secondary level, teachers have to be particularly resourceful in compiling information for use with these age groups. For example, commercially prepared textbook materials in any area of study rarely include recent statistics about female wages in comparison to males, numbers of women in various occupations and professions, or recent legal decisions affecting women. At the most, only token recognition is given to women in politics, work, sports, and religion. The historical role of women is rarely explored. The kinds of statistics and information just mentioned are often received by the students with indignation and a certain amount of incredulity. After reviewing such materials, students become more conscious of relevant stories in newspapers or on news broadcasts. They bring materials to class and begin compiling their own resource files.

Projects in addition to regular assignments help make the conditions surrounding contemporary women more graphic: make collages to illustrate concepts of stereotyped or liberated women and men, or of Ying and Yang; prepare imaginary accounts such as a speech announcing one's candidacy for the presidency of the United States, or a first-hand story of life as a concubine in traditional China; students can construct surveys and tabulate the results, thus gaining a firsthand understanding of the attitudes and perceptions of important others, for example, fellow students or the school staff. Some typical questions of student-constructed surveys include:

For males:

—how many times a week do you wash dishes?
—make beds?
—cook?
—do the washing?

For females:

—how often do you repair an appliance?
—cut the grass?
—take out the garbage?
—shovel the walks?

Interesting comparisons can be made between the responses of adults and high school students of each sex as well as between the responses of males and females. These relatively simple activities are extraordinarily facilitative in developing critical skills and an analytic approach to issues concerning women and in fostering development of consciousness raising.

ANCILLARY ACTIVITIES

As students and school staff take part in the actual women's studies courses or work toward incorporating feminist information within other existing courses, a cadre of experienced and knowledgeable people develops who begin to explore other ways of providing a focus on feminism. A particularly successful venture within some programs has been a schoolwide women's week. A typical and successful format is a series of seminars held throughout the school day involving speakers from the community and various professions including male and female nontraditional workers, important female policy makers in community government and organizations, women from other cultures, and the elderly and handicapped women. Topics can include:

—parenthood, if and when
—interfamily sexual abuse
—premenstrual syndrome—is it all in your head?
—changing roles in the family.

Presentations can involve speakers, panels, and films, often centering around a general theme for the week with a subtheme for each day. The most successful seminars are those that emphasize broadening options for both men and women. Students enrolled in the women's studies class during the semester of the special week-long activities play an active role in planning, inviting and introducing speakers, and participating in panel discussions.

In some schools staff and students have formed a standing sexism-in-education committee to monitor schoolwide announcements, analyze student handbooks for sexist language and illustrations, assist the staff of the school newspaper in avoiding sexism, investigate complaints about discrimination in the physical education department and in other areas, and develop alternative activities to the traditional homecoming court. Pupils have also served as resource persons for staff development programs on sex-role stereotyping, and they have developed support groups that meet outside of school hours in order to continue the consciousness raising that has occurred during their informal program of study.

PUPIL EVALUATIONS OF WOMEN'S STUDIES CURRICULUM

A carefully planned sequence of study will include procedures for evaluation. At the beginning of a course, for example, a pretest on attitudes toward sex roles is administered with the assurance that students may preserve their anonymity and that there are no right or wrong answers. The same instrument is administered at the end of the course, and a comparison of results is discussed with the class participants. Another useful tool at the end of a course of study is a series of open-ended questions; for example, what did you like most about the class? what did you like least? and how has study in this class changed your information or attitude toward countries and peoples we have discussed? toward your career? toward persons you admire?

Some comments have included:

—I've also started to wonder about many things. I have started to feel better about my desire to have a career, through this class.
—I really admire what a lot of other women and girls have to go through, how strong they must be.
—I also understand why women are starting things such as ERA. This class has opened the door to a whole new perspective.
—This class has also helped me see some things in a whole different way, such as men. I feel a lot more confident and secure with myself. I had better thinking going on, and a whole different outlook on life.
—This class has changed my career patterns because now I don't care what other people think; if I want to be something I'm going to try and be it.
—I now admire more women, not famous women, but normal women living everyday lives in these countries.
—It made me admire women even more. It seems that women all over the world put up with so much garbage and yet they can still hold their heads up and walk tall. I think sometimes that women here get so wrapped up in our fight for equality that they forget about the women in other countries who have it much worse.

As described, the basic principle for the development of women's studies at the secondary level is not only to offer courses specific to women's studies but to incorporate feminism within existing courses and areas of study. A remarkable example of the synthesis of economic and political information within the context of feminist concerns is demonstrated by the response of a female tenth-grade student to the following essay question: Do women in Communist countries hold more or fewer nonstereotypic jobs than in the United States? Does this give them an advantage over American women?

In Communist countries such as China and Cuba, women hold many more nonstereotypic jobs than they do in the United States. In fact, 34 percent of all Cuban workers are female, and 30-50 percent of the industrial labor in China is performed by women. All fields except those requiring great physical strength are open to women, and both China and Cuba have set up communal family care programs which free women from stereotypic housework.

This surge of female labor will probably be advantageous for these women, although it might not seem so now. At present, housework is considered nonproductive, and women are not allowed to be housewives even if they want to be. Today's Communist governments also dictate what jobs and training a woman will have, thus ignoring the ideals of free choice implied by the availability of nonstereotypic jobs. The long-term advantages outweigh the above disadvantages, though. For example, women now are getting the education long denied them, are coming out of seclusion, and can function economically without dependence on men, and if the present Communist government becomes totalitarian, there will be a generation of women present which will be educated enough to make truly free career choices. Educational programs set up for women today would be firmly established for future women, and society would have been conditioned to accept women in nonstereotypic roles. This governmentally forced integration of women into the work force should eventually overcome traditional attitudes towards women, but in the United States overcoming these attitudes is left to the women alone, who receive relatively little support from the government.

If anyone doubts the efficacy of women's studies at the secondary level, let them ponder this statement from a tenth-grade female pupil. Women's studies at the secondary level becomes a powerful political tool in the development of a generation of informed and concerned citizens who will in a few years become voters and taxpayers. The potential contributions of these adolescents so schooled in liberated nonsexist values and principles bodes well for the continuation of social policy and legislation protective of the rights of all regardless of sex.

PROGRAM EVALUATION AND RESEARCH

Far less is known about women's studies in secondary schools than in higher education, in part because the discipline has developed in a more idiosyncratic fashion, based largely upon the interest and commitment of individuals and not departments or school districts. A unique opportunity exists at the secondary level in contrast with women's studies in higher education. A difficulty in achieving discreet longitudinal data on the effects of women's studies in higher education is the difficulty in separating those who are studying the issues for the first time from those who have had previous courses or study. At the secondary level, in contrast, students have almost always not had any formal introduction to women's studies. There is a shared problem, however, between secondary schools and higher education, and that is the problem in distinguishing students who are self-selected and who enter the course with a high degree of awareness of issues from those who have little understanding of feminist concerns. A first necessary step in program evaluation, consequently, is the development of a longitudinal data base.

Evaluation specific to courses has been effectively accomplished using pretest and posttest assessment procedures. Within individual schools a data base is being developed including information on changes in self-concept and self-image among female pupils, an assessment of increased awareness of sexist practices in the school setting and the work place, attitudes of pupils toward women's issues, changed perceptions of career choices, and an increased awareness of problems and issues confronting male pupils. A useful standardized procedure for assessing changes in classroom interaction used in addition to the individually designed instruments is the classroom interaction analysis developed by Flanders (1960).

On a larger scale, moving beyond discrete courses with the developing data bases, it is possible to study the climate of an entire school as it has been affected by women's studies programs. Feasible research activities include an examination of the change in instructional methods and a determination of whether institutionalized sexism has been demonstratively decreased. It is now possible to study the effects upon teaching faculty members to see whether they show a greater awareness of the needs of women and of ethnic and racial minorities in their selection of materials, curriculum content, and methods of teaching.

There is a tremendous amount of work to be accomplished in all aspects of society—political, economic, social, and psychological—

before sexism is eradicated. Our secondary school systems represent the last point at which adolescent males and females are grouped for formal instruction. Some may continue on in various educational activities after leaving high school, but many will not. We cannot wait for post-high-school years in order to systematically inform our young people about issues of equality and equity for both men and women. The incorporation of women's studies content at the secondary level is critical to the development of nonprejudicial and nonsexist values and philosophies in our young adults. This is the importance of women's studies in secondary schools.

REFERENCES

Ahlum, Carol, and Fralley, Jacqueline, comps. *High School Feminist Studies.* Edited and with an introduction by Florence Howe. Old Westbury, N.Y.: Feminist Press, 1976.

Flanders, Ned A. *Teacher Influence, Pupil Attitudes, and Achievement.* Cooperative Research Project No. 397, Office of Education, U.S. Department of Health, Education, and Welfare. Minneapolis, Minn.: University of Minnesota, 1960.

Matthiasson, Carolyn J., ed. *Many Sisters: Women in Cross-Cultural Perspective.* New York: Free Press, 1974.

Smock, Audrey C. "Ghana: From Autonomy to Subordination." In *Women: Roles and Status in Eight Countries,* edited by Janet Z. Giele and Audrey C. Smock. New York: John Wiley, 1977.

8

Women's Education and Career Choice: Disparities Between Theory and Practice

Helen S. Astin and Mary Beth Snyder

In 1848 women gathered at Seneca Falls, New York, to discuss the social, civil, and religious rights of women, and it was then that many first demanded equal access for women to education, the trades, and the professions. By 1920, such efforts had won a major victory—the right to vote—but women were a long way from achieving equality with men in education and work. After a period of inactivity in the early 1960s efforts began again to revitalize feminism in order to achieve equality. In the early 1960s two significant events provided the background to the present struggle for equal rights. In 1963 President Kennedy appointed the Commission on the Status of Women, and its subsequent report, *American Women,* documented the low status of women in education and work. At about the same time, *The Feminine Mystique* by Betty Friedan presented the idea that American society had "imprisoned" women in their own homes by not encouraging them to pursue their talents and lead independent lives. This book helped to create a climate of awareness and dissatisfaction with the status quo.

Major legislation affecting women's rights has been enacted since early 1960.

—In the early 1960s "sex" was added to Title VII of the Civil Rights Act.

—The Equal Pay Act of 1963, amended to include institutions of higher education, prohibited discrimination in salaries on the basis of sex.

—In 1968 Executive Order 11246, which prohibits discrimination by all federal contractors on the basis of race, color, religion, and national origin, was amended to include sex.

—The Public Health Service Act of 1971, the first legislation forbidding sex discrimination against students, prohibited discrimination in admissions to medical schools and other health professional schools.

—Title IX of the Education Amendments of 1972 prohibited discrimination against students and employees on the basis of sex in all federally assisted education programs including admissions, financial aid, educational and guidance programs, and student services and facilities.

—In Section 408 of the Education Amendments of 1974, the Women's Education Equity Act, Congress declared that educational programs in the United States are frequently inequitable and limit the full participation of women in American society.

➤The purpose of Section 408 was to provide educational equity for women. This section authorized the commissioner of education to make grants and to enter into contracts for activities designed to carry out the purpose of the act at all educational levels with a charge to the commissioner to conduct a comprehensive review of sex discrimination in education.

As part of the required review, in 1975 the Higher Education Research Institute (HERI) undertook studies to assess the types and extent of sex discrimination in educational guidance and counseling programs and in policies and procedures which were intended to facilitate student access to postsecondary education (Harway and Astin 1977).

INSTITUTIONAL BARRIERS TO EQUALITY

An understanding of the problem of equality requires some knowledge of institutional practices that may act as barriers. These are, after all, presumably amenable to change. Such institutional practices include high school counseling and career choice information as well as postsecondary access.

High School Guidance Counseling and Career Choice

The first phase of the study by the Higher Education Research Institute (Harway and Astin 1977) was designed to examine discrimination in high school counseling and guidance programs that potentially served as major barriers to women's educational access and attainment. Sex bias in counseling was defined as any condition under which a client's options were limited by the counselor solely because of gender, that is, limiting the expression of certain kinds of behavior because they had not been traditionally appropriate for one or the other of the sexes. Sex bias in counseling could be overt, such as suggesting that a female high school student not enroll in a mathematics class because "women aren't good in math," thereby limiting her later options to enter scientific or professional careers. More frequently, however, sex bias was apt to be expressed covertly with subtle expectations or attitudes by a counselor that reflected certain stereotypic characteristics.

In high school, students draw on a number of sources for information as they are deciding what they will do after graduation—including that all-important decision of whether to continue their education and if so, where to go to college. The findings from the HERI study suggest that the role of high school counselors is somewhat ambiguous; counselors are underutilized by high school students, and students feel that counselors do not influence their plans to a great extent. Moreover, discussing plans with a guidance counselor does not appear to increase the student's satisfaction with the postsecondary decision.

A common source of information for high school students making college decisions is institutional catalogs, which can affect access in that they either attract or discourage students. A study of college catalogs in 1975 used a sample of catalogs from one hundred collegiate institutions and nineteen proprietary schools. This examination, utilizing a content-analysis technique, revealed that institutional catalogs from collegiate institutions rarely mentioned special services for women. For example, only 2 percent of the four-year colleges and 11 percent of the two-year colleges mentioned women's centers or child care services in the mid-1970s; only 6 percent of the four-year colleges provided gynecological services while no two-year college mentioned this service; 6 percent of the four-year colleges and 11 percent of the two-year colleges mentioned the availability of women's studies programs.

Related to the issue of sex biases in actual counseling practice, the question of sex bias in guidance and counseling theories that are taught in counselor training programs is important. Sex bias in guidance and counseling theory is a product of the combined effects of (a) the theoretical legacy of Freud, (b) the biological determinist view of gender and behavior implicit in nonpsychoanalytic theories, and (c) the therapeutic mission of traditional counseling, which is to help clients adjust to and perform certain cultural roles.

While non-Freudian theories reject a number of Freud's basic formulations of personality development, some assume a biological basis for sex differences in behavior with little or no thought that the culture might be the source of sex-role behaviors. Instead, professionals treat gender-related behavioral differences as confirmation of a biological basis of behavior.

Conceptualizing positive counseling outcomes as successful acquisition of, and adjustment to, culturally defined sex-role behaviors raises the question of whether the field of guidance and counseling may be a major perpetrator of sexist socialization. Psychotherapy has been viewed as a process for helping women to adjust to traditional roles and norms. The theoretical assumptions that the problem lies within the individual rather than within society (or that at least a portion of it is society based) becomes a further source of potential bias in therapy.

Guidance is typically vocational in nature, particularly at the secondary and postsecondary levels. In addition to familiarity with guidance and counseling theories, a counselor must have an understanding of vocational development. Osipow (1973) reflects the attitude of many early social scientists studying vocational development: "For many years, questions of career development concerning women were ignored or given cursory treatment partly out of lack of general social interest, and partly because the confusing nature of career development in women made the topic difficult to study" (p. 256).

A number of classical career development theories propagated in the early 1950s remain the guiding theoretical framework for counselors-in-training who are concerned with helping students make vocational choices. However, these theories suffer from the same malady as general counseling literature and theories: women's vocational development and concerns are either ignored or treated as trivial corollaries to men's career development. In these early conceptions, when views on women were incorporated they were primarily descriptive of the usual patterns observed in the career development of women. For example, women's careers differ from those of men in that they are characterized by discontinuities resulting from marriage and childbearing and rearing. No efforts were made to identify additional factors such as psychological determinants in women's career choice and vocational develop—ment.

In the late 1960s, two independent attempts at formulating theories about women's occupational development appeared. Psathas (1968) and Zytowski (1969) presented theoretical accounts similar in some ways to those presented in the 1950s. Psathas argued for the need to examine the occupational choices of women in the context of sex roles. He focused primarily on variables that specifically affect women's occupational choices as compared with men, for example, intention to marry, time of marriage, reasons for marriage, and husband's financial status. Zytowski was more concerned with women's vocational patterns and the interactions of women's roles as homemaker and worker. He emphasized such variables as age of entry into the occupational world and span and degree of participation in the labor force.

Even these early attempts at theoretical formulations of women and work had as the primary orientation and interest the occupational behavior of men. All had as their main goal a description of the differences between men and women in occupational choice and development and an emphasis on marriage and homemaking as the critical determinants in the career development of women. However, later literature on the occupational development of women that included research efforts by women social scientists interested in career development has a different focus (Baruch 1967, Tangri 1972, Harmon 1970, Almquist and Angrist 1971, and Astin and Myint 1971). These scholars were interested in isolating factors that differentiated women with certain career choices and commitments from women who were less likely to pursue or to persist in careers.

Women researchers have focused on intragroup variability. They report that some women exhibit characteristics early in their development that indicate strong career orientation. Other women show a weaker career orientation; while still others are primarily oriented toward family and homemaking. However, the majority of women make limited choices. The variables that do emerge as significant factors in differentiating women by career choice and commitment are psychological and sociocultural. Career-oriented women are more autonomous and appear to have been supported or encouraged by a significant man, for example, father, brother, boyfriend, or teacher, and they are more likely to have had working mothers. Career-oriented women also tend to value intrinsic rewards, to be less field dependent, and to exhibit more internality. They are quite likely to possess high mathematical aptitude.

Postsecondary Access

Educational access is a process by which an individual achieves a particular goal—a process comprised of all educational experiences leading up to and including postsecondary experiences. Equal access is defined as an equal opportunity to attend postsecondary institutions that can prepare a person for the occupation or life-style for which he or she is best suited by virtue of abilities, interests, and talents, and one that can provide the necessary services to foster self-realization among students.

This phase of the HERI study also paid particular attention to differences in the participation and experiences of women and men at different educational levels—high schools and postsecondary institutions (Harway and Astin 1977). It was found that in high school the sexes are sharply segregated among vocational and technical programs. Furthermore, women in high school have considerably better grades than men, but fewer of them, as compared with men, plan for bachelor's or higher degrees.

The rate of women attending institutions of higher education since the early 1970s has risen dramatically. By 1981 women surpassed men in proportions attending postsecondary schools by 2.8 percent (Astin 1981). An important question regarding educational equity is whether women attend the same types of institutions as do men. Do women who score about the same as men on aptitude tests enter high-quality institutions in the same proportions as do men? In 1975 and 1981 women, compared to men, were concentrated in smaller, less selective, and less affluent institutions. Among universities, men were represented in greater numbers than women: 51.3 versus 48.7 percent at public universities and 54.5 versus 45.5 percent at private universities. More distressing, however, was the fact that in the most selective private universities men outnumbered women by 23 percent. Furthermore, Astin (1977) concluded, in a longitudinal study of college students, that "although women earn higher grades than men in college, they are less likely to persist and to enroll in graduate or professional school" (p. 215).

Some studies (Davis 1969, Holmstrom and Holmstrom 1974) have dealt with the importance of role models and the impact of faculty attitudes toward women students in either inhibiting or enhancing the educational progress of women. These studies show that many women students believe that the male faculty members do not take them seriously (Holmstrom and Holmstrom 1974, Feldman 1974). Moreover, women graduate students considering withdrawal from school often cite pressure arising from this lack of acceptance as their reason. Women students do not usually have the same mentor-protégé relation with a professor that men students do, and they are, thus, deprived of an important support in their development as scholars and researchers. Epstein (1970) maintains that the male faculty member does not develop this relationship with his female students because he does not believe that women students are adequately committed or capable of becoming his successor.

Data collected in a national survey of faculty in 1980, however, suggest that women students have somewhat increased their status in the eyes of male faculty members. Faculty were asked to indicate their level of agreement with the statement "In my field, male students comprehend the material better than female students." About 92 percent of the male respondents expressed disagreement with the statement, indicating a positive outlook by male faculty on the intellectual abilities of their female students. Through affirmative action efforts, the percentage of women faculty members increased on most campuses during the last decade, yet their numbers remain far too low to provide a "critical mass" across all disciplines to serve as visible and effective role models for the women students in our higher education institutions.

A study of sex differences in academic administration (Astin 1977) found that by mid-1975 women accounted for .8 percent of the presidents and 1.1 percent of the chief officers of administrative divisions. Of the 156 women deans (15.7 percent of all deans in 1975), more than half were deans of either home economics or nursing schools. The study concluded that "... women are grossly underrepresented in all top administrative posts in American colleges and universities. What appears to be a modest representation of women among college presidents and academic deans turns out ... to be primarily attributable to the relatively high representation of women administrators in colleges for women." A more recent study (Astin and Snyder 1982), which examined the response by the higher education community to affirmative action regulations and guidelines since 1972, found that despite a nearly doubling of the available women with the Ph.D., women's representation among all academic personnel increased only 3.7 percent by 1982, up from 14.4 percent in 1972. This study also yielded the finding that women faculty continue to trail men in the proportion employed in the most selective institutions in this country; that is, 19 percent of all male academic personnel versus only 15 percent of all female academic personnel work in the elite colleges and universities.

A number of explanations have been offered for the continuing low number of women faculty among all ranks of academic personnel. Continuing salary differentials between men and women faculty may partially explain why some talented women Ph.D.s might seek employment outside academe. In the same study (Astin and Snyder 1982), which compared the status of women and men faculty in 1972 and again in 1980, a startling conclusion drawn was that overall the median salary differentials between men and women are the same today as a decade ago. Women in academe still earn only 77 percent of men's salaries.

In addition to the importance of role models and the lack of administrative and faculty models for women in colleges and universities, there are additional important considerations about women in college that need exploration. Instead of bringing about equity, the changes that occur in men and women during the college years result in further separation of the sexes in aspirations, interests, and competencies. For example, a study of college students' development (Astin 1977) reveals that women tend to lower their educational and occupational aspirations over time. Findings from this study indicate that women's educational aspirations for advanced degrees decline at a greater rate than men's. Additionally, compared with men, women are more likely to acquire general cultural knowledge than skills in athletics, original writing, technical and scientific skills (p. 129). The career implications of these findings are obvious.

In part, these differential patterns depend on the kinds of colleges attended by men and women. Whereas coeducational institutions do not affect men with respect to their aspirations, competencies, and leadership roles, women attending women's colleges are more likely to pursue postgraduate study and to participate in leadership roles while in college than are females at other types of universities or colleges.

There is no question that participation in leadership activities can lead to increased self-esteem within students. Women holding office or participating in administrative and faculty committees develop skills that can be useful in their occupational activities and roles later on. Astin and Kent (1983) report an important finding concerning the effect of extracurricular activity participation on other aspects of student development. In an eight-year follow-up study of women who had started college in 1971, women who had leadership experiences in college had developed greater self-esteem. The authors concluded that overall, leadership activities seem more beneficial to women's development of self-esteem than to men's.

The sources of financial support that a high school graduate has to draw on can be a barrier. Finances affect his or her decision to continue education, the choice of a particular institution, and his or her persistence once enrolled. Traditionally, a higher priority was given to educating men than to educating women, partly because of a belief that men are the sole breadwinners and, therefore, college education for women is frivolous because they will not "use" it. The damage that this belief has done is compounded by the fact that women rely more heavily on their parents for support to cover college expenses. Moreover, women are less successful than men at getting jobs to help pay for their education; and even when they do find jobs, they are underpaid in relation to men, and they are also less likely than men to receive military-related benefits.

PROGRAM AND POLICY IMPLICATIONS

These findings have implications for educators, administrators, and policy makers. It is evident that if women are to have the same educational and occupational opportunities as men do, steps must be taken by the secondary schools to insure that women have the necessary preparation. High school girls who take vocational curricula should be encouraged to diversify their fields of study from the typical female courses into technical programs that are now dominated by boys. High school girls enrolled in academic and college preparatory curricula should be counseled to complete advanced courses in mathematics and science in preparation for college mathematics and science majors.

Many young women continue to believe that postsecondary education bears little relation to their future lives. High school counselors have a multiple responsibility to help girls expand their attitudes about their future lives, provide detailed information about the financial costs of an education and sources of financial aid, and provide encouragement to tackle nontraditional subject matter while in school.

Programmatic guidance efforts can help high school girls change their perceptions about appropriate occupational roles for women and develop a better understanding of the multiple roles they are going to assume in the future. Specific efforts in assisting both sexes in preparing for the future might include specially designed courses on career development for both girls and boys. Such courses would have two components: self-assessment of interests and competencies and occupational information including the necessary preparation for various occupations as well as occupational rewards. Such courses would emphasize how sex-role socialization shapes occupational choices and would seek to free students from stereotypes.

A further recommendation is that women's studies be introduced in high school so that students of both sexes can study the images of the woman as depicted in literature, history, and art; this would also expose the student to important women writers, artists, and scientists. High school teachers and counselors are themselves products of socialization. Special efforts should be made to provide them with periodic in-service education in sex-role development and the role that socialization plays in shaping the self-perceptions, aspirations, and the educational and occupational choices of women.

Since parents obviously have a profound influence on their children, the high school should provide programs to assist parents in working with their sons and daughters on issues concerning education and career decisions. Not only must parents have complete information about college opportunities and costs, but they themselves must have experiences that encourage sex-role awareness.

A number of policy recommendations are also appropriate for postsecondary institutions. An examination of the data on women's participation in postsecondary education points to a few clear facts. Fewer women than men enter universities, especially among the more prestigious schools. Very few women attend technical institutions, and women in vocational education are likely to train for traditionally female occupations. Lastly, even though changes in the career interests of college women have occurred in the past few years, women undergraduates are still heavily concentrated in traditionally female fields such as education and the allied health professions.

The continuing concentration of women students in traditionally female fields can be attributed to their socialization in appropriate roles and occupations for women. Sex-role stereotypes are pervasive as women make decisions about their future lives. To overcome these stereotypes, which have become ingrained in high school, colleges—and, in particular, technological institutions—should develop *special efforts* to recruit high school girls and to provide them with tutorials and remediation in mathematics and science once they have been admitted to postsecondary institutions.

The cost of postsecondary education is perceived by many young women as a particular problem; and once in a postsecondary institution, women continue to have special concerns about financing. Because young women are typically more likely than men to depend on their parents for support, women whose parents do not value education for their daughters as much as for their sons may need at least as much financial aid as do the male students.

Work-study programs are an effective form of financial aid in that they encourage persistence. Women should be advised to participate in these programs, and efforts should be made to place them in jobs traditionally reserved primarily for men. Work experiences in nontraditional areas will help women to enlarge their options by developing new competencies and will help to make them personally and financially independent.

In graduate school, women should be encouraged to compete for research assistantships in addition to teaching assistantships since this experience offers the additional benefits of future learning, increased interaction with mentors, and future employment opportunities. Furthermore, women should be encouraged to apply for fellowships and grants, and professors should be encouraged to nominate women students for these in greater numbers.

Colleges should continue to support women's studies for the same reasons outlined earlier with respect to women's studies in high school. Moreover, since female role models are still rather scarce in higher education, particularly in male fields, special efforts are needed to give young women the opportunity to interact with role models in workshops and seminars.

The lack of gynecological facilities, day-care centers, and maternity benefits in student health insurance policies has been viewed as forms of sex discrimination in that many women need such support to continue their education without undue pressure. The provision of such facilities and services increases the woman's sense of belonging in the institution. Moreover, as long as a woman is expected by society to bear primary responsibility for her children, an effort should be made by institutions to provide for child-care services and to develop flexible policies for part-time study. Residency rules must be flexible enough to accommodate women who follow husbands to jobs in different states. Institutions must develop new and simpler ways of translating and accepting credit from other institutions so that these same women do not lose credit for previous college experience.

Even a decade after Title IX, implementing the spirit and letter of these regulations for the benefit of our young people continues to require the concerted efforts of states, local school districts, and postsecondary institutions. A more vigorous social commitment can lead to greater proportions of women persisting through college in nontraditional fields and occupations.

There is a need for institutions to reevaluate their recruitment practices for academic employment in ways that strengthen and improve the numbers and status of women personnel on college campuses. It is recommended that:

1. The record-keeping process for recruitment and hiring should be simplified, and the money saved should be rechanneled into developing a more effective recruitment process. Many institutions have invested significant funding on the maintenance of exceptionally detailed records on their recruitment and hiring process without significant affirmative action results. Prior to affirmative action, young men were recruited in the manner of star athletes. Affirmative action, unfortunately, has changed the one-on-one recruitment process. Potential candidates now respond to ads, send resumes, and arrive on campus for interviews together with five or six other candidates. Academic departments and personnel offices must join one another to provide a new emphasis that minimizes bureaucratic record keeping and maximizes the effort to identify and recruit promising women.

2. Systematic efforts are needed to insure that newcomers to our larger research-oriented campuses will quickly learn how one succeeds in such institutions. Senior faculty should be asked to provide guidance and mentoring for new faculty. Administra— tors should make released time and institutional research funds available for newly hired faculty.

3. The chief executive officers and governing boards of institutions should continue to pressure departments for improvements in affirmative action efforts. Departments should be required to engage in continuous self-study through assessment of the following criteria:
   a. demonstrable changes in the overall promotion of women and among the newly hired;

  b. promotion of women to higher ranks;
  c. monitoring of graduate school awards so as to maintain the balance between teaching and research for both men and women;
  d. expansion of funding and research opportunities for women.
4. Administrators must keep affirmative action in mind as they devise retrenchment plans. They should be particularly sensitive to the possibility that women might be asked to shoulder a disproportionate share of the burden of solving the financial problems of the institution.

The interests of educational enterprises and society as a whole will be served only if talent is nurtured and fully used regardless of one's gender.

REFERENCES

Almquist, Elizabeth M., and Angrist, Shirley S. "Role Model Influence on College Women's Career Aspirations." *Merrill-Palmer Quarterly* 17 (July 1971): 263-79.

Astin, Alexander W., *Four Critical Years*. San Francisco: Jossey-Bass, 1977.

Astin, Alexander W. "Academic Administration: The Hard Core of Sexism in Academe." *UCLA Educator* 19, no. 3 (1977): 60-66.

Astin, Alexander W., et al. *The American Freshman: National Norms for Fall 1981*. Los Angeles: University of California, 1981.

Astin, Alexander W., and Snyder, Mary Beth. "Affirmative Action 1972-1982: A Decade of Response." *Change* 14, no. 5 (1982): 26-31, 59.

Astin, Helen S., and Kent, Laura. "Gender Roles in Transition: Policy and Research Implications for Higher Education." *Journal of Higher Education* 54 (May-June 1983): 309-24.

Astin, Helen S., and Myint, Thelma. "Career Development and Stability of Young Women during the Post High-School Years." *Journal of Counseling Psychology* 18 (July 1971): 369-94.

Baruch, Rhoda. "The Achievement Motive in Women: Implications for Career Development." *Journal of Personality and Social Psychology* 5 (March 1967): 260-67.

Davis, Ann E. "Women as a Minority Group in Higher Academics." *American Sociologist* 4 (May 1969): 95-99.

Epstein, Cynthia F. "Encountering the Male Establishment: Sex-Status Limits on Women's Careers in the Professions." *American Journal of Sociology* 75 (May 1970): 965-82.

Feldman, Saul. *Escape from the Doll's House*. New York: McGraw-Hill, 1974.

Harmon, Lenore W. "Anatomy of Career Commitment in Women." *Journal of Counseling Psychology* 16 (January 1970): 77-80.

Harway, Michelle, and Astin, Helen S. *Sex Discrimination in Career Counseling and Education.* New York: Praeger, 1977.

Holmstrom, Engin Imel, and Holmstrom, Robert W. "The Plight of the Woman Doctoral Student." *American Educational Research Journal* 11 (Winter 1974): 1-17.

Osipow, Samuel H. *Theories of Career Development.* Englewood Cliffs, N.J.: Prentice-Hall, 1973.

Psathas, George. "Toward a Theory of Occupational Choice for Women." *Sociology and Social Research* 52 (January 1968): 253-68.

Tangri, Sandra S. "Determinants of Occupational Role Innovation among College Women." *Journal of Social Issues* 28, no. 2 (1972): 177-99.

Zytowski, Donald G. "Toward a Theory of Career Development for Women." *Personnel and Guidance Journal* 47 (March 1969): 660-64.

9

The Participation of Minority Women in Higher Education

Cora Bagley Marrett and Westina Matthews

INTRODUCTION

During the 1970s, the educational level of women in the United States rose rather dramatically. In the population as a whole, more women than men entered institutions of higher education, and the female share of advanced degrees grew for most disciplines. Although studies have traced these changes for the larger population (see especially Randour et al. 1982), few have examined trends for subgroups in the nation.[1] The present chapter seeks to fill the void by reviewing changing patterns in the education of women from minority backgrounds. We look especially at the status of minority women in science and engineering, given that (a) traditionally, few women have pursued these fields of study; (b)

---

1. For exceptions, see the reports from the following: Conference on the Educational and Occupational Needs of Black Women, held at the National Institute of Education, December 16-17, 1975, and the Conference on the Educational and Occupational Needs of Asian-Pacific-American Women, National Institute of Education, August 24-25, 1976.

there is considerable national interest in these areas;[2] and (c) these are fields in which prospects for employment remain favorable.

Our attention centers on four racial or ethnic minority groups: black Americans, Hispanic Americans, American Indians or Native Americans, and Asian Americans. We are interested in particular in the changes that have taken place since the beginning of the 1970s. Because we rely primarily on national data sources, the analysis is limited in certain respects. First, the sources do not allow us to examine in detail each of the groups and the different segments within them. Ideally, one should distinguish between Mexican-Americans, Puerto Ricans, and persons from various Latin American countries when reporting on the Hispanic population. Generally, however, the data are not adequate for such distinctions. Similarly, we know that the experience of foreign-born Asian women do not always parallel those of their counterparts born in the United States. Yet, we cannot turn to a large body of data to document those contrasts.[3] Indeed, in many instances we can reliably describe the experiences of only one of the four groups— black Americans—because the most detailed and complete educational record exists for this category of people.

Second, in many instances the sources present information for race or ethnicity and sex separately. With such information, one can trace changes among racial and ethnic groups or between males and females but not the course followed by men and women from different racial or ethnic backgrounds. As we shall document later, the differences among women and men from varying groups are large enough to warrant more study than they have received. Hence, we strongly endorse data collection strategies that make possible an understanding of the differences between men and women and the sources of these differences.

We compare contemporary minority women with their

---

2. Several national bodies have been formed to address the issue of mathematics and science education. They include the Commission on Pre-College Education in Mathematics, Science, and Technology, created in 1982 by the National Science Board; the Coalition of Affiliates for Science and Mathematics Education of the American Association for the Advancement of Science; and the National Action Council for Minorities in Engineering.

3. For a discussion of some of these differences, see Homma-True (1980).

predecessors, with nonminority women, and with men from both minority and nonminority backgrounds. This comparative approach is used quite commonly, but it is not without problems. Because the approach uses the levels achieved by other groups as the standard, it does not subject those levels themselves to close scrutiny. It might be, however, that against certain yardsticks—the needs of the nation, for example—the levels are far from ideal. Usually in such comparisons, differences in distributional patterns are taken as indicators of inequity, and the push is for parallel numbers. But numerical equity need not be the only or even the preferred goal. We do not explore in this discussion the matter of goal setting in measuring progress for minority women, but we recognize it as a topic that deserves widespread and systematic examination.

TRENDS IN THE EDUCATION OF MINORITY WOMEN

Enrollment at the Precollege Level

Throughout the 1970s, more women than men graduated from high school. This resulted primarily from the higher dropout rate for males. In 1980, about 17 percent of all men between eighteen and nineteen years of age as compared with about 15 percent of all women were high school dropouts (see Table 9.1). The 1980 figure for this group of men was not much different from what the 1970 figure had been, but it was slightly lower for women. Among white students, the dropout rate for men actually increased over the decade, while for women it declined somewhat. As a consequence of these countertrends, the white male-female difference was greater in 1980 than it had been in 1970.

The surveys provide dropout data on only one minority group, blacks. For blacks, as for whites, women in the younger age categories are more inclined to have remained in high school than are men. In 1980, about 20 percent of the eighteen- and nineteen-year-old women and 23 percent of the men were dropouts. For this category, the persistence rate for black men rose more sharply between 1970 and 1980 than did the persistence rate for black women, white men, and white women. But for an older age group—twenty-five to twenty-nine-year-olds—the rates for blacks of both sexes changed by about the same percentage points. High schools

Table 9.1 Percent High School Dropouts Among Persons Fourteen to Thirty-Four Years Old, by Race or Ethnicity and Sex: 1970 and 1980

Race or Ethnicity and Sex Total	Age Group and Year							
	14-34 years		18 and 19		25-29 years		30-34 years	
	1970	1980	1970	1980	1970	1980	1970	1980
Total	17.0	13.0	16.2	15.7	22.5	13.9	26.5	14.6
Males	16.2	13.2	16.0	16.9	21.4	13.8	26.2	14.0
Females	17.7	12.8	16.3	14.7	23.6	14.0	26.8	15.2
White: Both sexes	15.2	12.1	14.1	14.9	19.9	12.7	24.6	13.4
Males	14.4	12.4	13.3	16.1	19.0	12.7	24.2	13.1
Females	16.0	11.8	14.8	13.8	20.7	12.7	24.9	13.6
Black: Both sexes	30.0	18.8	31.2	21.2	44.4	22.6	43.9	23.5
Males	30.4	19.0	36.4	22.7	43.1	22.1	45.9	21.9
Females	29.5	18.7	26.6	19.8	45.6	22.9	41.5	24.8

Source: U.S. Department of Education, *Digest of Education Statistics*, 1982, Table 62.

retained more and more of their black students over the decade of the 1970s. Even though the gap narrowed, it was still wide enough in 1980 to indicate that schools still had greater success retaining white male and female students than black ones.

Enrollment in Higher Education

For the larger population, the most striking changes in male-female enrollment have taken place at the college level. In the early 1960s, far more men than women attended college; by 1980 participation rates had converged because of declining numbers of males in college and growing numbers of females. The representation of minority women also tended to increase over the period, but the outcomes were not always consistent with those for nonminority women. Consider the changes that took place between 1976 and 1980. Among blacks, women outnumbered men among the 1976 college enrollees, and because the male enrollment had dropped by 1980 while the female enrollment had risen quite noticeably, black women comprised an even larger share of the black college enrollees in 1980 (58 percent) than in 1976 (54 percent) (see Table 9.2).

Table 9.2 Enrollment in Institutions of Higher Education, by Race or Ethnicity and Sex: 1976 and 1980

Race or Ethnicity and Sex	Percent Enrolled		
	1976	1980	Percent Change, 1976-80[1]
Total	100.0	100.0	10.0
Men	52.8	48.6	1.3
Women	47.2	51.4	19.8
Non-Hispanic: white	100.0	100.0	8.3
Men	53.0	48.5	-0.1
Women	47.0	51.5	18.7
Non-Hispanic: black	100.0	100.0	7.1
Men	45.5	41.9	-1.3
Women	54.5	58.1	14.1
Hispanic	100.0	100.0	22.9
Men	54.7	49.1	10.4
Women	45.3	50.9	8.3
American Indian	100.0	100.0	12.2
Men	50.7	45.5	1.1
Women	49.3	54.6	24.6
Asian	100.0	100.0	44.7
Men	54.8	52.8	39.5
Women	45.2	47.2	51.1

Sources: 1976 data; U.S. Department of Education, *Digest of Education Statistics,* 1981, Table 93. 1980 data: *Digest of Education Statistics,* 1982, Table 92.

[1] Indicates the change in the number of people within the given category that occurred between 1976 and 1980. For example, the figure for the total shows that the number of students attending institutions of higher education was 10 percent higher in 1980 than it had been in 1976.

In contrast to the situation for black men, for Hispanic men the absolute numbers grew between 1976 and 1980. But because the growth was even greater for Hispanic women, women held a larger share of the Hispanic enrollment in 1980 (51 percent) than in 1976 (45 percent).

For American Indians, the nearly equal sex ratio of 1976 (49 percent female) had given way by 1980 to one that favored women (55 percent). In fact, the American Indian women represented one of the fastest growing college populations among the racial and ethnic men and women. We note, however, that the actual numbers were small: the nearly 47,000 American Indian women who were in college in 1980 constituted less than 1 percent of all college enrollees. At that time, American Indian women made up 2 percent of the total population in the United States.

Women of Asian or Pacific Island heritage had rates that surpassed those of American Indians. Between 1976 and 1980, the number of Asian women attending college grew from 89,000 to 135,000, an increase of over 50 percent. This count does not include nonresident alien students. The growth of the Asian female college population was associated with a rapid rise in the number of Asian males attending college. In fact, although the male rate grew a bit more slowly than the female rate, it was still fast enough to give Asian men a numerical edge over Asian women in the 1980 count of Asian college students.

In summary, nonminority women were not the only ones for whom college attendance became more widespread. For black women, Asian women, and American Indian women, college enrollment rose more noticeably than for men; in the last of these three groups, the difference in the female-male growth rate was even greater than it was for nonminority women. Black women increased their share of the black college enrollment, but we cannot determine if this was simply the continuation of a long-term trend. In other words, the change in some respects was less dramatic for black women, given the historical pattern in which more black females than males attended college. It appears that for the other groups, however, the changes that affected the education of nonminority women had clear effects on other groups of women.

Thus far, we have described changes in the size of the college population over time. We have not taken into account the size of the different bases from which students can be recruited. At this point, we turn our attention to the relationship between enrollment and the number of potential enrollees. We use as our data the percentage of two age groups—twenty- and twenty-one-year-olds and twenty-two to twenty-four-year-olds—enrolled in school. The figures cover all postsecondary institutions: nondegree-granting vocational and technical institutes as well as degree-granting two- and four-year colleges. Hence, the numbers are not strictly counts of college enrollment. But they approximate that enrollment quite closely as

70 percent of students enrolled in postsecondary programs are in two- and four-year institutions.

For both age categories more nonminority than minority students were enrolled in school in 1980. Of the six groups included in Table 9.3 white males were the group with the largest proportionate representation, while males of Spanish origin were the most poorly represented. The pattern for white females was closer to that of white males than to those of other females; among blacks, the male-female patterns in 1980 were nearly identical. Specifically, of men between the ages of twenty-two and twenty-four, 18 percent of the whites, 13 percent of the blacks, and 11 percent of the Hispanics were enrolled in school in 1980. For that same age group, the female figures were: white, 15 percent; black, 14 percent; and Hispanic, 13 percent. Among whites, a greater proportion of eligible men than eligible women were in college; for blacks, there was no sex gap; and for Hispanics, slightly more of the females than of the males were in college.

The changes between 1970 and 1980 were more noteworthy for women than for men. Among white men, the 1980 representation for both categories actually fell below what it had been in 1970. There

Table 9.3 Percent of Population in Selected Age Groups Enrolled in School, by Race or Ethnicity and Sex, 1970 and 1980

| Sex and Age | Race or Ethnicity and Year | | | | | | | |
| | Total | | White | | Black | | Hispanic | |
	1970	1980	1970	1980	1970	1980	1970	1980
Both Sexes								
20 and 21 years	34.1	31.0	35.4	31.9	25.7	23.4	23.3	19.5
22-24 years	15.4	16.3	16.2	16.4	10.0	13.6	8.6	11.7
Males								
20 and 21 years	46.5	32.6	48.9	33.7	30.8	23.0	28.4	21.4
22-24 years	11.4	17.8	24.2	18.2	13.2	13.3	10.7	10.7
Females								
20 and 21 years	25.3	29.5	25.8	30.2	22.1	23.7	19.6	17.6
22-24 years	9.1	14.9	9.4	14.8	7.4	13.9	6.9	12.6

Sources: 1970: U.S. Department of Education, *Digest of Education Statistics*, 1981, Table 4.
1980 data: *Digest of Education Statistics*, 1980, Table 4.

was a decline as well for twenty- and twenty-one-year-old black and Spanish males but no change among those between twenty-two and twenty-four years of age. Among women, however, for only one group—women of Spanish origin between twenty and twenty-one—were proportionally fewer enrolled in school in 1980 than in 1970.

The figures reinforce our earlier observation that the retention rates for women have continued to improve. Further, they suggest that should current trends continue, the gap between black women and white women will progressively narrow. It will take considerably longer, however, for Hispanic women to catch up with their white peers.

College completion patterns tend to converge with the enrollment trends just described. Black women received a larger share of the bachelor's degrees granted in 1979 than did black men; among Hispanics, American Indians, and Asians, no female-male differences appeared (see Table 9.4). Nor are the results different at the master's level. But the doctorate pool stands in sharp relief. First, far more white men than white women were granted doctorate degrees in 1979. Among minority group members, too, men outnumbered women, although the differences were not nearly so large as those for whites. Quite noteworthy is the male-female difference among blacks. Whereas more women than men were likely to obtain bachelor's and master's degrees, that was not the case for doctorates. In fact, there was a greater drop-off between the master's degree and the doctorate for black women than for Hispanic, American Indian, and Asian women; admittedly, there were very small numbers from these three categories at the first two degree levels.

Women have entered institutions of higher education in larger and larger numbers and have gained greater shares of the bachelor's and master's degrees granted by those institutions. But at the doctorate level, white men greatly outnumber all other groups, and while American Indian women do relatively well when compared with American Indian men, both sexes are greatly underrepresented among degree holders overall. It appears that at the first two degree levels, race is more of a barrier for black women than is sex. These women hold a smaller portion of bachelor's degrees than one might predict, based simply on high school graduation rates, but their

Table 9.4   Distribution of Earned Degrees at Each Level, by Race or Ethnicity and by Sex: 1978-79

Degree and Sex	Race or Ethnicity				
	Non-Hispanic White	Black	Hispanic	American Indian/ Alaskan Native	Asian or Pacific Islander
Bachelor's[1]					
Males	46.2	2.7	1.1	0.2	0.9
Females	42.8	4.0	1.1	0.2	0.8
Master's[1]					
Males	44.3	2.5	1.0	0.2	1.2
Females	44.8	4.4	1.0	0.2	0.8
Doctorates[1]					
Males	64.1	2.5	1.0	0.2	2.2
Females	26.8	1.8	0.5	0.1	0.6

[1] Percentages based on total number at this degree level.
Source: U.S. Department of Education, *Digest of Education Statistics*, 1981, Table 110.

portion exceeds that of black men. By the doctorate level, however, sex is the greater influence: women are more underrepresented than men. Even though one must interpret the small figures for Asian women quite cautiously, they seem to point to parallels between the experiences of these women and black women. Programs and policies established to increase the pool of doctoral degree holders among minority groups will undoubtedly affect the number of women doctorates from these groups. But unless there are deliberate efforts directed specifically at women, the programs are likely to expand the male doctorate pool more than the female one.

TRENDS IN THE FIELD CHOICES OF MINORITY WOMEN

Minority women have made significant gains in college attendance and completion rates when compared with minority men. But striking differences remain in the kinds of choices men and women make during their college careers. For all groups—whites, blacks, Hispanics, Native Americans, and Asians—far more men than women choose the physical sciences, the life sciences, engineering, and mathematics. The sex ratio is better balanced for the social sciences.

Sex differences appear for all groups, but they are not identical from one group to the next. Among whites, an equal number of men and women received bachelor's degrees in the social sciences in 1979; among Asians there were more women, while for blacks, Hispanics, and American Indians, the number was slightly higher for men (see Table 9.5). For whites, blacks, Hispanics, and American Indians, women received degrees in education at about twice the rate for men; among Asians, this was not a popular field for either sex. Asian women were better represented among biological science degree holders in 1979 than were women from all other backgrounds.

What emerges most clearly is the limited participation of women in programs with strong bases in mathematics. In engineering, for example, the number of women is extremely low for every racial and ethnic category. Participation in the physical sciences is higher, but in 1979 there was no group in which more women than men received physical science degrees. Nor was there marked movement towards quantitative fields between 1976 and 1979. Again, Asian women in engineering represent an exception, although their increased participation in that field was far outdistanced by that of Asian men.

The trends evident at the bachelor's level appear in the doctoral data as well. Asian women aside, one finds considerably fewer women than men among the doctoral degree holders in the physical sciences and mathematics (see Table 9.6). Black men who receive doctorates are likely to be in education; that is even more so for black women, although neither sex was as highly concentrated in education by 1979 as it had been in 1976. Between 1976 and 1979, Hispanic women moved away from education somewhat, but they gravitated towards the social sciences rather than to the physical sciences, the life sciences, and engineering. In contrast, Hispanic men made no major field shifts over that period.

The data on field choices lend further support to our contention that gender continues to be important to higher education in the United States. It is no longer a rigid barrier to participation in higher education, but it continues to shape the kinds of decisions that women and men make and the types of activities in which they engage. Perhaps most significantly, the trends outlined here indicate that gender effects are pervasive; they can be found for all categories of our population.

Table 9.5 Distribution of Bachelor's Degrees, by Field, Race or Ethnicity, and Sex: 1975-76 and 1978-79

Race or Ethnicity, Sex and Year		Total	Physical Sciences	Mathematics	Computer Sciences	Biological Sciences	Engineering	Social Sciences	Education	All Other
Whites:	Total, 1976	100.0	2.0	2.0	0.6	6.0	5.0	19.0	17.0	49.0
	Total, 1979	100.0	3.0	1.0	0.9	5.0	7.0	16.0	14.0	44.0
	Males, 1976	100.0	4.0	2.0	0.9	7.0	8.0	20.0	8.0	50.0
	Males, 1979	100.0	4.0	1.0	1.3	6.0	12.0	16.0	7.0	53.0
	Females, 1976	100.0	1.0	1.6	0.3	4.5	0.3	17.0	27.0	48.0
	Females, 1979	100.0	1.0	1.1	0.5	4.4	1.2	16.0	21.0	55.0
Blacks:	Total, 1976	100.0	1.0	1.0	0.6	4.0	2.0	24.0	24.0	43.0
	Total, 1979	100.0	1.0	1.0	0.8	4.0	3.0	20.0	19.0	50.0
	Males, 1976	100.0	2.0	1.0	0.8	5.5	5.6	27.0	14.0	45.0
	Males, 1979	100.0	2.0	1.0	1.1	5.5	6.0	22.0	12.0	51.0
	Females, 1976	100.0	0.6	1.3	0.4	3.5	0.2	22.0	31.0	41.0
	Females, 1979	100.0	0.8	0.9	0.7	3.8	0.6	19.0	24.0	50.0
Hispanics:	Total, 1976	100.0	1.0	1.0	0.4	6.0	5.0	22.0	17.0	47.0
	Total, 1979	100.0	2.0	1.0	0.7	6.0	5.0	19.0	16.0	50.0
	Males, 1976	100.0	2.0	2.0	0.6	6.0	9.0	24.0	10.0	47.0
	Males, 1979	100.0	2.0	1.0	1.0	7.0	10.0	20.0	10.0	49.0
	Females, 1976	100.0	0.7	1.1	0.2	5.3	0.4	20.0	24.0	48.0
	Females, 1979	100.0	0.9	0.9	0.4	5.7	0.8	18.0	22.0	51.0
American Indians:	Total, 1976	100.0	2.0	2.0	0.2	4.0	4.0	20.0	21.0	47.0
	Total, 1979	100.0	2.0	1.0	0.3	4.0	5.0	20.0	19.0	49.0
	Males, 1976	100.0	3.0	2.0	0.3	5.0	8.0	21.0	12.0	49.0
	Males, 1979	100.0	3.0	2.0	0.6	6.0	9.0	21.0	11.0	49.0
	Females, 1976	100.0	0.4	0.9	0.1	3.4	0.1	19.0	32.0	44.0
	Females, 1979	100.0	1.1	0.8	0.0	3.1	0.7	19.0	27.0	49.0
Asians:	Total, 1976	100.0	3.0	3.0	1.1	11.0	9.0	18.0	7.0	48.0
	Total, 1979	100.0	3.0	2.0	1.7	9.0	12.0	15.0	5.0	52.0

Table 9.5, continued

Race or Ethnicity, Sex and Year	Total	Physical Sciences	Mathematics	Computer Sciences	Biological Sciences	Engineering	Social Sciences	Education	All Other
Males, 1976	100.0	4.0	3.0	1.4	7.0	15.0	17.0	5.0	49.0
Males, 1979	100.0	4.0	2.0	2.1	10.0	20.0	14.0	4.0	45.0
Females, 1976	100.0	1.5	2.7	0.7	15.3	1.0	19.0	11.0	49.0
Females, 1979	100.0	1.7	2.1	1.3	8.9	3.0	17.0	7.0	59.0

Sources: 1975-76 data: U.S. Department of Health, Education and Welfare, *Data on Earned Degrees Conferred by Institutions of Higher Education by Race, Ethnicity, and Sex, Academic Year 1975-76.* 1978-79 data: *Data on Earned Degrees Conferred by Institutions of Higher Education by Race, Ethnicity, and Sex, Academic Year 1978-79.*

Table 9.6   Distribution of Doctorate Degrees, by Field, Race or Ethnicity, and Sex: 1975-76 and 1978-79

Race or Ethnicity, Sex and Year		Total	Physical Sciences	Mathematics	Computer Sciences	Biological Sciences	Engineering	Social Sciences	Education	All Other
Whites:	Total, 1976	100.0	10.0	2.0	0.7	10.0	6.0	21.0	24.0	26.0
	Total, 1979	100.0	9.0	2.0	0.7	11.0	5.0	19.0	24.0	28.0
	Males, 1976	100.0	12.0	3.0	0.8	11.0	8.0	20.0	21.0	25.0
	Males, 1979	100.0	12.0	2.0	0.8	12.0	7.0	18.0	20.0	27.0
	Females, 1976	100.0	3.0	1.1	0.3	9.0	0.8	23.0	32.0	22.0
	Females, 1979	100.0	3.0	1.2	0.4	10.0	0.7	22.0	35.0	28.0
Blacks:	Total, 1976	100.0	3.0	1.0	0.0	4.0	2.0	15.0	55.0	19.0
	Total, 1979	100.0	4.0	1.0	0.3	4.0	2.0	19.0	49.0	20.0
	Males, 1976	100.0	5.0	1.0	0.0	5.0	2.0	17.0	50.0	20.0
	Males, 1979	100.0	6.0	2.0	0.4	3.0	3.0	19.0	42.0	24.0
	Females, 1976	100.0	1.0	0.2	0.0	4.0	0.0	12.0	64.0	18.0
	Females, 1979	100.0	1.0	0.2	0.2	4.0	0.4	19.0	59.0	16.4
Hispanics:	Total, 1976	100.0	7.0	3.0	0.3	6.0	4.0	20.0	34.0	25.0
	Total, 1979	100.0	6.0	1.0	0.2	8.0	5.0	23.0	30.0	28.0
	Males, 1976	100.0	8.0	4.0	0.3	6.0	5.0	23.0	30.0	23.0
	Males, 1979	100.0	7.0	2.0	0.3	8.0	7.0	22.0	28.0	26.0
	Females, 1976	100.0	6.0	0.9	0.0	6.0	0.9	12.0	43.0	30.0
	Females, 1979	100.0	3.0	0.7	0.0	7.0	0.7	25.0	33.0	31.0

Table 9.6, continued

Race or Ethnicity, Sex and Year		Total	Physical Sciences	Mathematics	Computer Sciences	Biological Sciences	Engineering	Social Sciences	Education	All Other
American Indians:	Total, 1976	100.0	9.0	1.0	0.3	4.0	3.0	13.0	38.0	31.0
	Total, 1979	100.0	8.0	0.0	0.0	6.0	2.3	26.0	41.0	17.0
	Males, 1976	100.0	10.0	1.0	1.3	5.0	4.0	14.0	35.0	29.0
	Males, 1979	100.0	10.0	0.0	0.0	9.0	3.0	26.0	36.0	16.0
	Females, 1976	100.0	0.0	0.0	0.0	0.0	0.0	6.0	50.0	44.0
	Females, 1979	100.0	3.0	0.0	0.0	0.0	0.0	26.0	51.0	20.0
Asians:	Total, 1976	100.0	15.0	4.0	0.7	15.0	20.0	12.0	10.0	22.0
	Total, 1979	100.0	15.0	4.0	1.0	16.0	23.0	11.0	12.0	19.0
	Males, 1976	100.0	15.0	4.0	0.8	14.0	24.0	12.0	8.0	22.0
	Males, 1979	100.0	15.0	3.0	1.2	14.0	28.0	10.0	9.0	19.0
	Females, 1976	100.0	14.0	2.9	0.0	21.0	1.9	13.0	22.0	25.0
	Females, 1979	100.0	13.0	4.9	0.0	24.0	1.8	15.0	22.0	20.0

Sources: 1975-76 data: U.S. Department of Health, Education and Welfare, *Data on Earned Degrees Conferred by Institutions of Higher Education by Race, Ethnicity, and Sex, Academic Year 1975-76.* 1978-79 data: *Data on Earned Degrees Conferred by Institutions of Higher Education by Race, Ethnicity, and Sex, Academic Year 1978-79.*

THE UNDERREPRESENTATION OF MINORITY WOMEN IN QUANTITATIVE FIELDS

The data we have surveyed thus far show that women are underrepresented in those fields that require strong quantitative skills. To understand the sources of that underrepresentation we review here the situation for one group: black women. We have chosen this group because it has been covered by more studies than have other groups of minority women and because, at the college entry level, the participation rates of black women traditionally have exceeded those of black men.

Black women have been more likely than black men to attend college but less likely to choose quantitative majors. There are three possible explanations for this male-female difference. First, it could stem from differences in high school preparation: perhaps men enter college with more course work in mathematics and science, the prerequisites for many scientific and technical disciplines. Second, it might be the consequence of differences in initial choice of major: possibly, at the time of college entry men are more likely than women to choose a scientific or technical major. Third, perhaps males and females are equally likely to opt for technical fields, but males are more likely to persist in them through graduation. Let us consider the evidence for each.

Course Background

Entry into most scientific and technical majors demands a background in mathematics and often in science. If more black men than women earn degrees in mathematics, the physical and life sciences, and engineering, it could be that they bring different skills to college. Various studies, including our own, do not completely uphold this expectation, however. Let us look first at studies on course taking at the high school level.

Participation in Mathematics. In general, researchers have found more black females than black males in those mathematics courses that prepare students for college. A study of mathematics classes in four high schools located in a large West Coast city counted more black females than black males in courses at the level of algebra II and beyond (Matthews 1980). Of the 190 females, 43 percent were enrolled in those courses; the figure for the 140 males was 27 percent. A survey of over forty senior high schools throughout the nation uncovered a similar pattern (Marrett 1982). The four race-sex categories—black males, black females, white males, and white females—were rather evenly distributed in the sample. Of the 11,900 students, 24 percent were black males; 24 percent, black females; 25 percent, white females; and 27 percent, white males. Hypothetically, roughly one-quarter of the students in each category could have been enrolled in each course. Yet, that was not the result. Black males, for example, constituted well over one-third of the enrollees in general mathematics but only one-tenth of the students taking the most advanced courses. Whereas black females comprised nearly a third of the general mathematics students, they made up 16 percent of the students in advanced mathematics (see Table 9.7).

Consistently, black males were on the bottom rung of the course ladder and black females on the one just above them. Moreover, the

Table 9.7   Enrollment in Mathematics Within Course and Within Group Distribution

Course	Black Females	Black Males	White Females	White Males	Totals, Within Course
			Race and Sex		
General mathematics					
Within course	29.7%	35.3%	16.0%	19.0%	100% (N=4236)
Within group	43.8	52.9	22.7	25.0	
Beginning algebra					
Within course	27.5	23.9	22.9	25.8	100% (N=2666)
Within group	25.5	22.5	20.4	21.4	
Geometry					
Within course	18.4	14.4	34.6	32.5	100% (N=1999)
Within group	12.8	10.2	23.1	20.2	
Other intermediate					
Within course	24.6	23.0	29.7	22.6	100% (N=547)
Within group	4.7	4.4	5.0	4.1	
Algebra II					
Within course	15.6	11.5	37.2	35.8	100% (N=1630)
Within group	8.8	6.6	20.2	18.2	
Calculus; other advanced courses					
Within course	16.0	10.1	34.4	39.5	100% (N=821)
Within group	4.6	2.9	9.4	10.1	
Totals, Within Group	100%	100%	100%	100%	
	(N=2824)	(N=2870)	(N=2992)	(N=3213)	
Percent Each Group Represents in Schools	23.7	24.1	25.1	27.0	

Source: Cora Bagley Marrett, "Minority Females in High School Mathematics and Science." Report to the National Institute of Education, 1982.

female-male differences among blacks tended to be somewhat larger than they were among whites. In algebra II, for example, the number of females exceeded the number of males within the same racial group. Whereas among whites the figures differed by less than two percentage points, among blacks the spread was four points. At the most advanced level, there were more white males than white females, but the count for black females surpassed the one for black males.

The same outcomes appear if we use the group rather than the course as the base for calculations. Over half of the black males, compared with two-fifths of the black females, were in general mathematics. In contrast, a larger fraction of the females than of the males were taking calculus and other advanced courses. Although participation rates for black females declined from one level to the next in the sequence, in comparison with black males, black females were more likely to be in higher level courses. These studies point to greater participation in college-preparatory mathematics among black females than among males (also see Marrett and Gates 1981). But they do not belie the argument that males and females who enter college have different backgrounds in mathematics. Perhaps the males who go beyond the minimal mathematics requirements for high school graduation are more inclined to enter college than are the equivalent females. To determine the influence of course preparation, then, we must examine the college rather than the high school population.

Unfortunately, few studies have compared the mathematics background of college-bound black males and females. Surveys show us that the Scholastic Aptitude Test scores in mathematics are lower for college-bound blacks than whites, but they do not distinguish between black males and females.[4] The studies that have made the distinction are based on small samples. One such analysis, carried out among juniors and seniors at Wayne State University, found that black females who were majoring in the sciences had taken less mathematics than had all other science majors, including black males. In fact, the black females had had even fewer years of mathematics than had the white males who were majoring in nonscience fields (Sie et al. 1978). A study of the 1976 freshman class at the University of Washington found that black students had entered with less college-preparatory mathematics than white or Asian students, but there were no significant differences between black males and females. In fact, both sexes were more likely than

---

4. The Scholastic Aptitude Test scores in mathematics for college-bound seniors were as follows in 1976-77: whites, 490; Hispanics, 412; and blacks, 355 (Jacobsen 1980).

the other groups to have had at least one general or remedial mathematics course in high school (Remick and Miller 1977).

The University of Washington study, consistent with the research at the high school level, suggests that there is little if any difference between black female and male college students in the number of mathematics courses taken in high school. The Wayne State University study implies that even if a difference exists, it might not explain the differences in field choices that appear among degree holders. Recall that the women in that survey were actually majoring in science. It appears, consequently, that differences in mathematics courses taken in high school cannot fully account for differences in the field distribution of black men and women graduates.

Participation in Science. Perhaps the sharper contrasts show up in high school science preparation. Possibly, males take more science courses than do females. That was not the pattern the forty-school survey found, however. That survey compared the enrollment in advanced science courses with overall enrollment in the school and found that black females were proportionately more represented than were black males. There were fewer blacks of both sexes in the courses than one might have predicted based on their numbers in the schools; there were more white males, and the number of white females was proportionate to their distribution in the schools (Marrett 1982).

Other studies also report convergences in the science background of black males and females. One survey of secondary school students who were interested in science discovered that almost none of the black students had participated in honors or advanced-placement courses in science; but there were no disparities between the sexes (Erlick and Lebold 1977). The University of Washington analysis determined that about 90 percent of the black males and females had taken biology; about 50 percent, chemistry; and about 15 percent, physics. Again, the backgrounds of both sexes were nearly identical.

But the National Longitudinal Study of the Class of 1972 (NLS) uncovered noteworthy differences. Of the blacks in the 1972 senior class who entered college, females had taken fewer high school science courses than had males (Dunteman et al. 1979, Thomas 1981). Yet, the discrepancy seems to have had little effect on the field of study chosen; the females with the same course work in science as the males were not as likely to choose a science major. In summary, the data are limited, but they appear to indicate that the contrasts between females and males that might occur in high school science are not large enough nor influential enough to explain the different choices one sees among degree recipients.

Initial Selection of Major

Let us turn to the second possible explanation: males and females, whatever their high school coursework, have quite different plans for their careers when they enter college. The NLS data clearly uphold this view. Of the seniors who entered college, far fewer black women than men indicated an interest in a physical science, life science, or mathematics major (see Table 9.8). The divergence was especially pointed for engineering: none of the women but 9 percent of the men gave engineering as their planned major. One researcher who has examined the NLS data in detail reports that intended major, as chosen at the end of the high school career, had a greater effect on actual entry into quantitative fields than had such conditions as the number of mathematics and science courses taken or class rank (Thomas 1981). Women were simply less likely to contemplate majors based in the quantitative disciplines.

Persistence in Major

The male-female differences that one notes among freshmen could become even wider if there are sex differences in persistence in science. But the results of the NLS analyses hint that black women are no more likely than are black men to withdraw from science over their college careers. Nearly 36 percent of the black women expressed an interest in science—including social science—during their freshmen year. The same percentage of male freshmen made that selection. Four years later nearly 32 percent of the women but only 26 percent of the men either had graduated with a science degree or were still majoring in science. Others had withdrawn from school or had changed majors. Black females were more likely than black males to complete a science degree, but one should note that the figures include the social sciences, an area for which black female persistence was especially high.

Table 9.8 Intended Major—Freshman Year (Fall 1972), Class of 1972

Sex, Race, or Ethnicity	(N)	Physical Science	Engineering	Mathematics	Life Science	Social Science	Other Fields	No Intended Major	Unknown
Females	3334	2.0	.3	1.9	9.2	14.6	58.3	6.2	7.5
Black	433	3.0	0	1.9	9.1	22.5	54.2	2.3	6.9
White	2666	1.6	.3	1.9	9.2	13.7	59.3	6.5	7.4
Hispanic	98	3.1	.7	0	10.4	11.5	57.0	3.2	14.1
Males	3539	6.1	11.0	1.9	14.0	13.7	38.7	7.3	7.2
Black	278	5.4	9.0	1.7	8.7	12.3	49.0	4.8	9.1
White	2988	6.0	11.3	1.9	14.4	13.9	38.2	7.2	7.0
Hispanic	122	7.9	5.1	0	10.0	13.3	39.4	11.3	12.9
Total	6873	4.1	6.0	1.9	11.8	14.2	47.9	6.8	7.4

Source: George H. Dunteman, Joseph Wisenbaker, and Mary Ellen Taylor, "Race and Sex Differences in College Science Program Participation." Report to the National Science Foundation, 1979.

Strategies for Change

At present there are few longitudinal studies that trace black students as they move through their college years. But the available discussions seem to indicate that the precollege level must be the target if we expect to recruit more black women to scientific and technical fields. At a time when our country needs the highest levels of scientific and technological competence, large numbers of our youth are failing to develop even minimal levels of such competence. Although we highlight here the special case of minority females, growing numbers of minority males as well as are unprepared for a society that is as yet only a few paces into a great technological marathon that will expand for years to come.

Unless significant change takes place, only a handful of minority group members will compete in that marathon. It will be necessary to retain students in the courses that provide the training ground, but it will be just as important to encourage nontraditionalism among the students who take the courses. Until women begin to consider careers in technical fields, changes in course-taking patterns at the high school level will not invariably bring about changes in the composition of the scientific and technical labor force. Indeed, currently more black females are finishing high school with the prerequisites for scientific majors than choose such majors; and there are black women with master's degrees in quantitatively based fields who have not joined the population of doctoral level scientists. Minority women, like their nonminority counterparts, continue to embark on educational journeys that diverge from those pursued by males, particularly white males.

Minority women who enter quantitatively based fields are as likely to follow careers in them as are men. Most men (95 percent) who receive doctorates in science and engineering can be found in the labor force; that is, they are employed or are actively seeking employment. The same tendency appears for black women (88 percent) and Asian women (93 percent) as well as for white women (88 percent). The men are located primarily in the scientific and engineering (S/E) labor force; so are the women. Of every ten working men who hold doctorates in science or engineering, only one tends to have a non-S/E job. Likewise, the non-S/E labor force contains about one of every ten working white women, two of every ten black women, and one of every ten Asian women.[5] These facts should comfort observers who might fear that a rise in the number of women scientists and engineers would produce a drop in the size of the active S/E force. There are no signs that the nation would suffer severe losses in the number of persons committed to scientific work if the representation of women—including minority women—should surge.

MINORITY WOMEN AS PROFESSIONALS IN HIGHER EDUCATION

So far, we have considered changes in the status of minority women as students in higher education. The significant change has been in the number of these women, not in their fields of study. Minority women with doctorates in the physical and life sciences and in engineering are still few in number.

There is yet another area with limited minority female representation: higher education administration. According to a report in the *Chronicle of Higher Education* (3 February 1982), in 1978-79 minority women held less than 1 percent of the seven thousand posts at the level of dean and above in American colleges and universities. This figure excludes positions at historically black and single-sex institutions. Minority men fared somewhat better: they held 4 percent of the posts (see Table 9.9). The number of minority women administrators increased between 1975-76 and 1978-79 but at a rate (28 percent) below that for minority men (34 percent).

The seven thousand positions cited above include disciplines—agriculture, dentistry, and medicine, for example—that have small corps of minority women.But even if we count only those positions that (a) have no clear disciplinary base or (b) have sizable numbers of minority women, the situation remains rather unfavorable. In 1978-79, nonminority men held the bulk of the positions (74 percent); nonminority women, the next largest share (19 percent); minority men, only a handful (6 percent) and minority women, the smallest

---

5. See Appendix Tables 12a, 12b, 13, and 14 in *Women and Minorities in Science and Engineering* (Washington, D.C.: National Science Foundation, 1982).

Table 9.9 Higher Education Administrators, By Race/Ethnicity and Sex: 1975-76 and 1978-79

Posts, Race/Ethnicity and Sex	Year		
	1975-76	1978-79	Percent Change
All Posts	100.0 (N=6607)	100.0 (N=279)	5.9
Minority men	3.0 (N=200)	3.7 (N=279)	39.5
Minority women	0.1 (N=57)	0.1 (N=73)	28.1
Nonminority men	82.5 (N=5454)	80.4 (N=5982)	9.7
Nonminority women	13.6 (N=896)	14.8 (N=1102)	23.0
Selected Posts[1]	100.0 (N=2736)	100.0 (N=3153)	15.2
Minority men	4.3 (N=119)	5.7 (N=180)	51.3
Minority women	1.4 (N=39)	1.7 (N=54)	38.4
Nonminority men	78.3 (N=2142)	73.7 (N=2324)	8.5
Nonminority women	15.9 (N=436)	18.9 (N=595)	36.5

[1] Includes: Chief student affairs officer; Controller; Directors of affirmative action and equal employment, community services, food service, information office, institutional research, personnel, student counseling, student housing, student placement, and student union; and Deans of education, graduate programs, home economics, and social work.

Source: *Chronicle of Higher Education*, 3 February 1982.

fraction (2 percent). Moreover, minority women—even more than minority men—were concentrated in affirmative action and equal opportunity positions. Forty-eight percent of the minority women as compared with 22 percent of the men in the limited set of positions were affirmative action or equal opportunity officers.

Data based on historically black institutions follow the pattern in majority institutions. According to a review conducted on 86 of the 105 historically black institutions in the United States (Scott 1981), few women can be found in the higher administration ranks of these institutions. There were over 200 presidencies or vice-presidencies across these institutions in 1977; black women held six of those posts. Interestingly, the two colleges for women—Bennett and Spelman—had male presidents and vice-presidents. The author of the review concludes that at predominantly black institutions, as at predominantly white ones, sex is a barrier to full-scale participation.

Minority women—principally black women—in the professions have been concentrated in education, but they have not reached the topmost levels in that field. Unquestionably, motivational factors have impeded the academic progress of minority women. The same conditions that inhibit females from entering atypical fields prevent women from advancing in the educational hierarchy. But institutional barriers and roadblocks may be set up by other than the women themselves. The full-scale participation of minority women in all phases of American life demands that we understand the barricades that block involvement. Currently, the data sources give us only a limited view of these barricades. We call for the collection and aggregation of data on both race or ethnicity and sex and for attention in particular to categories in the population—Native American women, for example—who too often are overlooked or undercounted. Better data should enhance both the analyses that can be undertaken and the policies and strategies for change that can be instituted. Even without these data, we see clear indications that for minority women, minority status impedes progress. But sexism and sex-role socialization are additional forces the power of which should not be underestimated.

REFERENCES

Dunteman, George H.; Wisenbaker, Joseph; and Taylor, Mary Ellen. "Race and Sex Differences in College Science Program Participation." Report to the National Science Foundation, 1979.

Erlick, Arline C., and Lebold, William K. "Factors Affecting the Science Career Plans of Women and Minorities." Report to the National Science Foundation, 1977.

Homma-True, Reiko. "Mental Health Issues among Asian-American Women." In *Conference on the Educational and Occupational Needs of Asian-Pacific-American Women*. Washington, D.C.: National Institute of Education, 1980.

Jacobsen, Robert L. "Blacks Lag in SAT Scores." *Chronicle of Higher Education,* 7 January 1980, p. 5.

Marrett, Cora Bagley. "Minority Females in High School Mathematics and Science." Report to the National Institute of Education, 1982.

Marrett, Cora Bagley, and Gates, Harold. "Male-Female Enrollment across Mathematics Tracks in Predominantly Black High Schools." *Journal for Research in Mathematics Education* 14 (March 1983): 113-18.

Matthews, Westina. "Race- and Sex-Related Differences in High School Mathematics Enrollment." Doctoral dissertation, University of Chicago, 1980.

Randour, Mary Lou; Strausberg, Georgia L.; and Lipman-Blumen, Jean. "Women in Higher Education: Trends in Enrollment and Degrees Earned." *Harvard Educational Review* 52 (May 1982): 189-202.

Remick, Helen, and Miller, Kathy. "Participation Rates in High School Mathematics and Science Courses." Unpublished paper, 1977. ED 160-411.

Scott, Gloria Randle. "Balancing the Higher Education Equation with the Status Discrepant Black Professional Woman." Paper presented at a meeting of the National Association for Equal Opportunity in Higher Education, 1981.

Sie, Maureen A.; Markham, Barry S.; and Hillman, Stephen B. "Minority Groups and Science Careers." *Integrateducation* 93 (May-June 1978): 43-46.

Thomas, Gail. "Choosing a College Major in the Hard and Technical Sciences and the Professions: A Causal Explanation." Baltimore, Md.: Center for Social Organization of Schools, Johns Hopkins University, 1981.

U.S. Department of Education. *Digest of Education Statistics.* Washington, D.C.: National Center for Education Statistics, 1980; idem, *Digest of Education Statistics.* Washington, D.C.: National Center for Education Statistics, 1981; idem, *Digest of Education Statistics.* Washington, D.C.: National Center for Education Statistics, 1982.

U.S. Department of Health, Education, and Welfare. *Data on Earned Degrees Conferred by Institutions of Higher Education by Race, Ethnicity, and Sex, Academic Year 1975-76.* Washington, D.C.: Office of Civil Rights, 1978; idem, *Data on Earned Degrees Conferred by Institutions of Higher Education by Race, Ethnicity, and Sex, Academic Year 1978-79.* Washington, D.C.: Office of Civil Rights, 1981.

Women and Minorities in Science and Engineering. Washington, D.C.: National Science Foundation, 1982.

10

Women, Space, and Power in Higher Education

M. Jane Ayer

Despite the common occurrence of women in higher education and the longevity of women's colleges, the educational environment (of women) has not improved accordingly (Tidball 1976).

Twenty-five percent of full-time faculty are women, no increase from the 1970 statistics. The higher the rank the fewer the women; women's salaries remain 20 percent lower than males; the larger the institution the fewer the women; and women outnumber men in part-time positions including instructorships and lectureships. The proportion of women in top-level administrative positions has increased slightly since 1970, but they are still grossly underrepresented (Howard and Downey 1980).

Affirmative action programs have helped maintain a fairly consistent pattern in entry-level positions for women in higher education, but there continues to be a decline in the numbers of women at advanced levels. Often those brought in at entry-level positions leave before promotion to higher rank or before achieving a level of authority and influence. The best results of affirmative action programs have required undue monitoring and extensive administrative organization in order to assure even the least possible gains. Because of the stipulations of law governing equal employment, one would expect a more visible effect, if only at the lower or middle levels of academic rank, after ten years of effort. The combination of good intentions and the best legal efforts possible have not been sufficient to change practices and attitudes within the academy to provide equally for women and men in matters of career advancement and upward mobility as well as in all other conditions of employment. Women are exhorted to seize power, to move into the ranks of decision makers and budget planners, and to achieve voices and votes in order to better control that which happens to them. These are designed goals, but they represent a charge lacking a map of the educational milieu, a reading of the prevailing ethics and folkways within the academy that must be understood before charting a course of action. Over the centuries, this space of work and learning, so beautifully described by Virginia Woolf in *A Room of One's Own* (1929), has been defined by the male in all aspects: political, economic, psychological, and content of subject matter. It is the purpose of this essay to describe the fabric of the work space in academia, the nature of the space itself, and the roles of women and men within the space. Then it will be shown that the desired characteristics of able and productive leaders are neither restricted to one sex or the other, nor unattainable given the opportunity and circumstances.

The vying for role and power becomes a game, and if it were a game between competitors of both sexes one could say fair enough. But when it becomes a game between men, able or not, and all women, regardless of how capable, inequity is heaped upon inequity.

INHABITANTS OF THE WORK SPACE

There was no change within rank or in total numbers of women faculty from 1970-1980 (Howard and Downey 1980). Twenty-five percent of the full-time faculty were women; 8 percent were full professors; 16 percent were associate professors; 28 percent were assistant professors; and 49 percent were instructors. Salary descrepancies for women continued. Women's salaries were 20 percent lower than those for males, and the peculiar inversed pattern of the larger the institution the fewer the women employed also had not changed. Women continued to outnumber men at lower ranks and in part-time positions. The proportion of women in administration had increased only slightly, but it was still grossly underrepresentative and occurred primarily in the middle- and lower-level positions.

From among these slim ranks of women must emerge those who are to achieve visibility and power and to be leaders in changing the deeply ingrained career patterns of the academy. Given such limited numbers, how preposterous it is to think that any significant changes will occur within a reasonable span of time. Affirmative action programs are not effective enough to increase the numbers of women so that more effective leadership in changing the landscape of higher education can be achieved. Few in number, some women are lacking an understanding of the work place, expending commendable efforts and good intentions that are constantly rebuffed, unrewarded, and perceived as threatening. Certain conditions are the sine qua non for success in academics:

—an interplay of the role of a researcher and a scholar of note as evidenced by publications, success in obtaining and administering research grants or other forms of extramural support, and perceived status within a professional field.
—visibility as a leader in one's profession through national offices, committee appointments, speaking engagements, and consultancies.
—reputation as a good teacher, which is at once required while at the same time not being a sufficient reason for an elevated evaluation by one's peers. Good teaching is equal to only minimal publications in establishing a reputation.

These standard credentials are relatively objective and are established over time by the customary peer review in accord with the commonly shared definitions within academia.

An assumption underlying most studies of academic advancement is that higher-level achievement means moving from teaching-faculty into administration. Many academicians would take issue with this definition because the traditional hallmarks of academic success have been a rank of full professor and particularly a chaired professor, research grant awards and peer review assignments, and committee appointments or service by faculty election. In large research institutions, one's success is also measured by the number of one's doctoral students who have completed study, national offices held, and service on editorial boards or as editor for professional journals. These criteria for achievement remain the essential achievements in academia even though most authors have examined movement from teaching faculty to administration to demonstrate advancement.

Academic excellence and personal development are documented in individual vitae, records of achievement in teaching, research, and service. Supplementary to the highest levels of professional achievement, the movement by some individuals into administrative positions is to a certain extent a self-selection process. Certain personality characteristics prevail, and selected faculty experiences prepare one to be considered for administrative positions. Women are confronted by biased perceptions and are less likely to receive the same apprenticeship preparation for movement into administration.

CONDITIONS OF THE WORK SETTING

Institutions have a slowly developing and long-range effect on individuals and society. Social change is brought about primarily not by the institutions and their members, but by those who return to the larger society after periods of study and education. Members within the academy are conservative and more slowly changed.

Knowledge and the creation of knowledge are chiefly defined by an absence of temporality and an absence of response to what are viewed from within as the whims and vagaries of vox populi. Centuries of stereotyped role development of both men and women, behavior modification in its most pervasive and systematic form, continues to be expressed in the exclusion of women from authoritative participation as faculty and administrators. As is occurring in many occupational settings during these turbulent economic times, conditions have developed that impose yet another layer beyond individual control. The determinants of university decisions are accountability to various constituents, federal and state legislation as it affects educational priorities and funding patterns, and national economic conditions. Strategy becomes judgmental and changing as educational leaders seek the best resolution for maximum growth. For women and minorities, such strategies become antithetical to equality of educational opportunity as evidenced by little institutional interest in support programs for academic advancement. Judgmental strategy rarely works for the benefit of those who are apart from the common mold. Programs could, however, be set up to include time-shared positions, adjustable time limits for advancement to tenure, and flexibility in planning part-time study for professional advancement. These would work to foster women in the academy.

The larger the institution, the less likely one is to find women in the higher echelons of either rank or administrative structure. Demographic data skew the proportions by size of institution because of the many smaller private, and often religious, colleges that traditionally employ mostly women. Conversely, large institutions are, with a few exceptions, public and/or land-grant colleges; the differences in employment patterns between the types of institutions underscore the obvious pattern of discrimination in the larger settings.

The long-term effects of discrimination over the ages are born out in the career mobility of women within the tenure ranks. Until recent years, careers open to women have been teaching, nursing, and the helping professions, the so-called female disciplines. These fields are traditionally the nonpublishing, nonresearch areas of study with less autonomy for the practitioners than is so in most fields defined as male such as medicine, law, engineering, and business. Academic mobility, including movement into administration, has required strong faculty credentials that come about only through professional visibility, primarily research and publications. Ergo, few women qualify on these traditionally defined grounds for advancement. It is important to note that strong faculty credentials are required to achieve an administrative post, but once there, other skills and abilities are required to perform the job.

[At all steps of academic achievement, males have received more assistance and encouragement, the beginnings of a network and mentorship that start with the very first award of student financial aid, continue with project assistantships, coauthorships, and culminate in diverse sources of support for job placement.]The analysis by Centra (1974) of Ph.D. recipients graphically illustrates the relative ease with which males progress through various steps of what often becomes preparation for administrative leadership. Women who progress to the higher levels of administration do so by persistence and overachievement, commonly playing multiple roles and, hence, becoming the superwomen of the job place. True equality will have been achieved when as many mediocre women succeed as do mediocre men.

Mentorships that are available to women often occur for the wrong reasons. Mediocrity is rewarded and quality sacrificed for the sake of a woman who "can get along," resulting in an inevitable show of incompetence, which then becomes another link in the distorted reasoning that women as a group are inferior. Such actions, often based on a quota system, serve no one to the best advantage, least of all the woman put in the position, and they make ludicrous the use of population statistics as a basis for hiring and promotion. In an article that is in other ways an insult to informed attempts to assure equity, Ornstein (1976) uses demographic statistics from Chicago as an example of why affirmative action does not work. Based upon the available pool and Chicago population distributions, statistics would dictate that 35 percent of engineers employed by Chicago be black. In fact, the available national pool of black engineers is only 2 percent of all possible candidates.

A PERVASIVE BARRIER: SEX-ROLE STEREOTYPING

Sex-role stereotyping is the single most important barrier for women. It is the basis for most discrimination and lack of sponsorship and the primary reason for the slow rate of promotions resulting in a generally depressed career pattern. As long as a viewer accepts perceptions as valid, the die is cast for a range of behaviors, practices, attitudes, and emotions. Professions tend towards homogeneity by virtue of like abilities and patterns of interest, which become sources of bonding for members within. Most divisions within the academy are single sex, either predominantly male or female, but mostly male. Because of the control by one dominant group, in any analysis of career patterns for women in higher education, we must consider the impact of control on members from within. Members of many professional bodies create barriers against women who are excluded from attempting to join their ranks by earlier being excluded from educational opportunities and who then later face continued discrimination because of the lack of credentials. We have in this practice a very vicious circle:

women's lack of appropriate credentials is usually attributed to inadequate skills and abilities, which they were prohibited from learning or developing earlier in their careers.

The comfort within the homogeneous grouping, the sense of intimacy with like protégés, mitigates against women easily entering the inner circle of a profession. It must be remembered that the rite of passage for males has been a relatively homogeneous culture with bonding and sponsorship throughout by male mentors. This may have resulted in less spontaneity and diminished innovation, but this is less important and not even within the awareness of males because of the continued bonding. There is less need to be a supermale in order to succeed because the system itself is more likely to assure success.

It follows then that once having been allowed to enter the academy, women are not automatically accepted with the same enthusiasm and support as are newly arrived male colleagues. Personal contacts do help to diminish discrimination based on sex-role stereotyping, but another point of difficulty appears that has a bearing on professional advancement. Male students, especially in male-dominated fields, are likely to see women faculty as less effective teachers (Kaschak 1976), resulting in lowered ratings of performance. These ratings are, of course, used by the predominantly male faculty in determining salary and promotions. Thus, we add one more link in the chain of circumstances mitigating against professional advancement. Administrators in female fields are more likely to hire men than those in male fields are likely to hire women. It would be interesting to know if the ratings of teaching by males in traditionally female fields show the same opposite rankings of effectiveness, such as male nursing students.

Such differential treatment continues in committee assignments, institutional service opportunities, joint research collaboration, job recommendations, and in the many forms of informal support through networking. Exclusion begins in graduate study (Walsh 1974) to the point where the possibility of failure to complete a program becomes real. The same factors that later for married men with families and certain credentials are perceived as sufficient cause for more money, when present in women who request maternity leave result in lowered status and lesser expectations.

The rewards of the work place are as confused and mixed as are the uneven career patterns for women. Women are currently more likely to be stuck in position because of an unclear path combined with the now existing low ceilings for advancement. The typical route has been faculty credentials leading into low-level management positions that require certain technical skills. As one moves further up the hierarchy of positions, the requirements become more nebulous to the point that at the highest levels of management, there is little discernible correlation between faculty credentials and the requisite skills for the administrative position. This is to say that administrative skills are learned primarily on the job (Tuckman et al. 1976).

For the most part, only traditional areas and historically developed positions are possible avenues for advancement, this despite the programs and opportunities created by federal law combined with state and local efforts, for example, affirmative action, minority programming, or recently developed academic disciplines (such as African studies and women's studies). The proposition that institutions should continue to grow during bad times in innovative directions (Kanter 1979) does not bode well for the disenfranchised because even in good times with federal legislation as clout the disenfranchised were not accorded equitable treatment. It does not follow that in economically stringent times extraordinary effort will be made to provide equitable access for career advancement. Desires for advancement by the disenfranchised often reflect an accurate sense of one's abilities and worth; the more talented one is, the more apt one is to be frustrated by the dissonance between that which is and that which one has the potential to be.

If more individuals were better rewarded for extraordinary service to an institution as a supplement to other professional talents, we would be better able to create a different and acceptable reward structure. Many program areas require services of a type almost never rewarded but which are necessary for maintaining the quality of a program. For example, professional preparation in medicine, social services, and education includes instructional responsibilities that are essentially management skills. Group leadership, organizational abilities, and time management required by the programs could serve as apprenticeships for higher-level management positions. These professional responsibilities do not serve in that way, however; the individuals so assigned rarely gain tenure because they have not satisfied other scholarly requirements even though the instructional activities they performed were necessary and encouraged.

ACHIEVING POSITIONS OF INFLUENCE

In the previous section, it was shown that the traditional means of achievement in academia do not work in favor of women to the same extent that they do for men. Demonstrated competencies and adequate performance are often not sufficient for advancement, particularly at the higher levels of administration. Women have to more consciously learn the techniques of power and, in the positive sense, how to manipulate a system in order to achieve positions of distinction. We will now explore various techniques of power, analyze techniques within personality characteristics of men and women, and, finally, analyze the ways in which techniques of garnering power can be used for professional enhancement.

The Nature of Power in Higher Education

Power in private business is exercised more directly because of business structure and line authority. Higher education, in contrast, does not allow individual self-enhancement through uses of power in the same manner because of the controlling traditions of faculty governance. The first hurdle, then, to achieving a position of power is the control by a predominately male faculty. One can correctly say that control of a budget in academia is more similar to custodial care of a budget, and personnel decisions are collective rather than individual. Budget and personnel decisions are made at various levels of authority or governance, minimizing centralized control by any one individual or body of individuals.

At the same time, higher education has become more like big business due to the use of increasingly complex business management techniques. There are now requirements for fiscal accountability, facilities management, and the oversight of personnel policies, including union regulations governing grievance procedures, lines of authority, and staff benefits. The mixture of external funding in combination with public tax monies requires a legion of management experts who have academic titles, such as vice-chancellor, provost, or vice-president, but who are in actual practice business managers and fiscal officers. These positions receive support from staff specialists such as lawyers, budget planners, and trust officers. Input-output, feedback, data banks, and information processing are terms and concepts now as firmly entrenched in the lexicon of academia as they are in business. But no matter how closely higher education approximates private business, the controlling force will be the faculty as governed by faculty-approved policies and procedures. Thus, power and the enactment of power are shaped and controlled to a considerable extent by the collective whole.

The power in academia to curry favor by means of the distribution of money is minimized because of the successive levels of authority from the top down with chancellor, vice-chancellor, dean, department chairperson, and faculty. The greater amounts of money at the upper levels become parceled out in smaller sums at each successive level of administration. There are, to be sure, certain check points where key decisions determine how much of a total sum is to be distributed; it is very difficult if not impossible, however, for any person to play politics by assigning monies to an individual or individuals to be used for personal enhancement. In many instances in higher education, actual power is far less than perceived power.

Effectiveness in academia is rarely measured in terms of production quotas (read cost per credit or cost by level of instruction), but because of the national economic recession, business tools for assessing worth and efficiency are being used for the hard decisions such as faculty and staff reduction, facilities development, and problems precipitated by reduced enrollments. Despite the economic stringencies, however, performance evaluations focus primarily upon research and instructional effectiveness.

Given these contingencies of shared governance, academic power is perceived as an enabling force and not as restrictive or controlling. Power is diffused throughout levels of administration and is rarely centralized in any one person or at any one level.

A Style of Power

For purposes of our discussion, we will use the model of power analysis defined by Raven (1965), which was later put into operation by Johnson (1976). *Reward and coercion* (the ability to award positive or negative sanctions) are used judiciously, particularly coercion. Budget and personnel allocation are the foremost tools of both reward and punishment and the most conspicuous because of the observable impact upon people and programs. Money as reward takes the form of merit increases for research support activities, sabbatical leaves, and as special awards for instructional improvement. Often in these instances, the actual dollar amount is less important than the recognition of an individual's research and teaching efforts. Second to money as a tool of power and as providing status is the allocation of space and other physical resources.

Referent power is predicated on similarities, actual or perceived, and feelings of identification with a larger entity by individuals. Such associations often begin through commonly shared functions or areas of interest. Eventually the newer members in a group assume the attributes of the principal characters in behaviors, values, and folkways. Personal bonds are formed by shared scholarly activities and the honing of minds that is a natural outgrowth of intense study and concerted effort. Users of referent power are tied to the group for status identification and as a source for their own power. The common term *old boys club* with its images of informal fraternization and comradery belies the devastating effects upon outsiders of not belonging to this tightly woven network. The exclusive structure of these culpable societies has been a critical source of frustration and agony to women and minorities, latecomers to the academy who are unwelcome and rebuffed. Immense sources of power are localized within the informal network, and it is only with the approval of these networks that token women begin to appear in upper-level positions.

Expert power requires superior skills or knowledge and a perceived status of trustworthiness. Men are the acknowledged leaders in our society, and, conversely, it is out of character for a woman to be an expert or to be perceived as having power. Expert power is direct and impersonal.

Accomplishments in higher education are measured by success in teaching, scholarship, and service. Teaching and scholarship, in particular, require recognition as an expert, and one becomes an expert not only through individual efforts but also with the assistance of support systems, mentorships, and in being privy to informal sources of information. Informal information sources that facilitate image development as an expert are often withheld from women; no matter how accomplished a woman might be in her academic area, the special opportunities and prerogatives that come only by virtue of the informal system will negate her more formal accomplishments. The brightest and ablest of women will not move forward into successive and higher ranks without the informal support network. Given the numbers of women who successfully complete the Ph.D., who have presumably satisfied the same selection and retention requirements as for males, and who have fulfilled program requirements in a similar fashion, is it not strange that suddenly women appear to bottom out and fail to move forward professionally in ratio to males with the same apparent credentials?

Several years ago, at the national meeting of the American Council on Education, some women approached the doorway of a room where the opening reception was in progress. The sound of heavy male voices and male laughter was so overwhelming that some women moved away and initiated their own social hour, reminiscent of scenes described by Virginia Woolf in *A Room of One's Own*. It is puzzling that men are expected to bond with men and that women are also expected to, but are not allowed to, while at the same time the social expectation has been that women not bond with other women. This is a peculiar double standard for collegial relationships, which has the detrimental effect of retarding the professional careers of women.

Legitimate power relies on prior socialization wherein people feel that they have the right to influence, and the recipient must feel obligated to accept the influence. This form is commonly found within hierarchical structures such as president over vice-president and employer over employee. The hierarchical power of women has been most often expressed with children and in some nursing functions. Women often achieve a legitimate position by being helpless, a less direct form of power but one that fits the stereotyped female role. Males are made legitimate because of assumed and socially ascribed status wherein men act from a position of the right to influence regardless of whether they have been shown to have the skills and knowledges or more *expert power*. This form of power is perhaps the most frustrating to outsiders because actual expertness is not required.

Informational power is awarded to individuals perceived as being able to provide explanations for why another person should behave differently. This form is granted to women in many circumstances because of the social acceptance of certain female roles such as teacher, mother, or nurse. The same power, however, is not automatically ascribed when the person is out of role regardless of how well the person is known in role. Informational power outside of traditional roles is difficult to develop because women do not have access to the same sources of information or do not possess sufficient levels of detail in order for it to serve as a base of power.

Each category of power reflects a factual style and usually a component of personality that has become sex-identified. The only model that can be seen as a natural mode or style for women is that of *informational power;* women are not socialized to fit nor allowed to exert the remaining types of power, particularly *expert* and *reward and coercion.*

Women have been taught to conceal their knowledge and abilities so as not to be threatening (Moore and Wollitzer 1979). In so doing, women appear as less able, less assertive, and as less capable of leadership. Women's body language, words, and gestures create an aura of uncertainty. Consequently, women do in fact become less able, less assertive, and less experienced as leaders, all of which contributes to the development of low self-concepts and self-abnegation. Women are often judged to be ill-prepared because of their behavior, and it is only in recent times that a woman who displays traditionally masculine behaviors is viewed as healthy. Even though she is now more likely to be viewed as healthy, many males will continue to accept her as a peer with countless "yes-but (she is in some manner unusual)" reasons and rationalizations.

TO BECOME PERSUASIVE AND INFLUENTIAL

How does one learn to be persuasive and project influence? It is difficult for women to learn power acquisition behaviors because people who see themselves as being disenfrachised will not often assume a posture of force or persuasion. Some women project an image of apology, of qualification, and often fail to state a position with assertion or authority.

The reenforcement they receive often causes women to focus on detailed tasks rather than the larger picture and the implementation of ideas; through a process of acculturation, women become accommodative and passive, receiving ideas rather than initiating them. When they are expected to accomplish tasks requiring male-identified behaviors, such as administrative role behaviors, they are often penalized and isolated. It is usually required of women that they display "tactful femininity" and not "conspicuous confidence" (Weaver 1978). A conspicuously confident woman is, by various means, degraded and ostracized. Women are not necessarily superior to males, but they are not, by the same token, necessarily inferior. Masculine values, however, often preclude social and academic acceptance of the conspicuously confident women.

Women tend to underestimate their successes because, according to their own perceptions, they do not match the male definition of concreteness and accomplishment. Women do control in ways not obvious, often by conceptualization and inference, not by direct means of influence and control. Women are called devious, manipulative, and intuitive for good reason. They have become street-wise in academia, having learned over the years how to organize and control their environment in order to achieve their goals and satisfy needs, acting to provide for themselves in ways they themselves do not even recognize.

Women who do progress to higher-level administrative positions have difficulty in balancing two expected roles or ways of being. During the selection process, women are often chosen because of how they behave and not because of what they know. Presumably all candidates are required to have compiled a record of academic achievement defined in very valid and traditional ways for faculty leadership, exemplary teaching, research, and service. For women and men, these accomplishments are necessary but often not directly related to the administrative functions to be performed. At this juncture in the selection process, men are required to meet criteria of assertiveness, range of knowledge, organizational skills, and personal traits of self-assurance and authority. Women, in contrast, are more likely to be required to be complementary to the prevailing male characteristics and to be viewed within the context of a job on more personal dimensions. Qualifications of males are relatively straightforward, unqualified, and in direct reference to job responsibilities, whereas qualifications for women are personal: she must appear competent but not threatening, organized and concise but warm and supportive, assertive and effective but not castrating.

Thus, the first role requirement is satisfied: reasonable success so as to be acceptable to the faculty, but having the necessary female personality characteristic so as not to be a threatening woman. Ergo, the second requirement becomes difficult: a woman viewed as successful and competent for the job from the perspectives of both men and women, a no-win situation. It is not the truly accomplished, equally competent woman who often succeeds, but merely one who is acceptable for the wrong reasons to the prevailing power structure. There are obvious exceptions, especially in recent years with Title IX, affirmative action programs, the Equal Employment Opportunity Commission, the Women's Equity Action Council, National Organization for Women, and the varying degrees of success with state and national equal rights amendments. The increased numbers of women who have achieved the Ph.D. and who are in the available pool of applicants would seem to dictate that larger numbers would have achieved obvious measures of success in higher education. That they have not cannot be explained by any rational means.

Laws enacted for purposes of reversing discriminatory patterns have not been effective. The only possible avenue is to facilitate the movement of women and men supportive of women's advancement into decision-making positions where policy is enforced and where equitable treatment is an absolute requirement.

Universities and colleges are traditionally administered and governed by faculty. In recent years, there has been an increase in the numbers of nonfaculty, academic staff administrators who do not have faculty credentials but who have achieved higher-level administrative positions, often in business administration, as a fiscal officer, and in research grants administration. Most positions related to academic affairs, however, are held by academicians who are senior professors with established credentials. The route to such positions remains progress through professorial ranks. Mobility between institutions has always been a key element for advancement, with individuals sometimes coming full circle, having moved progressively through higher ranks at various institutions culminating in "coming home" as the highest ranking campus official. Despite retrenchment and a squeeze at the top, this mobility still occurs and serves to balance, to a limited extent, local choices. As is true in all elements of society during times of fiscal stress, fewer than the eligible will be able to move up.

Combined with economic and situational variables, women must circumvent situations peculiar to the female work environment. Typically women will be in careers that have no authority, most frequently the social sciences or the helping professions. Within these areas, women have most often been employed as specialists or supervisors, in staff positions and not as directors, principals, or senior professors (Bach 1976). It has been established in earlier sections of this paper that within professional ranks women are underrepresented at the higher levels. Thus, women are not in the appropriate positions for administrative advancement. The positions they do occupy are low profile, carry little influence to affect change, and are often on the periphery of the power structure. While there is probably less reason in academia for jobs to lose their meaning because of academic freedom and faculty autonomy, the conditions of employment and structure of the work place will not become more equitable until there are more women in positions of influence and power.

Peripheral positions do not provide the necessary learning experiences and administrative credentials for advancement. Women can become superwomen in committee functions and in meeting student needs, and they do achieve excellence in teaching and research, all of which provide the necessary and proper academic credentials. But unless they develop or possess key administrative attributes, often in the masculine mode, they will not be nurtured as administrators. Women who succeed are less similar to all other women than are men who succeed in comparison with other men. Women in nontraditional roles are likely to emphasize production or concrete accomplishments, have greater needs for achievement, and characterize themselves as more like managers (Moore 1977). A career-mindedness directs their activities and conveys an air of confidence and self-initiative. In addition to being less like other women, *by social definition* the successful executive woman will pursue selected goals at the expense of her family and not on behalf of her family. Being a family man means being a good provider, but there is no comparable accolade for a career woman (Prather 1971); careers are a legitimate masculine pursuit as defined by society, a definition which has had a devastating effect upon the psyche of women. Failure of our society to assure equal rights in the work place is a forceful restatement of this social value.

The need to achieve by men is ascribed to their role as provider and is viewed as an inappropriate need for women. The female stereotype is just beginning to change, allowing women similar assertive needs and role identifications. We are slowly accepting the fact that problem-solving skills and management techniques are not peculiar to the male species, but are instead learned social behaviors accessible to women as well as men. Similarly, we are only recently allowing men the freedom to choose domestic and service roles previously thought to be suitable only for women.

As women are allowed to be managerial and assertive, a range of new behaviors and set of identities become available. An early step is for women to develop access to concrete forms of power and resources and to project themselves as expert in various position responsibilities. It is necessary to attract attention to oneself by reputation as an expert and to be seen as possessing the desired skills and knowledges. Women cannot assume mentorships at the next highest levels, but men can, and such male-to-male support is expressed in committee assignments, joint research efforts, fishing expeditions, and golf games. Male bonding is assumed and will come about, but women have to exert more effort to attract even the most elementary forms of recognition. Women will not receive the same courtesies of position support because of role stereotyping, and the only answer is for women to achieve similar positions and to then play a conscious and similar role for other women at entry-level positions. The queen bee still exists; women who have achieved have an especial social and moral obligation to facilitate other women.

To foster feminine bonding and female support systems does not mean to be masculine or abrasive. Nurturance and empathy can be combined with goodly doses of assertiveness and active problem-solving abilities. Women have to learn the art of politics and what to do as well as what not to do. They must learn institutional folkways and informal networks of power and become skilled in manipulation of the formal power structure. To have such aspirations requires that a woman be androgynous, with a high spirit of adventure and a willingness to be nontraditional.

REFERENCES

Bach, Louise. "Of Women, School Administration, and Discipline." *Phi Delta Kappan* 57(7) (March 1976): 463-66.

Centra, John A., and Kuykendall, Nancy M. *Women, Men and the Doctorate.* Princeton, N.J.: Educational Testing Service, 1974.

Howard, Suzanne, and Downey, Peg. "Turning Job Burnout into Self-Renewal." *Educational Horizons* 58 (Spring 1980): 139-44. EJ 227 022.

Johnson, Paula. "Women and Power: Toward a Theory of Effectiveness." *Journal of Social Issues* 32(3) (Summer 1976): 99-110.

Kanter, Rosabeth M. "Changing the Shape of Work: Reform in Academe." In *Perspectives on Leadership, Current Issues in Higher Education,* No. 1, 1979. Washington, D.C.: American Association for Higher Education, 1979.

Kaschak, Ellyn. "The Effect of the Sex of Student and Professor on Student Evaluation of Professor's Methods of Teaching." Paper presented at the annual meeting of the Western Psychological Association, Los Angeles, April 1976.

Masters, Ruth R. "Perceptions of the Academic Community Concerning Selected Effective Teaching Behaviors of Women Professors in Masculinely-Stereotyped and Femininely-Stereotyped Teaching Disciplines." *Dissertation Abstracts International* 38 (April 1978): 5954A.

Moore, Kathryn M., and Wollitzer, Peter A. "Recent Trends in Research on Academic Women: A Bibliographic Review and Analysis." Paper presented at the annual meeting of the American Educational Research Association, San Francisco, 1979. ED 176 618.

Moore, Loretta M. "Distinguishing Characteristics of Women Managers." Doctoral Dissertation, Wayne State University, 1977.

Orstein, Allan C. "Quality, Not Quotas." *Society* 13 (January/February 1976): 25-28.

Prather, Jane. "Why Can't Women Be More Like Men: A Summary of the Socio-Psychological Factors Hindering Women's Advancement in the Professions." *American Behavioral Scientist* 15 (November/December 1971): 172-82.

Raven, Bertram H. "Social Influence and Power." In *Current Studies in Social Psychology.* Edited by Ivan D. Steiner and Martin Fishbein. New York: Holt, 1965.

Tidball, M. Elizabeth. "On Liberation and Confidence." *Educational Record* 57 (Spring 1976): 101-10. EJ 145 032.

Tuckman, Howard; Gapinski, James H.; and Hagemann, Robert. *Faculty Skills and the Reward Structure in Academe.* Washington, D.C.: National Science Foundation, 1976.

Walsh, J. "Women Entrepreneurs and Investments." In *Nontraditional Occupations for Women of the Hemisphere: The U.S. Experience.* Washington, D.C.: Women's Bureau, Employment Standards Administration, U.S. Department of Labor, 1974, pp. 25-29.

Weaver, Ellen C. "Implications of Giving Women a Greater Share of Academic Decision-Making." Paper presented at a conference on Expanding the Role of Women in the Sciences, March 6-8, 1978, ED 168 374.

Woolf, Virginia. *A Room of One's Own.* New York: Harcourt, Brace and World, 1929.

11

Studying Women's Studies: A Guide to Archival Research

Susan E. Searing

The advocates of women's studies have been remarkably inventive in establishing programs in North American colleges and universities. While successful program structures on different campuses largely reflect the specific character of individual institutions, they also share certain facets of organization that derive from the assumptions explicit in women's studies itself.

Women's studies is an overtly political enterprise, dedicated to improving the status of women in educational institutions and in society as a whole. Women's studies practitioners have incorporated that goal into the microstructures of their classes (through envisioning a "feminist pedagogy") and into the macrostructures of their department, programs, institutes, and research centers. Practical exigencies may prevent the full blossoming of alternative organizational paradigms, for compromise is ever necessary for academic legitimacy and viability, but there is evidence that women's studies programs have gone farther than many other innovative educational ventures in stressing the values of collective decision making, student involvement in planning, community participation, and service to women throughout the university, including nonteaching staff. As was so ably expressed in Rich's eloquent essay, "Toward a Woman-Centered University," women's studies aims to transform not only the content of classroom learning but the very nature of the academy (Rich 1975).

Given these goals, it is somewhat surprising that so little literature can be found in readily accessible sources on the particulars of program development. A primary focus of this essay is on the means of discovering and using the small but valuable pool of data and position papers that do exist and which can serve as guidelines for program development. Key studies that draw on primary documents and a synthesis of data will be highlighted, and the tools and methodology for further information gathering will be examined. The objective is to outline a path for present and future researchers on the development of women's studies.

To date the best survey of the literature on women's studies at the college level is Boxer's review essay (1982). Her heavily referenced article recounts the history of women's studies in considerable detail from the first isolated courses in the late 1960s to the exhilarating momentum of the present. The chronological narrative is followed by a discussion of internal political issues that challenge the practitioners of women's studies—notably, the integration of lesbians and women of color into women's studies and the National Women's Studies Association (NWSA) and the debate over "mainstreaming" women's studies into the liberal arts curriculum. The section titled "Theories" poses the question, "Is women's studies a discipline?" and touches on the notion of a feminist methodology.

Boxer also reviews the scant literature on program structures, delineates the arguments for and against departmentalization of women's studies, and provides examples of several organizational approaches. She takes pains to point out that "in many cases, however, no deliberate choice was made" (p. 688) and that "given the diversity of existing academic units, the forms of women's studies may be infinite" (p. 690). Boxer's sources of information are predominately articles and brief notes in periodical publications, although she also refers to government-sponsored studies, conference proceedings, and published reports by women's studies programs.

In reconstructing the early years of the movement, Boxer relies strongly, as any research must, on *Female Studies* (1970-76), a pioneer series that enabled women's studies faculty to share syllabi, teaching strategies, and political perspectives. *Female Studies* served as a critical communication channel in the early 1970s when women's studies first blossomed. Today, its ten volumes stand as the richest documentary source on courses and programs of that period.

Another reliable guide to the early days of women's studies is Robinson's federally funded study for the American Association for Higher Education (1973). Robinson draws her conclusions for thirty-two women's studies programs in existence in 1973, citing examples of program development, course offerings, and program organization and activities. For researchers, her eight-page bibliography is perhaps the most valuable portion of the document in which she cites in-house reports and proposals, plus conference and symposium papers, many of which are available as ERIC publications. A societal context is provided by articles from the popular press (for example, *Time*, the *New York Times*), local newspapers, campus newspapers and reports, and academic journals. These sources provide information about the development of women's studies within the context of the larger women's liberation movement from which the academic programs drew their inspiration, their advocates, and much of their subject matter.

Two surveys that trace the development of women's studies and its role on campus offer important analyses of institutional experiences with the new curriculum. In *Seven Years Later: Women's Studies Programs in 1976*, Howe (1977) studies fifteen mature women's studies programs that she categorized as being in "phase two" of development. These programs were characterized by "a line budget, a paid administrator, and a curriculum that moves through committees and is recognized in an official catalog" (p. 7). Most programs offered a major, minor, or certificate.

Among the several factors Howe examined in assessing the current state of mature women's studies programs were their internal governance structures and the administrative relations between the programs and the greater university. The study is useful for the presentation of alternatives or options for staffing and funding and for the appendices that permit comparison between institutions on selected variables such as enrollment, budget, degree-granting status, number of faculty involved, number of courses offered, and title and position allocation of the administrator. Howe's overview, based on interviews and observations, does not include bibliographic references as an aid to other investigators.

Of far greater use to researchers is the monograph entitled *The Impact of Women's Studies on the Campus and the Disciplines* (Howe and Lauter 1980). One of a series of reports sponsored by the National Institute of Education to address key questions posed in *Seven Years Later,* this work draws upon unpublished materials from 119 women's studies programs and about 57 professional societies, women's caucuses, and commissions, in addition to published writings. One chapter, a literature survey emphasizing recent and in-progress research and reviews of women's studies programs, focuses on data that will enable researchers and administrators to view the relationships between various aspects of program development (for example, enrollment, funding, administrative structure, course content), to judge the effectiveness of women's studies within a general curriculum, and to assess the impact on the personal and professional lives of faculty and students.

Appended to the Howe and Lauter study are substantial bibliographies on evaluation of women's studies programs and the impact of women's studies on professional associations. Also included are complete lists of the women's studies programs, committees, commissions, and caucuses that supplied information in the form of newsletters or unpublished documents. Special note is made of programs described in *Women's Studies Newsletter* 1-8 (1972-80).

Boxer, Robinson, and Howe and Lauter have provided a valuable service to researchers seeking background information about the development of women's studies programs. Less narrowly focused is the short-lived series *Resources in Women's Educational Equity* (1977-80), first published in 1977 and discontinued in 1980 when the federal government slashed funding for the Women's Educational Equity Act Program. Two special issues distributed in 1979 and 1980 extend coverage retrospectively to 1973. The series represented a unique approach to compiling a printed bibliography by creating an on-line tertiary data base. Abstracts were culled from twelve on-line bibliographic files encompassing the literature of history, education, medicine, business, psychology, and sociology, as well as files devoted to particular forms of publications such as dissertations, technical reports, and articles in popular magazines. The subject scope broadly encompassed women-related topics in education, legal status, careers, sex differences, life-styles, and health. The final volume included 1,650 references. Had the series been allowed to continue, it would have been a primary source for researchers. It remains a profitable resource for works from 1973 to 1980. Replication is expensive but not impossible; such efforts will probably lack a merged subject index and have a lesser scope of inclusions.

Women Studies Abstracts (1972-present), now in the eleventh year of publication, includes articles in women's studies, women's movement periodicals, and in scholarly journals of other fields. Unfortunately, *Women Studies Abstracts* is awkward to use. One serious drawback is the haphazard use of subject terminology compounded by the lack of cumulative indices for several years. To locate citations about women's studies programs, it is necessary to search under women's studies, women's studies programs, women's studies departments, college women's studies programs, women's studies curriculum, and college curriculum. A laborious search yields some citations of interest, but the total is small and includes only a few that could not be found in other, easier-to-use sources.

Beginning with the July 1972-June 1973 edition, the annual cumulative volume of *Education Index*, a standard educational index, includes an ever-increasing number of references under the rubric "Women's studies." Prior to 1972, a few references appear under "Curriculum—College and universities" or under "Women's liberation movement." Surprisingly few of the articles address the policy development and planning necessary to establish a women's studies program. This is also true of the ERIC data base, the on-line file from which records are extracted for publication in the two indexes, *Resources in Education* (1966—) and *Current Index to Journals in Education* (1969—). Few abstracts focus specifically on college-level women's studies programs; individual course syllabi and descriptions of content are better represented.

A QUESTION OF BEING HEARD

Clearly, women's studies faculty and administrators are not yet fully using the channels of communication afforded by journals in the fields of women's studies or education. Where, then, can scholars turn if they wish to study the brief history of women's studies in the United States? Where can faculty and administrators learn of their colleagues' experiences, the problems faced, and the solutions devised?

In *Women Studies Abstracts* and elsewhere, the most frequently cited source for information on women's studies programs is the *Women's Studies Quarterly* (1981-present), published initially as *Women's Studies Newsletter*. From 1977 to 1982, it was the official organ of the National Women's Studies Association. Other American journals such as *Signs, Feminist Studies, Frontiers,* and *Women's Studies* are primarily devoted to scholarly articles, whereas *Women's Studies Quarterly* focuses on pedagogical, organizational, and theoretical issues. A ten-year index to *Women's Studies Quarterly* is now available, facilitating inquiry into a decade of development and debate as portrayed in its pages.

On Campus with Women (1971-present), while offering briefer notes on women's studies programs and courses, has the added feature of carrying news relating to nontraditional careers, court rulings, employment, minority women, rape and violence on campus, sexual harassment, child care, women in sports, and other issues. Special papers from the Project on the Status and Education of Women are also included in the subscription.

STEPS IN THE STUDY OF WOMEN'S STUDIES

The published materials on program development only skim the surface of the brief but rich history of women's studies. The majority of institutions have nothing in print to chronicle choices and conflicts and their struggles and accomplishments in fostering the study of women in higher education. The researcher hoping to draw comparisons among the experiences of different colleges, or those seeking to examine the course of one institution's program, will inevitably be forced back to primary sources.

In a history of the establishment and entrenchment of women's studies programs, several types of formal and informal documents shed light on the processes and politics involved: internal proposals, reports, committee minutes, grant proposals, reports of outside evaluators, campus newspaper accounts, position papers, and memos. Some items have been deposited with the ERIC clearinghouses, but most exist solely on their originating campuses, in the files of the women's studies programs or key faculty members, or in academic departments and offices.

Researchers who desire to contact a broad spectrum of programs or to glean a representative sample are advised to use the annual directory of women's studies programs published in *Women's Studies Quarterly*. Each entry lists a contact person, address, and the degree(s) granted, if any. These listings update the more comprehensive *Who's Who and Where in Women's Studies* (Berkowitz et al. 1974). That publication listed individual teachers as well as programs; no more recent source has filled that function.

Another reference tool that provides comparative information is *Everywoman's Guide to Colleges and Universities* (1982). Although not complete because some schools did not return the lengthy questionnaire, the guide offers information about campus life, including curriculum, athletics, sex ratios among students and faculty, special services and programs for women, and minority enrollment. Institutions are rated in three key areas: women in leadership positions, women and the curriculum (in which women's studies programs carry significant weight), and women and athletics.

Everywoman's Guide is modeled after the standard handbooks that appeal to high school students and their parents, but the data are also useful to researchers. For example, one might ask whether colleges with women's studies programs offer specialized career counseling, programs for returning students, drop-in centers, or other special services for women. Are there more female administrators at schools where women's studies is strong? Are sports for women given greater emphasis where women also stand out in the curriculum? If any of these relationships seem significant, is there a discernible cause and effect?

A model for such studies can be seen in the work of Wood (1981), who measured certain organizational factors such as enrollment, selectivity in admissions, and proportion of female faculty, all figures easily obtainable from standard sources such as *The College Blue Book*, for schools offering women's studies programs and those that had not adopted them. Wood's is one of the few inquiries to make use of publicly accessible empirical data. As described by

Howe and Lauter (1980), most of the recent and relatively limited research on women's studies programs has been based on survey data. "It is not uncommon," they state, "to find comments by women's studies coordinators in their annual reports about the time they have devoted to filling out questionnaires" (p. 57), and they warn that the burden of fulfilling proliferating requests for information has begun to weigh on program coordinators, to the detriment of research. Yet they admit that the need of researchers cannot be met by data that are readily available:

> Apart from obvious areas such as enrollments and budgets, much of the program-supplied materials are not comparable across programs. Further, such materials, gathered at any one moment in time, may not offer a longitudinal view of a program's impact on a campus. Since the compilation of such data by researchers burdens programs excessively, few programs are consistently represented in studies, and at least half may not be represented at all (p. 24).

TOWARD A SYSTEMATIC HISTORY

Just why is the documentation on the development of women's studies programs so scanty? Is program development so tightly tied to institutional precedents and policies that feminists at one school cannot profit from the models of their colleagues elsewhere? Is program development and maintenance so political, in the nastiest sense of the word, that the full stories of the negotiations, committee battles, and compromises cannot be revealed without risk to the programs and their administrators? Or does the very rapid growth of women's studies, mirroring the ever-broadening impact of the women's movement, demand new tactics in each situation?

Reductions in federal funding, the prevailing back-to-basics philosophy, the increasing emphasis by students on career preparation, and other trends have altered the context within which women's studies programs exist. Earlier justifications, made in a climate of rising protest and based on an appeal to social fairness, may no longer hold sway. Instead women's studies may need to prove it can attract precious "FTE's" (full-time equivalents) in the marketplace of majors and electives.

There may be a grain of plausibility in these explanations, which argue against the desirability of sharing information and impressions, but it is doubtful that women's studies practitioners would thus defend their failure to document achievements. Rather, they would surely plead that they simply have had no time to construct records for posterity. Teachers and coordinators of women's studies programs, especially in the early stages, often take on the tasks as a "labor of love"; the released time (if any) granted by their home departments is seldom commensurate with the many responsibilites. Writing about experiences and organizing references for future use, particularly historical analyses, rarely seems as critical as are the more pressing matters of each day. Yet all would agree that there is a need for continued inventiveness and imagination in developing women's studies programs and courses and that to accomplish this teachers and administrators must be able to draw upon the full record of past endeavors.

The current debate over "mainstreaming" women's studies into the general liberal arts curriculum is a case in point. Many proponents of the integrated curriculum hark back to original manifestos, memos, articles, and speeches to prove that a total transformation of higher education has always been the goal of women's studies. Far from being reactionary and risking co-optation, they declare, the push for mainstreaming is more true to the original revolutionary objectives of women's studies instead of separate, "ghettoized" departments. Others, in particular women of color, Jewish women, lesbians, and other groups who are rightly insisting the women's studies courses and professional activities take account of their existence, see mainstreaming as little more than a reversion to the white, heterosexual, middle-class roots of study.

Only a critical reexamination of recent history can provide the knowledge and confidence to decide what direction women's studies must take on individual campuses. Only a sense of the past can enable feminist scholars to be true to the founding principles of women's studies, all the while critiquing earlier assumptions that failed to recognize the needs and contributions of *all* women.

It is too soon to fully judge the mainstreaming efforts underway, but it is certainly not too soon to begin gathering and preserving the documents generated by these pioneering experiments. Evaluations of faculty development seminars, the minutes of committees, and "before and after" syllabi may all be useful, not only to local administrators but also to researchers and policy makers trying to assess the nationwide effects of this trend. Moreover, future educational historians are likely to find the current debate intriguing, whatever its outcome.

The issues in women's studies have changed and matured, but the pressing need for information has remained constant. Robinson (1973) stated:

> There is also a lack of information from the programs themselves. Few programs have prepared lengthy descriptions of their history and development. Materials about specific programs are scarce and many times have been developed for purposes other than presenting an historical picture. Therefore, information about programs must be gleaned from bits and pieces of information found in widely scattered sources (p. 14).

Except for the blessing of the news notes and reports in *Women's Studies Quarterly*, the same lament can be sounded in 1983.

In *Seven Years Later*, Howe (1977) called for the creation of a communications network to distribute bibliographies, syllabi, and, "in monograph form, descriptions of women's studies programs, including documents submitted for official recognition and accreditation" (p. 73). She hoped that the Women's Education Equity Act Program would meet the need in part, but severe budget cuts have hampered the effectiveness of WEEA.

> Such documents would include program reports, course syllabi, external and internal evaluations, grant proposals, and key correspondence. Further, because there is no single institution responsible for collecting women's studies materials emanating from commissions, caucuses, and committees within and outside professional associations, the archive should also collect such materials. These would include reports, surveys, newsletters, and occasional publications, as well as convention programming (p. 79).

Howe and Lauter recommended the establishment of a natural archive of women's studies "in which those historical materials collected to date by groups and individuals can be deposited, indexed, and organized for use by teachers, researchers, and program directors" and which would "be organized so that it can continue to collect and make available new, annually solicited documents" (p. 79). The archive envisioned by Howe and Lauter would complement a longitudinal data base on women's studies programs and would include statistics on enrollments, degrees and certificates offered, courses, faculty, coordinators, support staff, space, budget, library resources, governance, and outreach.

The materials on file at the Feminist Press are the closest thing at this writing to a national archive of women's studies materials. In the research undertaken over the years by Florence Howe, the director, the Feminist Press now is the repository of an impressive array of primary documents on the development of women's studies in the United States and abroad. At present, however, it is closed to researchers. As a nonprofit organization with the primary mission of publishing materials for the study and teaching about women, the Feminist Press cannot devote its resources to cataloging these files. The Press is seeking a repository for the materials, preferably an established archive, that will catalog them and make them available to scholars and program planners. This will be a crucial step in preserving the history of women's studies and guaranteeing that the primary sources are not lost.

A national archive and a longitudinal data base are two worthy suggestions, but they are not the only possibilities to remedy the dearth of documentation and information of women's studies program development. Boxer (1982) closes her review essay with a plea for shorter, specialized conferences on practical single issues such as "integrating theory and practice in the classroom;... finding and creating job markets for graduates;... building a major or graduate program;... and surviving 'Reaganomics' and New Right attacks on academic freedom" (p. 695). This is an excellent proposal. Although an interchange of practical and pragmatic advice occurs at the annual National Women's Studies Association conferences, the information is not reflected in the descriptions of the formal sessions. A count of the small-group meetings at the third annual conference at Storrs, Connecticut, in 1981 identified only five sessions from a total of 272 that were explicitly described in the printed program as presenting information on women's studies programs and the struggles faced within institutions. A similar scanning of the program for the fourth annual conference in Arcata, California, in 1982 yields only nine sessions out of 149. There is a basic need to focus on the nitty-gritty of program development more forthrightly in conference settings where participants can share their triumphs, defeats, and novel strategies with other feminists in a supportive environment.

The development of a national on-line data base in women's studies also holds the promise of exerting some control over the literature of women's studies program development. Conceived originally by feminist librarians networking within the National Women's Studies Association and the American Library Association, the creation of a computerized data base has become a priority of the newly formed National Council for Research on Women, a coalition of women's research centers across the country. Presently, work is proceeding on the creation of a thesaurus of indexing terms. Because the council is particularly committed to capturing ephemeral materials—for example, the working papers issued by women's studies research institutes, small press publications, reports of research in progress, and the like—the data base may prove to be a perfect tool for consolidating bibliographic references with institutional source documents relating to program development.

Traditional printed forms of communication need not be abandoned, of course. The closing sentence of Boxer's essay suggests, "Perhaps it is also time for *Female Studies: Series Two,* for practitioners of the second decade to reach out and share, to deliberate over strategies and contend about tactics, but also to celebrate achievements and join hands for the long struggle to reform education and society in the image and interest of us all" (p. 696). The legend of *Female Studies* lives on in such recent publications as *Lesbian Studies: Present and Future* (Cruikshank 1982), *The Jewish Women's Studies Guide* (Elwell and Levenson 1982), and *All the Women are White, All the Blacks are Men, But Some of Us Are Brave: Black Women's Studies* (Hull et al. 1982). These valuable anthologies offer extensive bibliographies, syllabi, and encouragement to teachers and students exploring newer subareas of women's studies. Perhaps it is time to revive the general series as well, particularly as an aid to those newly converted to the mainstreaming movement.

Finally, it must be pointed out that women's studies has a vast oral history which has been barely tapped. Any archives of the movement should include tapes and/or transcriptions of interviews with the leading figures in the fight to legitimize research and teaching about women, as well as comments by students in women's studies programs.

This chapter is an attempt to assess the key secondary sources on the development of women's studies programs, emphasizing those that point to questions and to sources for further exploration; to draw attention to the meager primary materials available and to argue for an increase in their numbers and their accessibility; and to outline some proposals and current projects that might improve access to the primary literature. The information is of help to current practitioners who need information for decision making and planning, as well as to future historians of education.

Since its inception, women's studies has been concerned with making visible the realities of women's lives, which have been misinterpreted, ignored, or forgotten by scholars until recently. Let us not be guilty of the same sins. Although one cannot predict what future historians will make of the women's studies movement, we can state with assurance that feminism and women's studies will furnish the yeast for many dissertations and research projects in a variety of fields. It is our responsibility to preserve the historical files and raw materials for analysis.

REFERENCES

Berkowitz, Tamar; Mangi, Jean; and Williamson, Jane, eds. *Who's Who and Where in Women's Studies*. Old Westbury, N.Y.: Feminist Press, 1974.

Boxer, Marilyn J. "For and about Women: The Theory and Practice of Women's Studies in the United States." *Signs* 7 (Spring 1982): 661-95.

The College Blue Book. 18th ed. New York: Macmillan, 1981.

Cruikshank, Margaret, ed. *Lesbian Studies: Present and Future*. Old Westbury, N.Y.: Feminist Press, 1982.

Current Index to Journals in Education. New York: CCM Information Sciences, 1969-present.

Education Index. New York: H.W. Wilson Co., 1929-present.

Elwell, Ellen S.L., and Levenson, Edward R., eds. *The Jewish Women's Studies Guide*. Fresh Meadows, N.Y.: Biblio Press, 1982.

Everywoman's Guide to Colleges and Universities. Old Westbury, N.Y.: Feminist Press, 1982.

Female Studies, I-X. Old Westbury, N.Y.: Feminist Press, 1970-76.

Frontiers: A Journal of Women's Studies. Boulder, Colo.: Women's Studies Program, University of Colorado, 1975-present.

FS, Feminist Studies. College Park, Md.: Women's Studies Program, University of Maryland, 1972-present.

Howe, Florence. *Seven Years Later: Women's Studies Programs in 1976*. Washington, D.C.: National Advisory Council on Women's Educational Programs, 1977.

Howe, Florence, and Lauter, Paul. *The Impact of Women's Studies on the Campus and the Disciplines.* Washington, D.C.: National Institute of Education, Program on Teaching and Learning, 1980.

Hull, Gloria T.; Scott, P.B.; and Smith, B., eds. *All the Women Are White, All the Blacks Are Men, But Some of Us Are Brave: Black Women's Studies.* Old Westbury, N.Y.: Feminist Press, 1982.

National Women's Studies Association. Third National Conference: Women Respond to Racism. University of Connecticut, Storrs, May 31-June 4, 1981. (Conference program.)

National Women's Studies Association. Fourth National Conference: Feminist Connections Throughout Education. Humboldt State University, Arcata, Calif., June 16-20, 1982. (Conference program.)

On Campus with Women. Washington, D.C.: Project on the Status and Education of Women, Association of American Colleges, 1971-present.

Resources in Education. Washington, D.C.: Educational Resources Information Center, 1966-present. (Called *Research in Education,* 1966-74.)

Resources in Women's Educational Equity, 1-4 (with Special Issues 1-2). Washington, D.C.: U.S. Department of Health, Education, and Welfare, Office of Education, 1977-80.

Rich, Adrienne. "Toward a Woman-Centered University." In *Women and the Power to Change,* edited by Florence Howe. New York: McGraw-Hill, 1975.

Robinson, Lora H. *Women's Studies: Courses and Programs for Higher Education.* Washington, D.C.: American Association for Higher Education, 1973.

Signs: Journal of Women in Culture and Society. Chicago: University of Chicago Press, 1975-present.

Women's Studies. London: Gordon and Breach, 1972-present.

Women Studies Abstracts. Rush, N.Y.: Rush Publishing, 1972-present.

Women's Studies Newsletter. Old Westbury, N.Y.: Feminist Press, Clearinghouse on Women's Studies, Fall 1972-Fall/Winter 1980.

Women's Studies Quarterly. Old Westbury, N.Y.: Feminist Press, 1981-present.

Wood, Donna J. "Academic Women's Studies Programs: A Case of Organizational Innovation." *Journal of Higher Education* 52 (March-April 1981): 155-71.

12

Women's Studies: A Discipline Takes Shape

Karen Merritt

Women's studies courses sprang up on campuses across the country at the end of the 1960s and into the 1970s. They were the academic brain trust of the women's movement, the means for an intellectual analysis of the condition of women to which the women's movement was a political answer. College programs, including formal course sequences, certificate programs, minors and majors in the field emerged almost as rapidly, beginning with the approval of an autonomous program at San Diego State University in 1969. Black Studies suggested the model for early women's studies: overtly political, often separatist, confrontational of old-line academia. The first course offered by the University of Wisconsin-Madison in 1971 was paradigmatic. An outgrowth of a section of "Contemporary Trends," a course with volatile shifts in

---

Special note on sources: The author wishes to acknowledge the resources and information made available by oral reports made by University of Wisconsin-System Women's Studies Administrators and system documents. In particular, detailed information about the development of women's studies programs at Oshkosh and Whitewater campuses has come from the UW-Oshkosh Women's Studies Coordinator Barbara Sniffen and UW-Whitewater Women's Studies Coodinators Agate Krouse and Ruth Schauer.

topics, "Alice in Academe" was characterized by a spirit of ferment and new exploration.

Like the women's movement, however, women's studies from the start comprehended an essential conservatism. Early courses were, in a sense, profoundly revolutionary. Speaker after speaker looked deeply into her own discipline and marked the ragged fabrics of her venerable field: women omitted from research but who were used to characterize the discipline's understanding of human experience; findings about women that were either nudged into the familiar stereotypes or discarded as aberrations when they could not be made to fit; value placed on human activity and achievement according to the sex of the doer; and many unanswered questions about women, great holes in the disciplinary fabric caused by an epistemological void. For many faculty and students involved in these early courses, dedicated research on women became inevitable choices. Whatever the gap between what early practitioners had hoped would be achieved in the first decade of women's studies and what actually has been accomplished, the healthy evidence of revolutionary results is evident throughout the curriculum in higher education.

How, then, can one deduce from a decade of revolutionary progress a persistent conservatism? The equality-equity analysis in Chapter One gives an answer. The burden of the charge by feminist faculty was that the disciplines were deficient: biased, exclusive of female contributions and, therefore, incomplete. Revise traditional academic fields and curricular equality would follow and, by implication, educational equality would be achieved. The goal was compensatory. In short, though the feminist challenge to the epistemological basis of the disciplines was revolutionary, the goal of improving disciplinary content preserved the traditional curricular array and format. In the early 1970s, it was the hope of faculty at many colleges and universities that in years to come—ten, twenty, maybe fifty—successful women's studies programs would render themselves obsolete by virtue of their very success. Recommendations of a task force of a major public institution read:

> The traditional major and traditional department structure are not appropriate to women's studies. In order to consolidate research and knowledge about women, it is necessary to cut across traditional disciplinary lines. It is important that women's studies become neither isolated nor identified as a segregated area for women only; instead, courses about women must be an integral part of the entire university curriculum (System Task Force on Women's Studies 1974).

One may speculate that some conservative administrators who feared the potential for divisive separatism in the idea of women's studies or who were dubious of the substance of the field gave sanction to program development because the stated compensatory goals were a reasonable extension of the ideal search for truth.

The purpose of this essay is to trace the growth of women's studies programs, highlighting events that were indicative of trends which paralleled the national movement toward a permanent and independent disciplinary entity within a university. Women's studies remains unlike the older disciplines for many reasons. The field originated as the curricular arm of the American women's movement, seeking full social equality in the late 1960s. Some women's studies program development was tightly bound, in the early stages, to faculty women organizing and acting to end long-entrenched patterns of discrimination in universities. As women's studies programs have become institutionalized and recognizable counterparts to long-established academic programs, they have nevertheless maintained a special political identity that sets them apart. The separateness continues to make them suspect among faculty traditionalists in whose own disciplines an arguable political stance has become shaded through custom and which remains unanalyzed.

Women's studies programs have been unlike other programs in a university, too, because of the unusual role of administrators in program development, often acting as buffers against traditionalist faculty resistance to the field. In a few instances, administrators served as a barrier to any serious development of women's studies programming. Some programs have reflected a particular kind of conservatism that affects how deeply felt this field has made itself. The national discussion of opposing philosophies continues, whether to mainstream women's studies in the traditional curriculum or to maintain an independent interdisciplinary field.

By 1974, according to documentation by Howe (1974, 1975), only thirty-nine programs (degrees or minors) were in progress, but a total of 111 colleges, universities and consortia around the country were actively planning and offering women's studies courses. Early efforts at various campuses included the study of formal publications and internal working papers as well as recommendations for a path of program development that reflected a national perspective and a practical philosophy about the suitable purposes, content, and organization of women's studies. The humanistic purposes of women's studies were matched to the broad academic goals promulgated in various institutional mission statements and charters. One such mission statement could only be interpreted to assure support of a goal and was stated thusly: "developing in students heightened intellectual, cultural, and humane sensitivities; scientific, professional, and technological expertise; and a sense of purpose." The substance of the statement was directly associated with the political goal that has remained imbedded in the field:

In present society, the potential of women has been largely unrecognized and unencouraged. The "scientific, professional, and technological expertise" and the "intellectual, cultural, and humane sensitivities" of women have often been ignored, denigrated, or suppressed. One major purpose of women's studies is to raise the aspirations of women, expanding their sense of possible future alternatives and opportunities, and their appreciation of their own capabilities. The concurrent purpose is to enable men to widen their spheres of development, for they too have been limited by narrow traditional concepts of "women's roles" and "men's roles." One aim of women's studies will be achieved as women and men assume wider and more diverse roles in society (System Task Force on Women's Studies 1974).

Early programs were remedial and compensatory, offering a women's studies program at the level and of a nature that best matched the unique characteristics of each institution. Intercollege committees included teachers of women's studies courses, students, and the campus affirmative action officer (again, a reaffirmation of political context), who was to oversee the program rather than having it be dictated by an independent department. The preferred title of chief program administrator was "coordinator"; in addition to the academic duties of course and program development and management, coordinators were expected to serve as liaison with existing campus curriculum committees to facilitate cross fertilization.

In most instances the expectations from the beginning were that mainstreaming women's studies would be a major goal and that the political origins of women's studies would be embodied through cooperation with action-oriented groups inside and outside the institution. In all these respects, women's studies would diverge sharply from the great majority of other academic programs.

The coordinator-committee structure was a prevailing trend

across the country. Yet many specific assumptions about the future characteristics of women's studies were reflected in the urging that departments not be established but rather committees with some prerogatives of departments, eschewing the separatist strain in many minority studies programs. Without departments, women's studies faculty would not control hiring, promotion, or tenure, which has been disadvantageous and which has presented problems in various locations. The issue of curriculum control is complex because most programs and/or courses must be supported by departments. At the same time, however, if curricular deficiencies are to be remedied, an intercollege committee with members in many departments would have maximum flexibility. A department chairperson would be perceived as the defender of the department, by definition, and not as a collaborator, in contrast to a coordinator who is charged with responsibility to see that a program of pieces be coordinated. So, in theory, departments must keep their doors open to the coordinator. Under this formative structure, program committees and coordinators implicitly denied the hierarchy of the department. This surely had appeal to the political element in women's studies because the university hierarchy has historically been no friend of women. These early coordinator-committee structures served a useful purpose in that they suggested an impermanence that doubtlessly sugared the pill for dubious administrators: coordinatorships and committees could be dissolved far more easily than could departments. Thus, organizational structure codified an assumption that the ultimate sign of success would be a transformation of the curriculum so complete that women's studies as an independent entity embodied in the coordinator and committee would no longer be necessary.

THE PROCESS OF COMING OF AGE

From the beginning, the role of coordinator translated into a complex collection of duties that indeed did not much resemble those of a department chair. Programs often received budget and position support on a yearly basis only, and coordinators had to reconstitute arguments each spring to be assured of support for the following fall. Coordinators were heavily devoted to advocacy— arguing the necessity of women's studies courses to departments that should be offering them, pursuing curricular matters such as obtaining the appropriate *general education* credit designations for women's studies courses, or urging the library to purchase needed materials. Coordinators commonly had to defend the basic necessity for women's studies on campus. Given the origin of women's studies, demands for student counseling were more prevalent, and issues that were rarely taken to a department—for instance, sexism in the student newspaper—were taken to women's studies faculty. In addition to academic planning, a coordinator was usually expected to organize a variety of on-campus and outreach activities which a department would usually delegate to a committee. For all of these responsibilities, an institution would typically release the coordinator from one course, a .25 full-time equivalent (FTE) appointment. In some institutions, no administrative released time was given.

The development of courses, the methods in which they are listed, and jurisdiction over content presents an assorted history. Sometimes courses have remained based in departments and cross-listed with women's studies. In a few instances, particularly with the more mature and stable programs, women's studies is assigned a discrete "department" number, and the program becomes the primary sponsoring unit. Primary sponsorship means control over staff assignments, content, and sequence of offerings. Though some of these programs offer a major in women's studies, a minor or a certificate of program completion are the most common choices available to students. These program designations do not carry administrative autonomy as a major would because the control of course content and faculty typically remains with the department or instructional unit.

It is an advantage for a unit or college to obtain a discrete program designation because this has the psychological benefit of providing impetus for departments to develop courses that might be included in a certificate minor or major if for no other reason than to bolster departmental enrollments. To increase visibility and enhance political clout, on some campuses there has been an attempt to combine women's studies courses and programs under an umbrella structure encompassing a number of unrelated programs such as international, area, or ethnic studies. This arrangement is sometimes an advantage for reasons of economy and as a support network, but care must be taken to avoid a loss of identity and a possible erosion of staff positions because of the potential for shared duties within an interdisciplinary office.

Leadership of women's studies during the early formative years was often assigned to an individual who was simply interested in women's studies but who may not have had the necessary administrative credentials or who lacked credibility with the faculty, for example, adjunct appointments. Eventually some individuals were able to use faculty development awards as a means of developing skills as well as a means of gaining released time in order to devote more effort to program development. As faculty and staff worked at program development, there was a concurrent growth of student interest and participation; standards were developed for courses, and steering committees were appointed who were given more immediate control over program content. Typical programs now include, in addition to general issues of feminism, a focus on third-world women, political and economic issues, and an exploration of the contributions of women in specific fields of study, for example, history of science, French literature, or vocational and career development.

The crucial role campus administrators have played in women's studies program development has been a source of concern among women's studies administrators. Often, support is at best passive. For initiating programs, support from upper-level administrators is probably a major factor in shortening the time required for development. Supportive administrators also hold budgets stable or increase them in years when campuses are sustaining serious budgetary losses. Such efforts to accommodate women's studies course offerings while under pressure to give up dollars and positions to rapidly growing colleges such as business and engineering are key elements in the viability of these often popular programs. These special efforts have usually reflected the administrator's special perspective: successful women's studies programs are magnets for students, particularly women students, who often continue to be the most rapidly growing group of students on a campus. The problem of dependency on a single friendly administrator is obvious: If the administrator leaves, the program may suddenly be in jeopardy, particularly given the usual absence of department status.

Sharing resources in personnel is advantageous not only to preserve meager budget allocations but also for purposes of expanding a base of support and gaining visibility and credibility. For example, a women's studies librarian is an ideal floating position between units of a university system or on multidisciplinary campuses. This person can link program development between faculty and traditional library policies of aquisition. Position responsibilities include promoting materials acquisition and functioning as a resource person to faculty and students about the ever-expanding printed material in the field. Such a person can also facilitate cooperative activities such as conferences on library resource development, the compilation of various bibliographic materials, and the capacity to plan library acquisitions with programs as they are being developed and not after the programs have been initiated, a common occurrence.

Other collective activities include annual women's studies conferences, jointly prepared grant proposals, and consortia activities such as those sponsored by the Great Lakes College Associations, Women's Studies Consortium. The development of these activities in many states has paralleled the development and growth of the National Women's Studies Association.

WOMEN'S STUDIES AND POLITICAL ACTION

As women's studies programs have gained a degree of stability and familiarity on campuses, relationships with groups of organized women have changed. In previous years many groups, both on campus and in the community, had rallied and lobbied for certain issues such as equitable women's athletic programs, day-care centers, or flexible college admission policies. As women's studies programs developed and women gravitated to these centers of focus and support, participation in certain other groups or activities diminished. To some, this was a coming of age with the advent of women's studies; but to the more politically active, this was seen as a diluting of the strengths that come through collective political action. There is no less activity than in early years of the women's movement, but women are, in even greater numbers, expanding energies and using their talents within the context of specifically defined issues.

CONSERVATISM AND THE FUTURE

In many settings, undergraduate minors, special certificates, or majors are available in women's studies. But the majority of the more than 300 women's studies programs throughout the country continue to be under the direction of a coordinator or an interdisciplinary committee with a variety of offerings. The faculty development movement of the 1970s seemed tailor-made to the women's studies program goal of integrating research in the established curriculum. Major projects such as those in Montana, Arizona, and the Great Lakes College Association received national attention (*Women's Studies Quarterly* 1982). Networking among programs not only has facilitated the sharing of data banks but also has brought about visiting scholar programs and/or consultancies, for example, activities sponsored by the Wellesley Foundation and various projects financed by the Fund for the Improvement of Postsecondary Education.

The trends in current programming underscore an essential conservatism in most of the country: women's studies shall be made to fit into a well-established disciplinary mode, expanding the breadth of the traditional disciplines but neither displacing them nor creating pressure to reorganize them. It is true that the working of women's studies on a discipline can reorder the discipline in some fundamental way, as has been the case in the field of history. In recent years, however, writers in the field of women's studies have revealed a growing tension between the more conservative mainstreaming goal and the fact that women's studies as a discrete field has been developing in a direction which argues for its permanent independent status within academia.

From the beginning, the methodology of women's studies has been interdisciplinary and the pedagogy radical, particularly in validating personal experience as legitimate academic material. Practitioners in the field have been developing theory and practice peculiar to women's studies, as well as a vastly expanding body of knowledge that does not always fit into the disciplinary cubicles of the university curriculum. As a new way of knowing, the field shares the character of the disciplines. Yet the disciplinary trappings of the departmental hierarchy remain antithetical to the collective spirit of women's studies in which students, librarians, affirmative action officers, teaching assistants, and others are seen as legitimate contributors to the governing of programs.

The challenge for women's studies practitioners in the 1980s will be to harmonize mainstreaming programs with the continuing assertion by many as to the independence and uniqueness of the field. This will require searching out a permanent organization form that has institutional stability as protection against continuing fiscal hard times, but which continues to reflect the values of the women's movement from which the discipline of women's studies has grown. Women's studies programs may find a particular wave of opposition from administrators who have no quarrel with a solution for deficiencies in the curriculum, but who are suspicious of a permanent entity called *women's studies*. For those who have worked in women's studies, the experience has been one of profound revitalization, a sense of new excitement among venerable academic modes of knowing. The energy that this excitement has generated among faculty, students, and others in the academy is the strength by which the field will prevail.

REFERENCES

Howe, Florence. *Women's Studies Newsletter* 2 (Winter 1974) and 3 (Winter 1975).
System Task Force on Women's Studies. *Final Report*. Madison, Wis.: University of Wisconsin-System Administration, September 30, 1974.
Women's Studies Quarterly 10 (Fall 1982): 21-31.

Index